Tales of Quails 'n Such

Tales of Quails 'n Such

DECORATIONS BY WILLIAM J. SCHALDACH

by Havilah Babcock

WITH A POSTSCRIPT BY JAMES B. HOLDERMAN

UNIVERSITY OF SOUTH CAROLINA PRESS
COLUMBIA

Copyright 1951, by Greenberg: Publisher, a corporation.
Copyright © University of South Carolina 1985

Published in Columbia, South Carolina, by the
University of South Carolina Press

Manufactured in the United States of America

ISBN 0-87249-441-1

*Affectionately dedicated to two nice people
who have never met—
Ralph Terrill and my little granddaughter*

The stories in this volume have appeared in *American Forests, Field & Stream, Hunting and Fishing, National Sportsman, Outdoor Life,* and *Sports Afield.*

Contents

Foreword	ix
The Old Maid	3
The Parson Lied	11
Labor Trouble on the Punkin Vine	19
Slim Boggins' Mistake	29
The Smartest Thing	39
How Good Are Our Fishing Manners?	48
How to Miss Birds	58
When a Lady Undresses	68
You Can't Go Back Again	78
The Earthworm Cometh	88
Quail Hunting in the Old Dominion	97
When Fish Don't Bite	106
My Husband Is Slightly Off	115
I'm Betting on Bob	123
A Bird Hunter Must Walk	130
Minnows for Sale	137
"I Went to See a Man About a Dog"	146
Breamers Stop at Nothing	154
Good Bird Hunters Go to Heaven	162
Bird Hunting—Muleback and Otherwise	172
Let 'em Fall in Love First	180
Why Does a Bass Strike?	188
The Backsliders	197
Hell-Hound of the Sloughs	204
'Possum up de 'Simmon Tree	210
Hunting Bee-Trees	223
Stop-off for Turkeys	230
Postscript	239

Foreword

When John Bodette asked me to write a foreword for this book, an upsetting thought occurred to me: I had never written a foreword. In fact, I couldn't recall ever having *read* one. Forewording is apparently a trade for which I have small talent, and I hope that the reader will benevolently supply whatever a foreword is supposed to have that this one hasn't.

Twenty-five years ago I came to the University of South Carolina on a year's leave from the College of William and Mary, and found the country so entrancing and the people so hospitable that I have been here ever since. That must set some sort of record for leaves of absence. South Carolina is a fine place for a Virginian to live, and I hope the Old Dominion won't *sic semper tyrannis* me for saying that.

I was born in a certain year at Appomattox, Virginia, near the surrender ground, and I have been surrendering to one thing and another ever since. For twenty-five years now I have faithfully "fluctuated" between the two states with the hunting and fishing seasons. In fact, for a number of years—until I was caught up with—I was probably the only gent in the country who regularly voted in two states. I have also made occasional forays into such other Confederate strongholds as North Carolina, Georgia, and Tennessee for the redoubtable bigmouth bass, the saucy bluegill bream, and that artful dodger with a sense of humor, the Bob White partridge.

Since coming down here I have adopted many customs of the strange tribes that inhabit this region and have become, I hope, a passable South Carolinian. I have learned to eat rice and okra soup, sweet potatoes and baked 'possum, and Limping Kate and Hopping John when I'm hard up. I have also learned to imbibe limited quantities of that potent distillation of the swamps known as Berkely county corn.

I have conceived a profound respect for States Rights, although remaining somewhat vague as to what they are. I have learned to angle for the red-breasted bream of the serpentine creeks and black lagoons, the most mettlesome gamester, ounce for ounce, the Almighty ever put fins on, and the most delectable morsel an epicure ever licked his chops over. And perhaps most notable accomplishment of all, I have acquired a certain dexterity in turning catalpa worms inside out, a feat not dissimilar to that of cystoscoping a reluctant patient.

Schoolteaching has occasionally interferred with my hunting and fishing, but not too seriously. My motto has always been: work hard and quit suddenly. True South Carolinians never let their business interfere with their pleasure. With them hunting and fishing are not pastimes but passions, and they have proved charitable toward my frailties. The only time I ever got into hot water was when my enterprising and forward-looking secretary posted on my classroom door a notice which read: "Professor Babcock will be sick all next week."

The pieces which make up this book are lazy, loose-fingered and rambling accounts of my jaunts afoot. There is not one well organized and plotted tale among them. I suppose I ought to apologize for their formlessness, but that would be apologizing for deficiencies in my own character. A hunting or fishing trip is not by nature a closely planned and scheduled affair. You never know what is going to happen outdoors, for nature is more surprising than a woman.

I just go when I want to go, where I want to go, do what I want to do, and come back when I'm ready, which makes me about the only unbossed man in the country, unless it's you. I hate definiteness. I leave home to escape it. What's the use of going into the woods if you've got to take civilization with you? Can you imagine anything worse than knowing what's going to happen?

I am regarded as very eccentric by everybody who knows me. Nobody is shocked by anything I do, which enables me to get by with murder. My long-suffering spouse is hardened to the uncertainty of my goings and comings. Regardless of when I return to the ramshackle abode on Sumter Street, even if it's 2:30 at night, she calls imperturbably down: "Are you back *already?*"

Foreword

It was said of Dr. Oliver Wendell Holmes that he practiced medicine as an excuse for keeping horses. I have been accused of keeping dogs as an excuse for walking. In spite of being bony-shanked and bandy-legged, I can modestly describe myself as a good walker. Surely walking is a poor man's luxury, and one of the greatest gifts vouchsafed to ordinary mortals. How many times have I thanked Providence for a reliable pair of legs, whatever their esthetic shortcomings might be.

But I dislike paths, and the people who walk in them. I don't want to see things that other people have already worn out by looking at. Especially do I hate city-walking, and I am probably the world's worst pavement-pounder. Alice swears that I frequently walk 15 miles a day while hunting, and invariably drive the block and half to my classroom.

A good bird-hunter walks not merely for the sake of abridging distances and arriving at destinations. And he walks with all his senses, not just with his feet. As Whitman said, "Whoever walks a furlong without sympathy walks to his own funeral drest in his own shroud."

As I grow older I am inclined to thank God for simple things: for a bevy of quail scudding over tawny broom sedge; a staunch dog silhouetted against the setting sun; a night's untroubled sleep; the soft swish of a paddle at sunrise on the Ashepoo or Cumbahee; a cooling drink from a sequestered spring at noontide. If you give me these, you can keep the money. To go back to Holmes again:

"All I ask is that Fortune send,
A little more than I shall spend."

... And a few more puppies and grandsons to train before the carcass of this bandy-legged old bird hunter is hauled off to the cider press.

Havilah Babcock
Columbia, South Carolina.

Tales of Quails 'n Such

The Old Maid

Good covey dogs are, as Lincoln said of Civil War generals, "as plenty as blackberries." Hardy, spirited rangers that will put up whatever there is to be put up, and give you your money's worth day in and day out. That is, in good bird country.

But if you are ever fortunate enough to get your hands on a real single-bird dog, don't forget to say your prayers regularly. It's the only thing I'd steal without the slightest compunction of conscience—a really good one.

For a covey dog, give me a pointer—stamina, dash, derring-do. For a singles dog, give me a setter—patience, thoroughness, precision. Just one man's experience, and if it doesn't jibe with yours don't sue me for it. All you could get would be covey dogs, anyway. Single-bird dog is in my wife's name.

Also, if you care to, you can give me a setter that has been spayed. And I'll take my setter with a little age on her. Rare old Ben Franklin advised a young man to pick an old woman

4

to have his affairs with. The same consideration underlies my nomination of an oldish lady for singles hunting.

To carry the specifications a little farther, you can give me a slow dog, one that has plenty of time. There's no such thing as a fast singles dog and a good one.

Funny thing, too, I never saw a good singles dog with a fancy name. A friend of mine has a sedate and aging setter whose name is Bess, but whom we always refer to as the Old Maid, which just suits her mincing delicacy and fastidious thoroughness in the field. The Old Maid is not in the canine *Who's Who*. She has never been in a field trial, nor had her picture in the papers. And you have never heard of her. But I know a couple of hard-headed hunters who wouldn't trade her for a first cousin of the Grand Champion, once removed. Will Carrington is the other fellow. In fact, the Old Maid really belongs to Will, although he always refers to her as "ours." I have mainly a borrowing interest in her.

In golf, you drive for fun and putt for money. In bird shooting, you hunt coveys for excitement and singles for your game. This is truer now than ever before.

Time was when birds were so plentiful that covey hunting would give a man all that he wanted, and more than he was decently entitled to. I reckon such a time once was. If not, the old-timers I've listened to are a raft of unhallowed prevaricators.

I know a whimsical old gentleman who is fond of saying: "I ain't the man I used to be. Never was." Maybe it's that way with birds.

Time was when Bob was a self-contained and chancy fellow who held his ground until properly flushed. But he is not so stable as of old. He has become a bit jumpy here of late, often flushing at the least provocation. In fact, latter-day Bob is fast becoming an ungentlemanly trickster, full of sly ruses and pettifoggin' ways. Or to put it kindlier, Bob has developed a bad case of the d.t.'s. And pray who wouldn't have, what with the "reclamation" of his refuges by a benevolent and misguided Government, the encroach-

The Old Maid

ments of a more scientific agriculture, and a highly mobilized Coxey's army a-gunning for him day in and day out?

But for his twentieth-century nerves and growing slipperiness, he would have lost out in the unequal battle. Bob has learned that discretion is the better part of valor. His philosophy is not unlike that of a roguish old darky who "tote de game" for me and always gives as ample reason for running out on a free-for-all-fight: "Cap'n, I'd druther hear 'em say, 'Cain't dat nigger run!' than hear 'em say, 'Don't he look natchul.' "

For good and sufficient reasons, then, the singles dog is coming into his own. And sometimes local weather conditions join other factors to make such a specialist a prime necessity.

For instance, in low-country South Carolina, where I pay a few taxes and shoot a lot of birds, the 1939 hunting season opened in the middle of a drought. There had been no rainfall for more than two months. Fields, woods, even the devilish bays were as dry as tinder. Leaves rattled ominously wherever you stepped. There had been no rain to dissolve the dust from the undergrowth, and our dogs were forever sneezing and coughing. Trailing conditions were next to impossible. As the season advanced, the drought became more pronounced, and the birds more jittery and unstable.

Of the thirty-eight coveys that Will and I raised during the first week, twenty-seven flushed prematurely, slithering away at the first approach of the dogs and holing up in the impenetrable bays, where few bird hunters and *no gentlemen* will follow them. Singles hunting proved equally disastrous. The dogs would either run over the ground-hugging singles in the dusty straw, or flush them in the powder-dry, clattering leaves. It was not the fault of the dogs. Good hunters they were—Jackie, Pedro and High Pocket. Just too fast for dry-weather hunting.

During that unhappy first week, Will and I had one experience that will warm the cockles of any bird hunter's heart, however old and hardened a sinner he might be. A whopping big covey roared up from a pea patch ahead of

6

us and sailed away to a field of golden broomstraw. They didn't clump down in a body, but deployed nicely in two's and three's. As perfect a layout for singles shooting as a body could wish.

"That's the sort of thing that keeps a fellow huntin'," Will grinned. "The sort of thing that don't happen too often in this here modern society."

"Sure looks like the pay-off," I agreed. "And the answer to the bird supper that we've invited all those people to."

"Yes, sir," seconded Will as we strode confidently toward the field; "if a fellow can't fill his pockets with such a layout as that, he'd better quit."

But our hopes were short-lived. While we were still a hundred yards away, birds began to pop out of the dry straw and head for the distant and forbidding bay. We started to shout at the dogs and run—which a good bird hunter seldom does much of. But to no purpose.

Sweeping through the straw, our dogs routed those singles one by one. Even respectable dogs will sometimes lose their heads when things are popping too fast. When we got there, not a blessed bird was left. What can take an unruffled and philosophical spirit and tear it to tatters like that?

"And that's what makes a fellow quit huntin', I reckon." Will slumped forlornly on a log. "Twenty birds in that covey, and we got how many? Nary a one!"

"Pretty thorough job they made of it," I added dismally. "We hunted for that chance a whole week, and had it ruined in two minutes."

"Straw too dry."

"Dogs too fast."

"Birds nervous."

Thus we tersely diagnosed the case, and Will added the clincher: "Ain't goin' to be any better until it rains, and"—he looked toward the discouraged skies—"it ain't gonna rain no more."

"We got to do something about it," I ultimatumed.

"Yeh. Got to," Will dully agreed.

The Old Maid

"What you got in mind?"

"Nothing."

I chewed a sassafras twig and wondered if I could put a notion in Will's head without his suspecting my authorship.

"By the way," I said, trying hard to sound honest, "how old is the Old Maid?"

"She's pushin' eleven."

"Too old to hunt, of course."

"Yeh. Too old."

"Fattish, too, I reckon."

"Yeh. Fattish, too."

"We agreed last year not to hunt her any more, besides."

"Sure. Shook hands on it and promised Mary."

"Never do to lie to Mary."

A pretty satisfactory conference, I figured, knowing Will as I do. And when we met the next morning, there was the Old Maid in person, an amiable old blue-ticked Llewellin, squatting like a fat dowager on the front seat of the car. And there was Will, looking happy and sort of sheepish.

"Got her, but had to stand for a lot of kidding from Mary. Said we ought to be ashamed of falling back on an old pensioner, us with our two-hundred-dollar dogs. But my pride is gettin' easy to swallow here lately."

"Of course, we've got to favor her," I conceded, fondling a shaggy ear.

But it was soon apparent that the Old Maid would do her own favoring. Quietly she trotted behind us, contenting herself with an occasional excursion to check up on a likely thicket or a tentative clue that the other dogs had found and abandoned. Nothing could induce her to try her fortunes with the rollicking trio that swept the fields ahead. The Old Maid knew why she had been brought along, and she knew her own limitations, which is about the finest thing either dog or man can learn.

Within half an hour the other dogs had raised a fine covey, the birds flushing wild as usual and sailing off into an overgrown field.

"Now let's call those rambunctious hellions in, tie them to a sapling, and let the Old Maid speak her piece," decided Will.

So saying, he produced three lengths of rope and tied up the traveling trio, much to their disgust and the jeopardy of the sapling.

The Old Maid had seen the covey and watched it down. As we approached she trotted sedately ahead of us and began to insinuate herself through the undergrowth. Step by step she minced along, sneaking through the dry weeds and straw like a ghost. "Walking on pins and needles," Will called it. And presently she announced a single, which Will brought down and which she retrieved with the same daintiness, carefully retracing her steps on the retrieve to prevent invading untested ground.

"Notice how she came out the same way she went in? Old thing doesn't mean to risk a flush," beamed Will.

"I don't need a guide-book to the Old Maid's virtues, thank you," I answered, and bagged the next bird myself.

Back she went unbidden to her task, tiptoeing tediously about, warily testing every clump of weeds for her high-strung quarry. Once she pointed a single with a bird in her mouth—a heart-warming sight however often you have seen it. And once again she brought in a twosome—not to be dramatic, but because common sense dictated such a procedure when two birds lay side by side.

When her tedious job was done, bless my soul if the Old Maid hadn't pointed and retrieved nine of those singles without a mishap or accidental flush!

One of her traits that had particularly struck me was her quiet self-sufficiency. Not once had she let her anxiety to retrieve betray her into rashness, as might well have happened with a less practiced hand. Not once did she require instructions as to her job. We never talk much when the Old Maid is on a hard case. Matter of fact, she never thinks such a touchy situation appropriate for idle chatter. When a bird was downed, Will simply announced the fact. In him she

The Old Maid

had complete faith, never requiring reassurance and never relaxing her quest.

That very thoroughness of hers cost us an hour's delay the next day and gave me a side-light on Will's training methods. Will has a way of his own with dogs, and the incident, although a trifle irritating at the time, was highly revealing.

A wing-tipped bird had scurried into a hollow log and baffled the Old Maid's efforts to extricate it. Valiantly she laid siege to that log, prying, scratching and jamming her muzzle into the hollow, but to no avail. Nor did our added efforts help any. I tried to talk her into resigning the case, but no amount of persuasion could induce her to abandon the beleaguered quarry.

"We can't do anything with that derned dog, Will. We've lost fifteen minutes already. Tell her to be reasonable and come on."

"Just against her principles to leave a wounded bird, I reckon," replied Will.

"Heck! Pitch another one near the log and let her retrieve that. Maybe that'll satisfy the fussy old dame."

"That would hardly be honest, would it?" demurred Will. "A dog should be taught not to lie. Best way to teach 'em that is not to lie to them. I taught her that same thoroughness when she was a puppy, and I'm not goin' to fuss with her now. She's right and we're wrong, only she has more time than we have."

With that, Will smiled indulgently and stalked off across the field. A quarter of an hour later he was back with an ax and a wedge, and we fell to splitting that log so that the Old Maid could satisfy her conscience.

"That's what comes of having too good a dog," I chided peevishly. "And damned if you ain't as stubborn as she is."

But in my heart I felt a sneaking admiration for the pair of them.

For the next four weeks, as long as the dry weather lasted, we followed the same procedure: letting the other dogs hunt the coveys and the Old Maid the singles, especially when conditions called for delicate maneuvering. They were altogether the most restful and satisfying hunts I've ever had. And three-fourths of the birds we bagged during that time we owed to the patience and finesse of the old lady.

"That dame is a genius, and nothing else," I conceded after a particularly fine day. "Just as an academic question, Will: what will you take for your half of her?"

"Well, there's my car, my gun and the other dogs. There's the farm, the mules and the kitchen stove. And there's my wife, maybe. But the Old Maid, I reckon she's about the only thing on the place that ain't for sale."

"Think I'll put her in a story," I ventured.

"If you do, be sure to say she ain't for sale."

"No dogs like her nowadays, Will," I insisted, caressing a ragged ear. "Sometimes I think that nothing is as good as it used to be, anyway."

"Oh, you're just getting mellow over your shootin' these last few days. Matter of fact, that puppy I'm workin' on now will be just as good as the old lady in time. It's not hard, if a fellow has the patience, time, the birds—and a dog to start with. But unless a man is cut out by Providence to fool with dogs, I reckon he'd better hire his trainin' done. Best money he ever spent. Or buy one already trained. If he's an important fellow that gets off just now and then, he'd better buy a dog that's set in his ways, an old dog that's got more sense than he has—one he can't ruin. And I don't mean any harm by that. A fellow has got to be out of a job and not worried about it to train a dog right, I reckon."

The Parson Lied

I often wondered how the Parson stood the society of two such shop-worn angels as Rick and Wes. The rough-and-ready ways of this unrivaled pair must have taxed his Christian forebearance, as their tales sometimes taxed his credulity. There was the night, for instance, I spent with them on the Little Pedee.

"The smartest thing I ever saw," Rick stretched his long legs before the hickory fire and began, "was an old buck deer we used to hunt on the Savannah River. That buck would jump a five-foot fence just to get himself chased now and then. Just for the fun of the thing."

"You mean," put in Wes, the skeptic, "to set there and tell me . . ."

"I mean to set here and tell you that old son-of-a-gun naturally *enjoyed* it. He holed up on Take Notice Jones' place where he knew he was safe, because old man Jones had the place fenced on the swamp side and kept out-riders to drive hunters off. Well, whenever we'd turn the dogs loose in the swamp, that buck would sail over the fence, give them dogs a little settin' up exercise, and then sail back and go on about his business as ca'm as a cucumber."

"What do you think of that one, Parson?" challenged Wes. "A little strong, wouldn't you say?"

"My profession," replied the Parson judicially, "has taught me to be reluctant about impeaching the statement of another."

"You see, Rick? He's callin' you one, plain as day."

"No," corrected the Parson gently. "I had never heard of a deer that smart, it is true. Must have been a remarkable old buck, I'd say, but in a state as fine and big as South Carolina you'd expect to find an outstandin' deer here and there."

"Well," Wes was not to be outdone, "the smartest thing *I* ever saw was a wild turkey. An old gobbler that could read."

"You mean to set there and tell me . . ." bristled Rick.

"I mean to set here and tell you that gobbler could read," continued Wes unruffled. "And we'll let the Parson be the judge. A tremenjous old gobbler he was, with an eight-inch beard and as smart as a steel-trap. Stayed in the Four Hole swamp and always kept a big flock with him. But whenever we'd take our turkey dogs in there and flush the gang so we could yelp 'em to our blinds, you know what that bearded old gent would do? Well, I'll tell you. He'd fly across the border and light up in a big dead pine, just above a big sign that read: GAME REFUGE: NO TRESPASSIN'. Then like a preacher in a pulpit, he'd call out every blessed turkey in that part of the swamp. Now, Parson, didn't my turkey have more sense than Rick's deer?"

"I'm not an authority on turkeys, but I'd say off-hand that was a remarkable old gobbler, a very remarkable one, in fact, but in a sovereign state like South Carolina chances are there would be an outstandin' gobbler here and there," the Parson wisely evaded.

"If you want *my* opinion," interjected Rick with virtuous warmth.

The Parson Lied

"Now, boys," the Parson lifted his hand in a pacificatory gesture, "when it comes to deciding between such intellectual giants as Rick's buck and Wes' gobbler, I hate to sit in judgment. Who am I to pass on a sportive old buck's idea of self-enjoyment, or to impugn the capabilities of an embattled gobbler when the welfare of his followers is at stake? Animals are sometimes not so smart as we think they are, and perhaps sometimes much smarter. We all know that they often *bluff* one another, for instance, and I wonder whether they don't bluff us too, more than we suspect. I knew a dog, for example, that completely bluffed its owner and came within a gnat's nose, to use one of Rick's locutions, of bluffing me."

"July hound, wasn't it?" Wes sat up. "I had one once . . ."

"No. Bird-dog. An Irish setter, in fact."

"Let's have the story," encouraged Rick.

"Sure. Your turn anyway," seconded Wes.

"I'd rather not recall the incident," the Parson demurred. "In a way, it brings up unpleasant memories. Fact is, gentlemen, that old bluffer caused me to deviate from the high regard for truth which wearers of my cloth are supposed to exemplify, and perhaps the story had better remain untold."

"You mean a dog made you tell a lie?" hopefully asked Wes.

"Wes, you are such a literalist!" chided the Parson. "I said he caused me to deviate. In other words, to fall into a voluntary verbal inexactitude."

"A voluntary verbal inexactitude," repeated Rick, smacking his lips over the edifying phrase. "If that ain't a masterpiece. The next time anybody calls me a liar. . . ."

"Oh, dry up, Rick, and let the Parson tell his story."

"Since I am among friends," agreed the Parson, "and since both principals concerned are now dead, I see no reason for withholding it. Throw a log on the fire, Wes, and I'll try to reconstruct my experience.

"It was some twenty years ago, I should say. I was then a young preacher, on my first charge up in Virginia, and somewhat more interested, I am afraid, in bird-hunting than in the spiritual well-being of my small congregation. I accounted myself lucky, therefore, when I received a hunting invitation from an old Judge Bagby, who had been a great crony and shooting companion of my father's in their younger days.

"The Judge lived in a historic and half-forgotten old county, as famed for its fine hunting as the Judge for his fine dogs. So, as you can imagine, I lost little time in crating up my two young setters and heading for the old homestead. On reaching the county, I engaged an affable young fellow, whom I had chanced to meet, to conduct me over the meandering red roads that led back to the Judge's hereditary seat.

"My guide, who knew my host well, proved chatty and informative. I learned among other things that the Judge, who was of a distinguished Virginia family, was held in great affection throughout the country, and that in spite of his advancing years, he was as ardent a sportsman and lover-of-fine-dogs as ever. Indeed, that he now owned a particularly fine hunter for whom a rich Northerner had offered him a thousand dollars, and that it had looked for a time that the Judge would have to sell the dog to prevent foreclosure on his homestead. But, my guide further informed, the Judge had instead hit upon the happy expedient of selling his ancestors."

"Did you say *selling his ancestors,* Parson?" Rick asked.

"Yes, not so complicated as it sounds, perhaps. The Judge was of distinguished lineage but impoverished. That is, he had a family but no money. A newly-elected Congressman had money but no family, so the Judge sold the fellow his family portraits. The fellow took them to Washington and hung them up in his own fine house, and the Judge extinguished the mortgage."

"That ain't so strange," offered Wes. "I got two half-uncles I'd swap for a middlin'-good coon dog any day, and they ain't hung up yet either."

"Before you can sell ancestors," observed Rick not im-

The Parson Lied

personally, "you got to have some there's a market for."

"Anyway," resumed the Parson, used to such unflattering exchanges between the two, "I was mightily pleased with the prospect of hunting with a dog held in such esteem by so discerning a judge. When I arrived, the old gentleman welcomed me with great heartiness, but when he noticed my setters he was momentarily taken back."

" 'Young man, I neglected to write that you needn't bring any dogs. Didn't you know, sir, that I still have the Senator? Since you've brought yours along, it would be a shame not to hunt them, but you must not judge them by tomorrow's hunt. They will be competing with the Senator, you know,' the Judge said, with simple sufficiency.

"As if in answer to his name, there strode forward a great red dog. He was magnificently-coated, with a splendid sweep of tail and a majestic head—altogether the handsomest figure of a dog I ever saw.

"That night the talk ran strongly to dogs in general and the Senator in particular. From an old trunk the Judge brought out a pile of yellowing papers, and with these as a text, gave me such a masterful disquisition on the Senator's family tree that I reflected rather shakily upon my own. You know what a genius those elder Virginians have for tracing kinship, what with first cousin second-removed and such intricacies. And all that time the big dog stretched gravely before the fire as if such laudatory proceedings were to be taken for granted.

" 'What I want you especially to notice tomorrow, which will be the only hunt I've taken this year, is the Senator's great nose. It's nose that makes a dog, you know. I've bred for that, and I've got it,' " he concluded proudly.

"As soon as the sun melted the frost the next morning, we took the field. It was a beautiful place. The farm lay in a great bend of the river, its wide fields rolling away to the lazy James that glinted in the distance. And were there birds in those overgrown fields! Within fifteen minutes we topped a slight rise to find all three dogs dead on a covey. At the apex of the triangle stood a great red statue, with head and tail proudly aloft, a picture that an artist might have traveled far to see.

"Remarking that coveys were plentiful, the Judge suggested that we forego the singles. And, indeed, before another thirty minutes had passed, we crossed a hedgerow to find all three dogs piled up again, with the Senator dead on and my dogs backing close behind as before. Here, I said, is such a dog as a man is seldom privileged to hunt, and when within the hour the identical performance was repeated, I began to wonder whether the Judge wasn't right: that my dogs or anybody else's were useless when the Senator took the field.

"My dogs were good—I've never had better to this day—but here was an old master who had beaten them three times in a row. The technique of a dog that could do that was worth watching. I stepped up on a stump to watch proceedings in the rank ragweed ahead. In a moment I observed something that made me a little curious. All three dogs were hunting actively enough, but the Senator was continually hunting *behind* mine. And when one of mine tested the air and pointed, the big Irishman, to my increasing puzzlement, glanced guardedly about, then sneaked forward and boldly planted himself just ahead of my dogs. The thieving old reprobate! Had he been doing that all along? Well, I would find out definitely.

"Thereafter I walked ahead, so I wouldn't miss too many tricks. My enterprise was soon rewarded. When my dogs began to make game, the big red dropped cautiously behind them, fussing around busily and making a great pretense of hunting, but carefully avoiding any territory not already covered. Apparently he was *afraid* to find birds.

"When my dogs located the covey, he again glanced covertly around, slunk guiltily ahead, and imperiously planted himself. That tragi-comedy kept up a better part of the day. Each time the Judge walked up proudly and magnanimously reassured me that my dogs could not be judged fairly in such competition, that they would doubtless

The Parson Lied

show up well under other circumstances. And every time this scene was reenacted, my blood pressure climbed higher and higher.

"There was another thing, too, that struck me as peculiar. Instead of picking out his birds, the Judge invariably shot into the coveys, sometimes missing altogether. This, coupled with his unwillingness to follow the singles, puzzled me no little, since the Judge had the reputation of being a crack wing-shot. Watching him narrowly, I finally divined the truth: his eyes were so bad he couldn't follow the singles, yet throughout the day he stoutly refused to allude to his shooting or to offer his impaired vision as an alibi. Matter of fact, I doubt whether he could distinguish one dog from another at any distance.

"When birds fell, which was most often to my own gun, the possessive way in which he ordered the Senator to retrieve somehow conveyed the idea that he was trying to protect his secret of failing vision from the dog as well.

"But it was the conduct of the dog that puzzled me most. About him I had a suspicion as wide as a barn door, but one I couldn't confirm unless I should have an opportunity of hunting him alone. Late in the afternoon I contrived such an opportunity. As we reached the river and turned back, the Judge considered a moment which route to follow, remarking that the two hunts were equally good. I promptly suggested that we separate so I could have the pleasure of hunting the Senator alone. He assented at once, but the dog hung reluctantly back, an act so out-of-character as to call forth the wondering comment of the Judge. Only after peremptory orders from his master did he consent to go at all.

"Alone with me, the Senator was in a quandary, and his every manner showed it. The old fellow made a few half-hearted excursions from the path, sniffed importantly, then fell back as if he expected to get by with it. When I forced him into the field, there was an embarrassed uncertainty in every movement. Presently, to his deep mortification he walked smack into a feeding covey. He had not smelled them at all. During the rest of the afternoon he blundered into two other coveys and any number of singles. Then, as if recognizing the uselessness of further pretense, he quit cold and refused to budge from the path. Now that the Judge was not along to witness his infamy, the masquerade was abandoned.

"The Senator had lost his nose, as I had suspected. Lost it completely, either from the encroachment of age or some bodily illness such as the attack of pneumonia he had survived that winter. As you know, an impairment of the sense of smell often accompanies age. All the morning he had been bluffing high-handedly. I sat down and called him to me.

" 'Senator,' I said, 'you are nothing but a hypocritical old scalawag. My dogs have found every bird, while you piously appropriated every point they made, put them in a false light, and had the Judge sympathizing with me. I am going to expose you as soon as I get back. I am going to denounce you to the Judge as the swindler and grand rascal you are, sir!'

"The more I thought about it, the madder I got. I was a younger man, then," the Parson put in parenthetically, "and I could hardly wait to unmask the old fraud and vindicate my own dogs. When I arrived, I found that the Judge had preceded me, and that supper was waiting.

"Across the table the old gentleman beamed pridefully at me.

" 'Well, how did you and the Senator get along?' he asked.

" 'There is something I must tell you about that dog, sir. The Senator is nothing but a —'

"I was aware of a movement under the table, of the pressure of a big muzzle against my knee, and of a warm tongue caressing the hand in my lap. I glanced indecisively at the tell-tale little rectangles on the wall, where the portraits had hung, then I resolutely finished:

" 'The Senator, sir, is nothing but a genius!'

"And I left the two old frauds to bluff each other awhile longer. There are times, my friends," the Parson gravely relighted his pipe, "when the truth must be used with moderation."

Labor Trouble on the Punkin Vine

I always had a sneaking suspicion that the custom of hank-holding was devised to give my grandfather somebody to talk to. My captivity gave him a guaranteed audience.

"Did I ever tell you that one about Cap'n Billy Mahood of the old Punkin Vine?" he once began with a tentative lift of his shaggy eyebrows. "Cap'n Billy and his bird dog, and them hot boxes we had one too many of?"

I glanced at the hank of yarn on my upraised hands with an appraising eye. The tale might outlast the yarn, I figured, and I was about to enter a mild demurrer when an admonishing nudge from my mother reminded me of my duty in such matters.

"No sir," I answered resignedly. "Don't recollect as you ever did."

It was back around '99 (my grandfather said), when I was firin' on the Punkin Vine for Cap'n Billy. The Punkin hauled mostly lumber. We'd run down to Wileysville one day and back to Hadleyburg the next, about a hundred mile each way, and what with one thing and another, it took us nigh onto a day to make it.

The Molasses Special, they called the old Punkin. She warn't very fast, for a fact. I mind one day we pulled into Wileysville on the minute, and them smart-alecks down there thought they'd have some fun with us. "We come down to congratulate you for gettin' in on time." they said. "Hell," answered Cap'n Billy, "we ain't on time. This here's yestiddy's train!"

A mighty likeable fellow was Cap'n any way you took him. And a great bird hunter in especial. None better in his day, I don't reckon. Had a big pointer by the name of Preacher that was a powerful smart dog. Would bring Cap'n Billy's dinner and climb right up in the cab with it, he would. Sometimes Cap'n would take him along to hunt between runs, and finally Preacher took to ridin' the engine regular.

One day we pulled up with a hot journal box down in that growed-up country they called Po' Chance. While we was jackin' up to put in a brass, Preacher disappeared. Presently he barked. Cap'n dropped his tools.

"Hish, Johnny! That dog don't never bark that way unless—"

We climbed onto a flat cyar and looked across the field. There was old Preacher daid on a point, a-beggin' somebody to shoot his birds.

"You boys just take your time about puttin' that brass in," Cap'n grinned. "Got my gun in the cab."

In a few minutes we heard him shootin', and after a while he was back with his pockets a-bulgin' with birds. He and Preacher was both as pleased with each other as two mortal souls could be.

After that whenever we passed through Po' Chance, Cap'n and old Preacher was a-lookin' out the cab window. Kind of grieved them to run through without stoppin', I reckon. One day Cap'n said to me:

Labor Trouble on the Punkin Vine

"Johnny, is there anybody important-lookin' back there on the cyar?"

"No sir," I said. "Nobody but a lumber-inspector and a cattle-buyer a-playin' cyards with the brakeman."

Then he looked at me with a beseechin' sort of grin and called me "Johnny, me boy," and I knew what was coming.

"Johnny, me boy, don't you smell a hot-box back there somewhere?"

"Might be able to find one. But don't let old Q. catch you!" I hollered playful-like, as Cap'n gave her the brakes and slipped off into the field with Preacher.

"That old hellion ain't apt to show up around here," he laughed. "Anyway, what old Q. don't know won't hurt him."

Q. Peddebaum was who we meant—old "Q" we called him, though we never figured out what the Q. stood for. But that one letter put the fear of the devil in the heart of every man-jack that worked for the A. F. & P. system, of which the Punkin was a branch.

An old-time trainmaster he was. There were trainmasters and trainmasters, but Q. had a aidge on them all. He was meddlesome and mean as a snake. Always a-sneakin' and a-pryin' around, ridin' blind and hidin' under water tanks, to catch a lad noddin' and report him. My, he was a mean 'un, though!

Well, before long we was having hot-boxes two-three times a week. That Po' Chance country was alive with birds, howsomeover it looked so poor it would take three peas to sprout—two to grunt and one to push. After a while the lumber company got to complainin' their blasted logs rotted on the train, and the head-office was gettin' curious about the epidemic of breakdowns we was having all of a sudden.

"Suppose we give them a little variety, Johnny," Cap'n suggested. "Maybe a leakin' flue, or a broken eccentric, or a spreadin' tire."

But Cap'n Billy's idea about giving them a little variety didn't help much. I told him we'd better hold up a while and let our luck catch up with us. Cap'n was gettin' along in years, with a passel of children to support, and I was oneasy about him losin' his job. But it just looked like he couldn't bear to run through Po' Chance. And old Preacher just as bad. Don't reckon a body could rightly hold it agin them two. But I mistrusted things was gettin' shaky, and I jumped on Cap'n about it.

"Shucks, Johnny," he said. "When the huntin' season closes we'll go back to runnin' on time. Anyway, ain't we dividin' the birds? Who's a-kickin'? Maybe we have been ridin' our luck a little hard, but I brought the puppy along today, and I want to see what she'll do. After today we'll quit. What do you say, Johnny, me boy?"

Now I should have argued with Cap'n. But a mighty pretty puppy she was, the very spittin' image of old Preacher, and the eagerest little thing you ever saw. And Cap'n a-settin' there in the cab with her muzzle in his lap a-confidin' to her.

"Johnny, who's a-ridin' with us today aside them drunk lumber-jacks?" Cap'n asked as we got near Po' Chance.

"Nobody much," I said. "Two lightnin' rod agents is all, and one of 'em's asleep."

"Well, they ain't no immediate danger of anythin' gettin' struck by lightnin', is they? So you might look into that hot-box matter while me and the puppy look around. If anythin' pops you can blow for me as usual."

Son, you've heard about the pitcher that went to the well once too often. There I set in the cab window a-watchin' that puppy friskin' about and waggin' her tail like she was mighty anxious to please Cap'n, if she could figure out how to do it. And Billy was a-fondlin' her with his voice in a way you wouldn't a-known, it was that gentle and comfortin'.

All at once a fellow swung up into the cab. A tall, raw-boned sort of fellow with a black beard, he was, and I recognized him as one of them lightnin' rod agents.

"What's a-holdin' this train up, my good man?" he asked. "And where's the engineer, sir?"

That "my good man" should have warned me, but it didn't.

Labor Trouble on the Punkin Vine

"He's gone back to see about a hot-box, sir," I answered.
"So it's another hot-box, is it?"
"Yessir. Another hot-box," I said, a-stickin' to my guns.

Well, sir, about that time there comes a *Boom! Boom!* from the field as Cap'n unlimbered that old twelve gauge of his'n. Never heard a gun shoot so almighty loud in my life. *Boom! Boom!* It was worse'n Bull Run.

And when I turned around, I near jumped out of my skin. A-towerin' in the doorway stood—well, who do you reckon it was of all people. It was Q. Peddebaum, sir. Yessir, old Q. himself, with his false beard danglin' in his hand. And he was a-purrin' and a-smirkin' like a toothless old tiger.

"So Cap'n Mahood is a-fixin' a hot-box, is he? Well! *Well!* I must congratulate him on attendin' to the company's business, a-lookin' after hot-boxes out there in the field. That's where he's been having most of his broken eccentrics and leakin' flues, too, I understand. I'll just step out and lend him a hand."

He was rubbin' his hands together like he was enjoyin' himself powerful, which I reckon he was, and his voice was a-drippin' with pizen. Billy's goose was cooked, but I reached for the whistle rope anyway.

"That's thoughtful of you, my man, but you needn't bother about warnin' him," he said, still purrin' and rubbin' his hands. Then he stopped his purrin' and barked at me. "If your hand so much as tetches that whistle, you're fired, sir!"

With that he stepped off the engine, his face as black as a cloud. Cap'n was a-goin' to catch the very old Harry, and he warn't a man to take it layin' down. So I stepped off the engine, too, and made for the field. But old Q. got there first. I looked through the bushes, son, and there was a beautiful sight. There was that puppy daid on a covey of birds. She was a-tremble all over, with haid and tail up and one foot h'isted delicate-like. It was a elegant sight. Cap'n Billy was walkin' slow toward the puppy and talkin' husky-like to her, and he didn't see Q. Peddebaum till he was right behind him.

"Well, well, Cap'n Mahood. It's so nice to find you a-lookin' after the A. F. & P.'s interests thisaway. Now if you will condescend to return to your engine, sir, you'll find a gentleman waitin' there to convey the gratitude of the company to you in person—and help you get to Wileysville on time for once."

You've seen a cat projectin' with a mouse. Well, that's what old Q. would have put you in mind of, he was that pizen and smiley inside. Cap'n winced and his hat sort of settled back on his haid when he saw the trainmaster. Then he stood stock-still, ca'm as a cucumber, which is always dangerous in a man. Kept watchin' that puppy as if he didn't have eyes for nothing else. After what looked like forever he spoke.

"That's as may be, sir. I'll return to my engine as soon as I honor her point."

My lands, but Cap'n was a cool one! Old Q. jumped like he had been rattler-bit. "You'll go back now!" he roared, a-shakin' his bony arms. "You been pullin' the wool over my eyes long enough. You'll go back to your engine now, or you won't have any to go back to!"

"I told you," Cap'n answered quiet-like, without takin' his eyes off that puppy, "I told you I'll go back as soon as I shoot over her. I won't go back afore, and there ain't enough trainmasters on the A. F. & P. to make me, sir!"

When Cap'n challen'ed him thataway, old Q. got hoppin' mad. Right off, hell popped open. Yessir. Wide open. Peddebaum grabbed up a piece of fence-rail and raised it over the pointin' puppy. It would a-broken her back at the first lick, but she just stood there a-tremblin'. I reckon she loved Cap'n more than she was a-feared of dyin'.

"Stop!" Cap'n's voice snapped the air like a black-snake whip. "You can abuse me, and you may have cause, but if you tetch a hair of that dog, so help me God, I'll drap you in your very tracks, sir."

By thunders, but it was a ticklish case! After all, the Cap'n had a gun in his hands, and to this day I b'lieve he'd a swung it on Q. if the trainmaster'd twitched an eyebrow.

Labor Trouble on the Punkin Vine

Peddebaum stood sort of paralyzed for a minute. Nobody had ever challen'ed him thataway before, and he didn't know how to take it. He looked at Cap'n and then down at the puppy, and he must have seen it was a ground-hog case, for he stepped back and dropped the stick. I could see the sweat a-glistenin' on his face. My, but he was an all-fired angry man!

"You're fired, sir!" he bellowed at Cap'n. "And you'll never get another job on the railroad. I'll have you blacklisted on every road in the country, and I'll hound you out of every job you ever get. You're fired. Do you hear me? Fired! *Fired!*"

Was that old lobo in a tantrum! It was a fearsome sight, son, a fearsome sight. And just then—

"Watch what you're doing, Junior, and hold that hank right!" my business-like mother interrupted.

—And just then (my grandfather resumed) I heard somethin' movin' in the hedge below me. I glanced around, and there stood the other fellow that I had taken to be a lightnin' rod agent, too. In the excitement he had slipped my mind entire. A oldish, white-haired little gent he was, with a game leg. Hobblin' out in the open, he faced old Q. Peddebaum.

"I am in the habit of doin' my own hirin' and firin', Mr. Peddebaum, and you should have learned that by this time," he said. "Since when do I have to depend on a trainmaster to tell an employee what the A. F. & P. thinks of him? You may return to the train, sir, and allow me to dispose of this matter."

And did old Q. tuck his tail and slink off!

"My name is C. K. Wingard, sir, president of the A. F. & P.," he turned to Cap'n. "You might have heard tell of me before."

"My Caesars!" I said to myself. "The president himself! One ain't enough to fire a man. They got to have two to tell Cap'n how low-down he is!" I never felt so sorry for a man in my life. Just stood there with his big shoulders saggin' and him a-lookin' at the ground.

And the way the president marched into him! He told Cap'n the A. F. & P. had had many a man lay down on the job, but never before a engineer who left a whole train to go bird-huntin', and I don't know what-all he didn't tell him. A real eloquent old gent he was. The air was fair cracklin' around Cap'n, who was just a-standin' there absorbin' his miseries.

Presently I saw the old gent wink at Cap'n and glance at the retreatin' back of the trainmaster. Then he dropped his voice, and you could have knocked me down with a feather, I was that surprised by what he said.

"Looky here, Cap'n, ain't that a puppy a-pointin' yonder?"

"Yessir," said Cap'n, without lookin' up.

"How old is the little thing, Cap'n?"

"She ain't a year yet, sir."

"And has she been a-holdin' stanch through all that rumpus, Cap'n?"

"Yessir," said Billy.

"Think of that! Scared to death she is, too, and no wonder. Well! Well! She puts me in mind of a strain of pointers I used to hunt—same kind of tickin' and all. Old man Pettit from over in Nebo county raised 'em and—"

"Then that there puppy is from the same stock," said Cap'n, forgettin' his miseries all of a sudden. "She comes straight down from My Lady Sue and—"

"Mister, you don't have to tell me any more. *I owned My Lady Sue!*" he said kind of hushed-like. Pretty quick both of them was a-shakin' hands and sayin' nothing, and the little old gent blew his nose powerful hard. After a while he looked sort of sidelong at the Cap'n.

"Sir," he said, "I ain't shot over a dog for twenty year, since I got that leg cracked up, and I'd be a mighty proud man if—but shucks, I probably couldn't hit a shock o' fodder now."

"And I'd be a mighty proud man to have you do it for her, sir," said Billy, a-handin' his gun over. He was red and grinnin' all over, he was that happy.

Labor Trouble on the Punkin Vine

"Oh, you shouldn't do that!" the little gent protested, all blushery and eager like a girl. "I might miss, and a puppy is entitled to have her first birds killed for her."

But he took the gun just the same and stepped up right peart, forgettin' about his game leg in the excitement. A fine covey of birds sallied out in front of the puppy and headed through a scraggly oak. It was hard shootin', and I was mortally afeared he might miss. But he didn't. Dropped them as neat as a pin, by thunders, one with each barrel.

The puppy give an eager little yelp and fetched both birds back with hardly any coaxin'. Climbed right up and handed them to the president, she did. Well, sir, you never saw a man so powerful pleased. He set right down there in the broomstraw, the president of the A. F. & P. himself, and hugged and petted that puppy like she was his own baby, a-sayin' words to her that I couldn't hear. Cap'n had turned his face away, to keep from makin' a fool of himself, I reckon. In a few minutes they walked across the field together, with the old gent totin' the gun, and the two of them a-talkin' like school boys.

All that time, mind you, I had been squattin' there in the hedgerow, takin' it all in. And just as I started to get up, a lumber inspector come a-stridin' out. He was mad as two hornets, and I knew he didn't know what was what, but them inspectors was troublesome anyway, so I set still.

Not noticin' the little gent, the inspector lit into Cap'n unmerciful for holdin' up the train. Said the Punkin Vine warn't nothing but a dinky line noway, and I don't know what-all. And about that time the little president straightened up his head and tossed back his mane, he did.

"Humph!" he snorted. "Can't you respect a hot-box when you see one, sir? And furthermore, you tell your lumber company if they don't like the way I run this railroad they can kiss Aunt Jinny and build one themselves. And another thing, sir. The Punkin Vine may not be very long, but she's just as wide as the New York Central, i-God!"

"Father!" chided my mother. "You shouldn't use such shocking language around Junior."

"Marthy," he answered with solemn reproach, "I didn't say it myself. I was a-quotin' the president of the A. F. & P., i-God!"

"What happened after that?" I demanded, as the last round of yarn raced from my uplifted hands.

"Well, Cap'n kept his job, and the president took to inspectin' the Punkin Vine sort of regular, 'specially in the huntin' season. But for some reason or other," chuckled my grandfather, "the service didn't improve much."

Slim Boggins' Mistake

A big covey exploded from the brown fern and went corkscrewing through the tree-tops. Only a jumping-jack could have drawn bead on those pettifogging politicians. I got one bird and thanked providence for its kindly intercession.

"How did you come out?" I turned to my companion.

"Short and simple are the annals of the poor," he answered, glancing wryly at the interlacing tree-tops. "When I zigged, they zagged. And vice versa. There are too many bones in the human body for that sort of shooting. Even my head got in my way."

Then as we stood by, explaining our misses to each other's entire satisfaction, a fat cock lifted leisurely from the fern and loafed tantalizingly away through the only opening in the thicket. We looked ruefully at our empty guns.

"Could have knocked him down with a second-hand washboard," was Cliff's unhappy comment. "Third time that's happened this morning. Hereafter I'm going to save a shell for the sleeper, so help me Hannah!"

I have never figured out the psychology of the sleeper, that saucy jackanapes who gets up belatedly and flies provokingly low and straight away while the gunner stands like a simpleton with an empty gravel-shooter. Is his tardy take-off due to wariness or to unwariness? Is he a dastardly fellow who deliberately lets his compatriots take the rap? Is he a slow-coach and addle-pated dunce who requires an extra interval to think things out? Or is he the Phi Beta Kappa of the class who figures thus to disadvantage the gunner?

That morning I was shooting indifferently because of the sleepless night I had spent. Regularly, for a quarter of a century, inability to sleep the night before has made a wreck of me on Thanksgiving, the traditional opening day for quail in South Carolina. I doubt that I have slept twenty-five winks in twenty-five years during that particular night.

I count everything that can jump a fence or go through a gap, and wear out every sleep-inducing device known. "I could be bounded in a nutshell and count myself a king of infinite space were it not that I had bad dreams," I quote Shakespeare, who was something of a hunter himself.

"Tomorrow is an important day," I spend the night reminding myself. "If I don't get some sleep, I'll feel like the wreck of the Hesperus and shoot worse than a constipated owl with a crooked shotgun." Maybe I make it too important. I'm a bird hunter, not a psychologist. Finally, I deliver an ultimatum to my uncooperative body: "Now, damn your hide, you can sleep or stay awake just as you like, but you are going to catch the devil tomorrow and you needn't expect any sympathy from me. So if I were you—"

You'd think an old codger like me would have too much gumption to behave like this. But if you are a born bird hunter and had rather hunt birds than do anything else on this slightly flattened and somewhat cock-eyed globe, you might discover in your heart a modicum of sympathy.

For twenty-five years I have hunted with the same companion, which must establish some sort of record for mutual tolerance! Now, there are both advantages and disadvantages

Slim Boggins' Mistake

in having the same side-kick so long. We know the idiosyncrasies of our dogs, which enhances the pleasure of the hunt. We also know the idiosyncrasies of each other, which *sometimes* enhances the pleasure of the hunt.

During twenty-five years of companionship any two men will accumulate a fund of experiences to talk about, but long association tends to reduce the necessity of conversation. We know each other so well that we don't have to talk. A monosyllable may effect a meeting of minds, a meaningful glance may recall some experience memorable to both. Even a wide grin becomes an adequate reminder.

But such intimate companionship makes bragging next to impossible. How can you embroider some past exploit with glowing details if your audience was there when it happened? It's like gilding the lily in the presence of your mother-in-law, like having an extra conscience always following you around.

"No man is a hero to his valet," remarked Carlyle. And seldom to his hunting companion. When I inventory my deficiencies as a side-kick, I realize that only a great and magnanimous gentleman would put up with me for twenty-five years. But calling Cliff a gentleman doesn't keep him from bossing me around at times.

"Havilah!" his voice boomed through the flatwoods. "Why don't you quit wool-gathering and look after your dog?"

Fleet, my sedate little setter, was trailing in a patch of beggar's-lice near a cornfield. Cliff's slim-legged pointer raced in, verified Fleet's discovery, and seconded the motion. But neither was dead yet. Every quail dog has some mannerism that advertises the proximity of game and tells the discerning owner how the quest is progressing.

I never cock a gun over Fleet, however imminent things look, until her merry tail stiffens and curls at the tip. Cliff never slips the safety over Carrie until her right hind foot is lifted gingerly from the ground. The beggar's-lice was seven feet tall and seed showered down as we passed through.

"Why do people import food for birds when this native

beggar's-lice is unbeatable? There's enough food here for ten coveys," remarked Cliff.

"True," I replied. "But in a few weeks it will be plowed under. After all, that's the greatest single enemy of quail—the plow."

At the far end of the patch both dogs dropped dead, a big bevy hurtled up, and we downed three birds on the rise. One of the secrets of bird hunting is marking the flight of a decamping covey, an art at which Cliff is especially adept. But this time we both saw it: fully twenty birds deploying beautifully in the broomstraw 350 yards away.

"Lovely! Lovely!" rhapsodized Cliff. "The enchanted dream of every bird hunter. Your masterpieces of art, your fabled beauties of the boudoir, your deathless symphonies—what can hold a candle to a picture like this?"

"First one like that I've seen for quite a spell," I admitted, "except on a patent-medicine calendar."

"Button up your shootin' britches and shake a leg," Cliff relapsed into English. "Let's go down and take up collection before they start socializin' and get together."

We did. And that's one of the things I like about quail shooting in the Carolina low country: You can usually see where your birds go down. That is, approximately where. I don't mean you can saunter nonchalantly down and spit on their tails, and I'm not guaranteeing you can hit them when you get there. That's a horse of another complexion.

But the gunner's vision is often unobstructed for a quarter of a mile, and he gets at least a general idea as to the line of flight. He doesn't have to tramp over half a county to exhaust the possibilities, as he must often do in broken terrain where singles shooting is little more than a process of elimination: you just look everywhere they *could* have flown.

This flat country is also friendly to my aging legs. Indeed, my old underpinnings have a deep affection for the gentle terrain of this half-forgotten kingdom. But how they do argue and upbraid me when they have to propel my *corpus delicti* up and down the red hills of my native Virginia, as they do

Slim Boggins' Mistake

ten days every season! Yes, mine is definitely a flat-country species of leg.

I like the low-country too because it is unfenced—one of the few unenclosed and unspoiled provinces left on the map. It is said that barbed-wire did more to tame the Wild West than did the six-guns of the United States marshals, but I don't want anything tamed. Don't fence me in! On the sprawling plantations I can walk or ride the livelong day without encountering a single fence. Yes, sir, I've hunted bobwhite over a fair segment of his range, and I'll take mine in the South Carolina low-country every time.

"By the way," I asked after we had pocketed enough singles from the beggar's-lice bevy, "where was Timrod while the other dogs were trailing back there? I completely forgot the pup."

"Timrod was excusin' himself from the proceedings," laughed Cliff. "He stalked stiff-legged forty yards behind the other dogs, with his ears pricked up and an awfully worried look on his face. He figured something was going to pop, and he didn't want to be caught with his suspenders down."

Carrie is Cliff's dog, and Fleet is mine, but Timrod, a six-month-old setter pup, is *our* dog. We had taught him the backyard rudiments before the season opened, but this was his first day in school, his maiden voyage afield. Nearly every season we have a stripling coming along, not only as an eventual replacement, but for the pleasure of watching a youngster discover himself. We have a theory too that teaching a pup his a-b-c's keeps a hunter's heart young.

A mighty hunter is Timrod, and the world is full of wonderful things to be pointed. During the morning he must have pointed a full twenty times, stretching out on everything from stink sparrows to terrapins. And at noon he wound up in a blaze of glory by dropping as dead as chiseled granite on a yoke of oxen plowing in a field.

Not only have I hunted for twenty-five years with the same companion, but over the same territory, and in many instances the identical coveys themselves. Indeed, it would not be inaccurate to say that I have been shooting at the same birds for a quarter of a century! Successive generations have brought me both pleasure and embarrassment. Bob is a durable fellow and a great begetter of his kind. And he is a stable freeholder who sticks to the old homestead as long as it remains congenial to his tenancy.

Down through the years many of these coveys have earned pet names for themselves, such as Lazy Mule, Barking Dog, Foolish Virgins, Mother-in-Law, Po' Chance and Handshake. Years ago—it must have been in the late 'twenties—Cliff and I each downed three birds with a single shot and spent the rest of the afternoon admiring each other. It was an epic event, one enshrined in the memory of two men who are no longer spring chickens. Thus the covey we still call Handshake won a niche in our affections.

There are practical advantages in hunting the same territory and the same coveys year after year. We have learned the flight habits of many families, and how to dispose ourselves to best advantage before a rise. We have learned their range, their probable feeding ground and their sanctuaries, because we have read their diaries from season to season. We know when and where to hunt a particular covey. Such information can be a very present help in time of need.

It was in the Po' Chance country that we found ourselves on Thanksgiving afternoon, and here we ran into one Slim Boggins, a neighborhood character famed for his shooting prowess and not in the least averse to demonstrating it.

"Have you gents ever heard of a fellow who can drap fo' birds on a rise?" he pushed his cap back and asked.

We didn't think we had. With an occasional fluke shot maybe, but certainly not with any measure of consistency. Was there such a fellow?

"You air talkin' to him now. Slim Boggins by name. My ole she-bitch is trailin' yonder. Come on over and I'll give y'all a demonstratin'."

Striding loose-jointedly behind his dog, he kicked up a covey and neatly dropped four birds on a simultaneous flush.

Slim Boggins' Mistake

Furthermore, he made it look easy, almost inevitable, in fact.

"That air is what I mean, gents. And I ain't usin' no fancy autymatic neither. Jes' this here ole flippity-flop pump gun. Shucks, 'tain't nothin'," he discounted.

I looked at Cliff and Cliff looked at me, and we conveyed a lot without saying anything. This cocky, self-contained and unbookish fellow, this gangling son of the swamp, was the nearest thing to a natural shot we had ever seen. And the ancient pump which he fondled was as nerveless and supple-jointed as its owner. Never tell me that a repeater can't compete with an automatic in speed!

"Two birds fromped down in that broomstraw yonder. Come on over and I'll give you gents another demonstratin'," our uninvited guest announced.

A few minutes later the gaunt "ole she-bitch" pointed and her gangling master beckoned to us. "Now I'll th'ow this ole gun on the ground till the birds get up. Then I'll grab her and politely drap 'em both."

Two birds hurtled away toward a pine thicket. Slim swooped down, retrieved his gun and dropped them both. And they were as dead as a quarter past four when they hit.

"'Tain't nothin'," he manfully deprecated. "Also shoots 'em from the hip. If you gents want a free sample—"

Cliff and I were impressed by this backwoods paragon. We were also scared. If this "demonstratin' " kept up, there would be precious few birds left in Po' Chance. This two-legged epidemic that called himself Slim Boggins had to be curbed in some way.

With his usual resourcefulness, Cliff launched the attack. A flank attack it proved to be, and its very simplicity at first baffled me.

"Most wonderful shooting we have ever seen, and we are indebted to you for the exhibition," Cliff laid the groundwork. "It probably won't improve our shooting any, but may I ask you one question?"

"Shore, shore. Anything to oblige," expansively offered our Mr. Boggins.

"Do you practice monocular or binocular shooting?"

"Says how much?" Slim blinked.

"Do you shoot with one eye closed, or with both open?" Cliff pursued.

"Aw, that. Funny thing, I ain't never noticed. Never crossed my mind till you brung it up. Funny, ain't it? Tell you what, I'll take notice and let you gents know. It mout help y'all some. That's me, Slim Boggins."

Fleet had a single at the base of a cypress stump. I raised my gun, but Cliff shook his head. The bird flew as straight as a martin to its gourd. Slim raised his gun and confidently banged away. Then he banged again, but the bird reached the haven of the swamp untouched. A frown of perplexity gathered on Slim's face, but it was quickly dissipated.

"Shucks. Had my left eye closed that time. That ain't the way I been doing it. I shoot with both eyes open. It's come to me now. Show you gents next time," he quickly reassured himself.

A few minutes later Carrie froze at the edge of a pea-patch. Two birds got up and sauntered straight down main street. Slim pumped away four times, but nary a feather did he cut. Stock-still he stood, enveloped in an awful silence. The shadow of amazed disbelief crept over his face. Picking up an empty cartridge, he absently fingered it, then shook his head as if to dispel a grisly vision.

"Great balls of fire! I helt both eyes open that time. That must not be the way I do it either!"

An awful doubt had insinuated itself into the soul of Slim Boggins. He eyed his dog distrustfully and regarded his faithful old pump with new-found suspicion, as if the wife of his bosom had unaccountably betrayed him.

"Jes' happened to think," he explained limply. "Got fo' cows to milk when I get home. If you gents will excuse me—" And he sloped off across the field.

That's the last we saw of Slim Boggins. But not the last we heard. A hundred yards away he must have stepped into a single, because we heard a rapid succession of shots and

Slim Boggins' Mistake

then, "Great balls of fire!" Three hundred yards away another fusillade rent the air, and the word "fire!" resounded through the hushed flatwoods and died away in the swamp.

"Cliff, the devil's going to get you for sure!" I said. "For a trick like that, your carcass should be hanged, quartered and dried on a 'simmen bush. Besides, there's a constitutional amendment about cruel and unusual punishments."

"I haven't done a thing, not a blessed thing!" Cliff protested with a twinkle discernible at fifty feet. "Our Mister Boggins just made the mistake of thinking. He shot well because he shot unconsciously, in a manner of speaking. He was not handicapped by a college education. But he made the mistake of thinking, and that's sometimes fatal. Now let that teach you a lesson, son," he admonished with a solemn chuckle.

"Well, our friend will recover in time, but chances are he won't insist on demonstrating to us again," I said. "And these Po' Chance birds will give you the thanks of the republic. They've had enough for one day. We have only an hour or so before dark. Let's amble over to the Mother-in-Law covey and see how they fared this summer."

It was in the Mother-in-Law country that Timrod won his spurs. These birds are great gadabouts, and it was nearing nightfall before Carrie and Fleet found their names on the society page. Then they trailed across a bog, through a field of wild partridge-peas, and into an uncultivated strip fingering out from the swamp. There both dogs came to a peremptory halt.

But we instantly lowered our guns and looked at each other for swift confirmation. There, slightly ahead of the other dogs, was little Timrod on point. He had intercepted the homeward-bound covey and pinned it down in the brown cinnamon fern, under whose friendly canopy Bob so loves to doze. And there stood Timrod, with both eyes resolutely shut, rigid as a bisque figurine.

"I'll just be damned!" breathed Cliff. "Do you see what I see?"

"Shut up! Ain't you got no manners?" I grinned back.

As we eased forward Timrod covertly opened his eyes and glanced at Carrie, his guardian and preceptor. Her right hind foot delicately scorned the ground. Carefully Timrod lifted his foot to conform. Carrie's muzzle angled sharply to the left. Timrod, who had been manfully pointing the whole world more or less, shifted his muzzle to match. Then he sort of looked over his glasses at us and ventured: "Is this something like it, *mister*?"

Lowering his gun, Cliff nodded to me and lifted one finger. I shot once at the scudding bevy, and we held the other dogs while Timrod proudly retrieved the bird. Then we danced a jig around the newest member of our family, playfully pommeled him in the fern and called him "old horse." The starry-eyed Timrod pranced around and yipped his great pleasure. "Come on, let's find some more!" he barked.

"We've got a dog in the family now," Cliff said. "When you get home, write that down in your diary."

And I did. I wrote: "On this day Timrod, a pup of whom I have high hopes, graduated from the first grade and received his diploma."

It was nightfall now, and the hunt was over. Another Thanksgiving had come and gone. It had been a pleasant but somewhat arduous day, and as I climbed gratefully into the car I fervently sighed: "May the Lord be thanked for putting a night between every two days!"

The Smartest Thing

What is the smartest thing you ever saw a bird-dog do?

A dictionary defines reasoning as "a surrogate manipulation of the environment in a manner that facilitates overt adaptation." It is an open question whether a dog or even a Democrat can do that, but then the same dictionary defines man as "a featherless and tailless biped." Call it reasoning, rationalizing or whatever you will, most observing hunters who have followed good dogs afield have seen them think their way out of situations in a way that inspires pleasurable recollections down through the years.

One of the canniest tricks I ever saw was pulled by Judge, a grizzled setter belonging to a dog-loving doctor in low-country South Carolina. The genial practitioner encouraged his dogs to retrieve by the homeopathic method of feeding them bird-heads, a practice as time-honored in the South as giving 'coon-hounds a dosage of gunpowder to make them rambunctious. Regardless of the merits of the doctor's system,

Judge had come to consider the heads of the birds he retrieved his personal and indefeasible property.

One day the doctor, while accompanied by Judge and a younger dog, managed to drop three birds on a rise. Judge, who chanced to be across a ditch from his master and the other dog, dutifully set about retrieving the trio. But as he picked up the first and prepared to hurtle the ditch, he saw the younger dog standing by the master and licking his chops in anticipation. Here was a case that called for a little self-consultation, so old Judge put on his thinking cap. After a moment's indecision he evolved a solution that, whatever its weaknesses as a piece of abstract reasoning, proved a masterpiece of practicality.

Dropping the bird on *his* side of the ditch, he successively returned for the other two, laying the trio side by side. Then he sat down, neatly decapitated the birds and devoured their heads. His dainty repast over, he gravely delivered the unruffled carcasses to his amused and amazed master, eyeing the younger dog with a superior air all the while. "Stick around, small fry, and you might learn a thing or two."

Nip and Tuck, roistering pointer blades, were both precocious pupils, becoming adept retrievers at a tender age. But Tuck, the boss of the brace, soon exhibited a trait that showed real executive ability. When I threw a ball, he would station himself in front of me like a safety man near his own goal line, until Nip made the retrieve. Then he would intercept Nip, grab the booty, and swagger toward me as if his technique had been unimpeachable.

Tuck never outgrew his inclination to steal the show. Even after he became a seasoned campaigner, I dared not praise another retriever too effusively. If I did, Tuck would hoist the Jolly Roger, tackle and dispossess the upstart as he approached me with a bird. But the long-suffering Nip finally found a way to checkmate his roguish brother.

If he found a bird when Tuck was between us, he would often ignore the discovery and continue pottering about until the coast was clear, then trot cautiously toward me with the

The Smartest Thing

prize. Time and again I have watched him bide his time and judicially weigh his chances of negotiating the enemy's lines unobserved. And when sorely harassed, he was not above hiding the bird until Tuck, the highwayman, had betaken himself elsewhere. Yet they say that man is the only reasoning animal.

The biggest fake I ever met was old Trounce, a huge pointer whose acquaintance I made while spending a summer in a country hotel in Virginia. Trounce had sustained a broken leg trying to dodge a churn-dasher in the hands of an irate housewife, and everybody at the friendly little hotel took to petting him and rubbing the splinted member. The old reprobate fell in love with the life of Riley. Squatting on his rotund rump, he would station himself in front of the hotel and court the compassion of all passers-by.

The damaged leg healed quickly, but old Trounce had discovered a racket that was too good to be lightly abandoned. Whenever he was ordered out of the kitchen or caught in one of his unsavory escapades, he would pull a tragic face, roll his eyes like a dying martyr, and limp his way out of a licking.

When I went back to shoot birds that fall I found Trounce to be a potentially fine hunter, but a most damnable malingerer. Whenever I chided him for some peccadillo afield, he would put on that dying swan act and limp his way out of doing whatever he didn't want to do. But one day I ordered him into a briar patch, and the sanctimonious old fraud insulted my intelligence by limping on the wrong foot! Then it was that I went after him with a sassafras brush.

That brought about a sort of gentlemen's agreement between us and Trounce quit malingering in the field. But whenever he got back to the hotel and was caught robbing a hen's nest or something, he would resume his tragic role and limp all over the place. "Mister," he wanted me to know, "if you don't give me away around the house, everything will be O. K. in the field."

Having passed his three-score-and-ten afield, Mike was now an old pensioner. His hunting days were over and he knew it, but how hard he tried to bluff me into thinking that he expected to be taken along! Something—maybe a touch of clairvoyance but probably the portentous bustle about the house—always told Mike when I was getting ready for a hunting trip, and he would make a laughable attempt to hide in my car beforehand.

His attempts at hiding were always laughable because his requirements seemed to be met as long as not more than nine-tenths of his hulking carcass was visible! Whenever I opened the car to let the younger dogs in, I was sure to find a fat rump protruding a mile high, with only his head buried under a hunting jacket or floor rug. A great-uncle of his must have had an affair with an ostrich once.

Mike was not trying to fool himself, and he was really not trying to fool me. Just playing a dumb game with himself, I guess, and dreaming of his yesterdays. But when we returned at nightfall he subjected all hands to a searching inspection. Bullying his grandsons around, he sniffed each in turn and pumped whatever information he could from them. He clambered into the car and collected whatever clews were there. Then he sniffed my gun and my boots, winding up his inventory with a prodigious sniff at my hunting jacket. Having put together the scraps of an old newspaper as well as he could, he retired with dignity to his corner. If he couldn't do it, he could at least read about it.

I seldom think of Mike without thinking of Major LaRue, a gentleman of a bygone age and a bygone elegance, and the hero of my boyhood. At the advent of every hunting season the Major would appear in the little Virginia town where I grew up—the Major with his pedigreed dogs, hand-loaded shells and imported fowling-piece. Every morning he would dress up in full hunting regalia, get an early breakfast, bustle around with dogs and gun, and—send me hunting.

Like Mike, the Major's hunting days were over. Like Mike, there yet burned within him an unquenchable love of the hunt. The only price I paid for the luxury of his gun, shells and dogs was a fumbling chronicle of the day's hunt while

The Smartest Thing

the Major sat, his bottle of digitalis on the table beside him, and listened with the half-shut eyes of a virtuoso. I hunted during the day, while Major LaRue, like some Ulysses grown too old for the wars, hunted at night before the smoldering fire in the deserted lobby of the little hotel.

Even as a spraddly-legged puppy, Roebuck was the most unfenceable dog I ever saw. Tractable enough in other respects, he had an insuperable aversion to being on the inside looking out. Some kennel knaves emulate the mole and escape by the subterranean route. Others take French leave by the aerial route. Such finicky tactics as these Roebuck disdained. He merely barged through, under the working hypothesis that the only difference between a little hole and a big one was a matter of time and energy. I spent the better part of one summer repairing his ravages on an old fence and trying to anticipate his next eruption, in which Roebuck refused to cooperate. Cocking his head sidewise, he would sit on his haunches and calmly appraise my handiwork, as if to say: "Pretty thorough job, boss, but if a fellow went at it the right way—"

As long as I was in evidence or anywhere about the premises, Roebuck showed not the least disposition to break out. But within a few minutes after my car pulled away, my wife would invariably telephone me that he was out and overrunning the household. Roebuck was just too smart to show his hand—to point out the weak spots in the fence for my benefit. But he taught me one thing: the way to keep a dog from breaking pen is—never to let him start.

Whenever and wherever old hunters foregather and the subject of retrieving comes up, "Now let me tell you what my dog did!" becomes the preamble to many a prideful tale. It is in retrieving, where conditions are highly variable and reactions often unpredictable, that a dog individualizes himself. Finding a lost bird or overhauling a wounded one is an unstandarized and unstandardizable business.

One of my boyhood recollections is of Boss, a big Irish mugwump and a magnificent retriever. I remember once seeing Boss in the act of picking up a wounded bird when his nose called a halt and he stopped short on another single. As he stood pointing, the wounded bird began to flutter noisily in the leaves in front of him. As if fearful the fluttering would rout the single, Boss gingerly extended a big paw and held the wounded bird still. His action might not have been dictated by reason, but it was certainly reasonable.

One of the finest instances of a dog's rationalizing on a retrieve was that of Lady, a demure little setter bitch in her second season. Walking down a slippery log with a dead bird in her mouth, Lady suddenly saw a wounded bird scurrying to safety in the morass below her, with her master in frantic pursuit. Stopping short and retaining her precarious footing on the log, Lady considered the proprieties of the occasion. Was a bird in hand worth two in the bush? Should she relinquish a certainty for an uncertainty?

After weighing the matter a moment, she laid the dead bird on the log, sprang into the morass, captured the escaping bird and took it to her master. Then, deliberately and without a word from her owner, she returned for the bird she had deposited on the log. Regard it as you will, that dog thought her way through a difficulty and hit upon the solution.

An almost equally remarkable case of a retriever thinking her way out of a dilemma was related to me by a distinguished diagnostician: "Two dead birds fell together, possibly six inches apart. My old bitch picked up one, but as she did so a puppy started in to get the other. Quickly Snow dropped her bird beside the other, squatted growling over them, and tried to browbeat the puppy. Again she picked up the bird, and again the puppy made a break for the other. Snow was in a quandary. After successive attempts to bring one bird to me without exposing the other to the interloper, she sat and revolved the matter in her brain. Then she got up, calmly took both birds in her mouth, and trotted toward me. She had never retrieved double before. If that was not a clear-cut case of brain-action, what was it?"

The Smartest Thing

Some dogs, as if they have a little Chesapeake in them, will retrieve with alacrity in the coldest water. I have a German pointer who had just as lief fetch a water-fallen bird as anything else.

Bess, however, was like the cat in the adage: she abhorred getting her dainty feet wet. So when a bird fell at the edge of a savanna, three or four feet from the bank, she was in a pickle. She trotted worriedly from one side to the other. Finally she solved her problem by "paddling" the water toward her with first one front foot and then the other, setting up a slight suction that wafted the bird to her, much as a cat does a dead fish.

After an unsuccessful quest for a dead bird at the outset of a hunt, Speed was called off by his master. Two hours later, during which the party had put up several coveys and and traversed several miles, they returned to the car. But as Speed was climbing in he suddenly bethought himself. Trotting back to the near-by covert in which the bird had been lost, he resumed his interrupted quest and eventually found the bird. Considering the time that had elapsed and the coveys that had been raised in the interim, one would hardly convict Speed of amnesia.

Now and then I have seen dogs that were smart enough to abandon a point when lost, report to their masters and escort them back to the birds.

Fortunate is the broken-country hunter with such a dog. I recently heard of one that will invariably return to his owner, attract his attention by scratching at his leg, and lead him to the bevy. I have never had a dog with such an intelligence quotient as that.

But I have hunted with a graying and sagacious old setter who, whenever he was lost on point, would emit a single bark without budging one jot or batting an eyelid. If we still had trouble in locating him, he would wait a prudent interval and bark again. Old Joe was gathered to his fathers three years ago. *Requiescat in pace.*

Among the old wives' tales my grandfather used to tell

about the saddle-hunting days was one of a dog that came to a dead point under the belly of his standing horse, a single having found doubtful refuge in a tuft of grass beneath. Neither the dog nor the horse, runneth the tale, budged until he had climbed from the saddle and shot the bird. The same dog would allegedly climb up against the side of a horse to hand his master a bird.

We sometimes fail to appreciate the physical and nervous distress which prolonged pointing may cause a dog, particularly if the point is made from an awkward position. A stanch dog may stand with the immobility of alabaster, often in a strained position and with one foot uplifted, for an hour or more. Yet I can't hold one arm out at right angles to my body for five minutes without acute discomfort.

I once saw a nimble debutante, Virginia Dare, scramble over a low rail fence and drop to a tense point with her forefeet on the ground and her hind feet still atop the fence, in almost a perpendicular position. The nearness of the quarry made any attempt to change her position risky, and she knew it. Rather inhumanely, perhaps, I waited to see how long she would hold the unique posture. She held for ten minutes—until her front legs buckled under her.

Alabama Bill was as pot-bellied as Falstaff and a bit wabbly on his pins, but a steadfast old gent at that. One day he was lost for an hour in a cane savanna. When I finally found him, it looked as if the old codger had shuffled off and *rigor mortis* had already set in. He was lying flat on his big belly, composedly pointing a covey. Whether that was a case of laziness or intelligence I am not quite sure. There isn't much difference, anyway you look at it.

From Mississippi comes a touching story of a fine dog reluctantly offered for sale by its owner. A prospective purchaser, a man of undemonstrative habits and clipped speech, took the dog out for a trial. But to the chagrin of the owner, who was along, the dog proceeded deliberately to break every commandment in the decalogue and make a miserable spectacle of himself—to prevent being sold.

The Smartest Thing

As to the truth of this the deponent sayeth not because he knoweth not, and because it was also from Mississippi that he received the offer of a dog that is Phi Beta Kappa material. After enumerating the dog's points, the would-be seller postscripted: "He also barks whenever you miss a shot, unless you're shooting in a thick place, when he makes allowances." I declined the offer. When I buy a bird dog, I want one with sense enough to keep his mouth shut, not a smart-aleck.

How Good Are Our Fishing Manners?

"The surest way to tell whether a fellow's a gentleman is to take him fishing," the head of a manufacturing firm told me recently. "If a man has any inherent rascally traits, they are sure to come to the surface. Whenever a bright youngster comes up for promotion, I take him fishing before committing myself. It's the touchstone of good breeding."

"I have four daughters," another acquaintance said. "Whenever one of them gets serious designs on a young fellow, I don't hire a genealogist to look up his family tree. No sir. I just take my prospective son-in-law on a fishing trip. Not primarily to see how good a fisherman he is, but to see how good his fishing manners are. I want no surer index to a man's character than his conduct on a fishing trip."

"You know what's a fact?" a third acquaintance contributed. "When fishing season opens, there will be more fishing in this country than ever before in history. Shorter hours, bigger incomes, faster transportation, and a backlog of pent-

How Good Are Our Fishing Manners?

up fishing urges will cause our lakes and streams to be jammed as never before. Even places that we used to regard as remote and inaccessible. And what I'm thinking is this: *Unless the fishing manners of a lot of people improve,* we are going to be getting into each other's hair something awful!"

Such pronouncements as these, which one hears frequently nowadays, have set me to ruminating a bit. What exhibitions of bad manners have I seen, and peradventure been guilty of? What breaches of piscatorial etiquette are most annoying to others? What *are* good fishing manners? I ask myself. How good are my own? And, mister, how good are yours? I know you and I haven't been guilty of arson, malfeasance, felony and such heinous things, and we are no doubt exemplary husbands and fathers, but just how good are our fishing manners?

Fishermen are in general an amiable set of folks. Although they may occasionally deviate from the straight and narrow, as a whole they are a charitable, uncomplaining, and warm-hearted lot. You won't find many arch malefactors among them. It is true, however, that from time immemorial fishermen have been regarded as fabricators of fibs. And because of their unsavory reputation, they sometimes find it necessary to lie in self-defense.

May I illustrate. You catch a bass that actually weighs seven pounds. But however unimpeachable your reputation may be, your friends will forthwith discount the size of your catch and give you grudging credit for a mere five-pounder. Now this is a palpable error. Indeed it is a vile slander, and you smart under the indignity thereof.

Thereafter you anticipate the skepticism of your friends and add the discount in advance, calling your bass a *nine* pounder. When your cynical cronies have finished their dastardly discounting, the net result is the beauteous and shining truth, namely, a seven-pound bass. The skepticism of his friends may thus make it necessary for a fisherman to tell a lie *to get the truth believed.*

Have you ever taken a friend fishing and sworn by the

eternal never to take him again? What is the surest way a man can make himself *persona non grata* on a fishing trip? Whom do you nominate as Public Nuisance Number One? What is the most discourteous thing a fisherman can do? What, in short, is the unpardonable sin on the part of a fellow angler?

One unpardonable sin is abusing the confidence of a host. You probably have your own version, but here is what I mean. After much questing, you finally ferret out a secret fishing place, some secluded and unhaunted spot which always yields you a handsome string. It is your own virginal and inviolate secret, and you hug it complacently to your bosom.

Then one day brotherly love wells up within you. You get to feeling sorry for the henpecked and luckless fellow next door, so you take him to your secret place. Of course, you enjoin him to secrecy, implicitly trusting his innate sense of honor. Both of you have a grand time, and you come home laden with fish and fellowship. For days you feel noble and public-spirited.

But when you go back to the selfsame spot, there sits your erstwhile friend with two of *his* friends. He has been sneaking back unbeknownst to you and bringing his cronies, who in turn have been bringing their cronies. Now your secret place has become a mecca for the hoi polloi. Your virginal spot has been ravished.

You suppress the resentment in your manly bosom and pretend not to notice. But deep inside is an unshakable conviction that your erstwhile friend is an adder-in-the-bosom and a snake-in-the-grass. Also an unshakable resolution to let the fellow severely alone for the rest of your normal life. A fellow who thus abuses a friend's confidence will not, I am afraid, ever glimpse the Pearly Gates.

Have you ever had a companion drop his hook right beside yours while you were getting a bite, or right in the precise spot where you had just caught a fish? That is the severest test of friendship known. It's perfectly legal, to be sure, but

How Good Are Our Fishing Manners?

to heck with legality. It is certainly not an evidence of good breeding. I've been telling my wife this for years.

"That's the most unethical thing anybody can do," I am continually saying to her. "No lady will do it."

But she ignores my dissertations on outdoor ethics and blithely continues her poaching. A man's wife is a privileged character, I suppose, but I sometimes wish Alice had more chivalry in her make-up.

There are few things a hook-and-line fisherman resents more than having somebody else tell him when to pull. It is always construed as a reflection on the puller's intelligence. Besides, it's a bootless sort of kibitzing. If the fellow pulls and lands his fish, he tells himself that he was going to do it anyway. If he pulls and misses, he reproaches you with an *et tu, Brute* look, wonders how your wife puts up with such a busybody, and resolves not to vote for you at the next election.

Right here I want to make a confession. Herein lies a cardinal weakness in my own character, a shortcoming that my tolerant friends are all too familiar with. I seldom offer gratuitous advice, and am not generally regarded as a meddler or buttinski. But to save my life I can't resist telling the other fellow when to pull. Whenever a cork starts down, all the king's horses and all the king's men couldn't keep me from blurting out:

"Pull 'im! Pull 'im! You got 'im!"

I always repent me of my folly and offer a shamefaced apology to my friends. And I always resolve to be silent and strong-willed thereafter. But I invariably repeat my graceless performance at the next opportunity. I sometimes apprise my companions of this idiosyncrasy in advance.

"Now I'll probably butt in and tell you when to pull," I forewarn. "But don't pay the least attention to me. I'm just a sap that way. Use your own judgment, regardless of any advice I might give you."

Fishing is like hunting: the commonest fault is being too quick on the trigger. Yet few mortals can resist kibitzing when the other fellow is getting a bite. It is one of the weaknesses to which human flesh is heir to, and it is to be ardently hoped that the Great Supervisor of Scales and Balances will smile understandingly at such mortal frailty when the day of reckoning comes.

Telling a companion when to pull is bad enough, but when he pulls and misses, never, *never* say: "You didn't give him time enough. If you had just waited a second longer—" That's an invitation to justifiable homicide!

"The other day I hung a nine-pound bass on a flyrod," a hapless acquaintance of mine said, "and I lost him. Know why?"

"No," I confessed, not being omniscient.

"Too much advice," he said succinctly.

"What happened?"

"Well, I'll tell you. Ten other fishermen were watching me at the time. Instantly all ten began to shout advice—ten different kinds of advice. Now every man there was a friend of mine, every man there wanted me to land the bass, yet collectively they were doing their best to prevent it. The bass wasn't handicapped by advice."

"I see."

"And another thing," he resumed. "Let a man hang a fish, and everybody within a mile and a quarter hollers: 'Hold him! Hold him! Don't let him get a-loose!' As if the poor harassed fellow wasn't already doing his damnedest. That's the most dim-witted, buffle-headed and witless thing an onlooker can say."

"But suppose it's just meant as moral encouragement," I suggested.

"When you've got a nine-pounder on your line, you don't need any moral encouragement." And he stalked away, firmly convinced that he had lost a prize quarry through the over-solicitude of his well-wishers.

It is also unmannerly to question the weight of a companion's fish. One who has the instincts of a gentleman accepts the other fellow's estimate. When you haul in a fish, heft it gleefully and say, "Five pounds or I'm a Dutchman,"

How Good Are Our Fishing Manners?

you have every moral right to expect a gentlemanly confirmation from your companion.

If your companion cocks his head critically, narrowly scans your prize, rubs his chin reflectively and begrudges, "Nice fish, but I'd say not over three," what sentiments well up in your tolerant bosom? Well, you aren't sure whether you want the fellow to go to heaven or not. Never take a mathematician on a fishing trip. Or a pair of scales.

The converse is equally true. If you want a fellow to be your friend for life, if you want to marry his youngest daughter, if you want to be made the beneficiary under his will, just say: "Sorry to differ, old man, but you are underestimating the weight of your fish. He'll go nearer seven than five. And did the son of a gun fight!"

It is also not cricket to bring up invidious comparisons. When you land a gleaming seven-pounder, it is hardly chivalrous for your companion to say: "Nice fish. By the way, did I ever tell you about the time I caught three nine-pounders in 30 minutes down in Florida?" Such a remark is legal enough, but it's hardly conducive to an abiding friendship. In fact, it's hardly conducive to longevity.

"If you are going to write a piece about bad manners, put this in," a fellow townsman insisted. "After a two-day search, I found a bream bed in the Santee and cautiously anchored my boat on the outer fringe. Another boat barged unceremoniously up, brushing my gunwale as it passed, and dropped their hooks alongside mine. They were blundering clowns whose antics soon wised up the bream, and none of us caught anything. When I suggested that we keep our boats away from the bed, one of them said: 'Hell, this is public property, ain't it?' I hope I'll be on the jury when those guys come up for murder."

I have acceded to the request of my fellow townsman and inserted the incident, but I am well aware that some estimable folks don't consider fishing a bream bed altogether good manners either, however time-honored the practice may be in the solid South.

I had a similar experience on Lake Murray a few years back. Catching the water low one fall, I spent half a day piling and weighting brush in a cove to make a crappie rendezvous. Six months later I drifted quietly over my brush pile and began to collect dividends. But before I had strung the third crappie, a passing motorboat came up with full throttle and rammed its prow into my precious brush pile.

Then three men brought out an armful of canes and dropped a dozen minnows alongside mine. In a few minutes their hooks were entangled in the submerged debris. Instead of rigging up other lines, they began to tug, yank, and swear. In ten minutes there was not a crappie within a hundred yards. And not much of my brush pile.

When I gently remonstrated, they unanimously invited me to take a trip, an invitation which I unanimously declined. For a moment I considered a boarding party, but there was only one of me and there were three of them. It was clearly a situation that called for discretion rather than valor. After all, what was a mess of crappies compared to a compound fracture of something or other?

Anybody who would muss up another's fishing like that would skin a flea for its hide and tallow and gallop its carcass through hell for the chitterlings. I hope the cheap skates read what I'm saying about them, but I don't think they are literate enough. It was public water, and they were legally within their rights, as they reminded me. But mere legality is not enough. You can utterly spoil the other man's fishing and be as legal as you please. Mutual consideration and common decency begin where the law ends.

I've seen some notable exhibitions of bad manners on the part of trollers too. I am not, of course, indicting trollers as a whole. But time and again have I seen them roar thoughtlessly into a placid cove-tip where the hook-and-line gentry were plying their trade in frail craft; or where a hopeful bait caster was doing his best to seduce that big lunker into striking again; or mayhap a solitary fly caster was on the verge of enticing a reluctant virgin from the lily pads.

How Good Are Our Fishing Manners?

The cove-tip should be sacred and inviolate to these, our serenity-loving brothers. But up come the trollers, tearing the water into tatters, scaring the fish into the next county, and almost capsizing the small boats of the fisherfolk in the cove. And leaving behind them the maledictions of an erstwhile contented citizenry.

And worse still, I once saw a careless troller swerve so closely inshore that his propeller cut a caster's line in two. It was during the war when casting lines were precious. The aggrieved caster dolefully reeled in his scrap of line and stared fixedly at the retreating boat. Then he slowly shook his head. That gesture alone was a sad commentary on man's inhumanity to man. How many of you have had your feelings ruffled by the unmannerly acts of trollers?

Now people who commit such moral misdemeanors are not necessarily hardened sinners. They may be thoughtless rather than unneighborly. But obviously a little etiquette would not be amiss. I once heard an elegant old gentleman say:

"That young cut-up in the motorboat is having himself a grand time, although he has ruined the fishing of a dozen other people. But he is not necessarily criminal. A body is not born with good manners, you know. Good manners have to be learned, which means they have to be taught. That young fellow's behavior is a reflection on his elders, on those who started him fishing. When we teach our grandsons how to catch fish, we must also teach them how to make friends. Otherwise we are leaving them half-civilized, for what is civilization but good manners?"

Have you ever, while casting contentedly along a shore line, had another boat come from behind and cut in ahead of you? Did you chide the interloper for his barbarous manners, or did you just sit still and let your pancreatic juices run amuck? A fellow who will do a trick like that doesn't know an ethic from a pillowcase.

Any boatman who has an ounce of courtesy also respects the rights and the privacy of bank fishermen. He considerately circles them, not coming close enough to cause them discomfort, to harrow their feelings, or to impair their fishing. A courteous boatman says to himself: If our positions were reversed and they were in the boat, how close would I want them to come? If 20 million of us are going to fish together in harmony, each of us must say to himself: I am going to treat the other fellow as I want him to treat me.

"The unpardonable sin in a fishing companion is grouchiness," one angler contributed. "The first requisite of a companion is companionship. The churlish member who is forever bellyaching can ruin an otherwise pleasant trip."

It is true that grumbling and griping because fish don't bite will hardly endear a man to his companions. I once had a greathearted friend, Reed Smith, whose philosophy I shall not soon forget. Whenever we returned from a bootless trip, he always smiled and said: "The weather was fine, the society pleasant, the conversation brilliant. Thanks for letting me go along."

Whenever I apologized for some particularly fruitless safari, he always said: "It could have been much worse. I once drove 500 miles to shoot ducks and never got a shot." Reed was verily a gentleman and a scholar. May his tribe increase. He is a poor fisherman, indeed, whose pleasure depends solely upon the number of fish he catches.

"The unpardonable sin," said another, "is gluttony. I'm talking about the fellow who takes more than the law allows, more than he needs, or more than his share. I'm talking about the unregenerate hog and show-off that you find now and then in all sports. The man whose sole ambition is to see how much he can catch or kill, with no thought of the morrow or the other fellow. His motto is: 'To hell with everybody but me.'"

"I nominate the gold-bricker," suggested another angler. "The man who doesn't pull his part of the load, who doesn't tote fair with his fellows. I mean the congenital tightwad in every party who is forever sponging on the rest. His wife is always using *his* car, he is always flashing a bill that he knows

How Good Are Our Fishing Manners?

nobody can change, or he always leaves his wallet in his other pants, which he thoughtfully leaves at home."

"No, the unpardonable sin is none of these," sagely remarked a ruddy-cheeked old gentleman with a merry twinkle in his eye.

"What is it, then?"

"The unpardonable sin is breaking the *unwritten law*," he said cryptically.

"And what, may I ask, is the unwritten law?"

"When you go fishing with me, don't catch more fish than I do!"

How to Miss Birds
(In a Few Easy Lessons)

In case you haven't heard, I had a missing streak during the past quail season, a streak that made all others in my long and graceless career look puny by comparison. If you didn't hear about it you were in the minority, because I asked everybody and his Uncle John for advice. I finally recovered from my historic slump, but the remedy was so drastic and unorthodox that it should be recommended only in last-ditch cases.

"Just how bad is your slump?" asked the first friend to whom I repaired for counsel.

"Well, I couldn't hit a taurine in the poopdeck with a horticultural implement," I said, or words to that effect with a minor syntactical substitution here and there. "During the past week I shot 35 times and got 7 birds. A dozen beautifully pointed covies I missed with both barrels, and in the wide open. The 7 birds I did get were unannounced singles that I accidentally knocked up in the thickets. That's the most insulting thing about my slump."

How to Miss Birds

"Right much of a come-down for you," he clucked sympathetically. "Last time we hunted together you clipped 9 out of 10."

"Now don't go harking back to used-to-be's! That's like reminding a fellow with lumbago how good his back felt before he got it."

"Very well. Suppose we get down to brass tacks," he suggested with a professional air. "Are you using the same gun?"

"Same gun."

"Same shells?"

"Same shells. Also same birds," I added as a bitter afterthought.

"Then you must be doing something different," he announced with the finality of a great diagnostician putting his finger on the pathological spot.

"The invincibility of your logic touches me deeply," I said. And I picked up my slump and left. I hoped the touch of old-world courtliness with which I bowed myself out did not go unobserved.

The next day I heard about another gunwise acquaintance. And a very thorough workman he proved to be. Meticulously he measured me from forelock to fetlock and back again, methodically jotting his discoveries in a little book. He measured my hands, my arms, my neck, my shoulders. Even my cubit, which I had never had measured before. And all with an air of professional preoccupation. A doctor would have charged me 25 bucks for such a going-over. Many a jaybird has been classified 1A on less.

With equal thoroughness he addressed his mathematical inquiries to my gun. This fellow would make a crack foreman of a coroner's jury, I thought. Having satisfied himself about the gun, he directed his researches toward my torso again. Arranging me before a large mirror, he said:

"Now aim the gun at your forehead and pull both triggers."

"Won't one trigger be enough?" I asked, demurring a bit. "That left barrel—"

During this suicidal scene he stood behind me, with head cocked like an art connoisseur on the verge of a great discovery. Having never practiced shooting at myself, I am afraid I didn't score too high on this part of the quiz, evincing no doubt a cowardly tendency to flinch. But a generous and perceptive gent he was.

"Well, old man," he beamed, "I have discovered your trouble."

"You have?"

"Precisely. Too much drop."

"Too much drop?"

"Your gun has too much drop for a middling-short neck like yours," he amplified.

"Then what I need is another gun with—"

"My dear fellow," he waxed benevolent, "why incur such needless expense? You see, I happen to be something of a gunsmith, with a little workshop here in my own home. If you'll just leave your gun with me a few days—"

A strange hunger crept into the fellow's eyes. It was a sort of chop-licking gleam somewhere between that of a corporation lawyer sensing a fat fee, and a Bluebeard about to seduce his 15th blonde. With maybe a dash of Oh-Grandmother-what-makes-your-ears-so-big thrown in. I thanked him for his altruism and promised to leave the gun with him later, but I knew I was telling the biggest lie in history.

Funny thing about amateur gunsmiths. Fine people they are the world over—good neighbors who will lend you the very paste off their toothbrushes, upstanding Rotarians with here and there a deacon thrown in, good solid folks who vote the straight ticket and all that. In short, you can trust an amateur gunsmith with your lawnmower, your mandolin, and your wife's shoe-trees. *But never with your gun.*

"Might as well face the facts," I said on my way home. "Looks like I need a new gun. Or a new neck. But I'll give them both another trial before I decide anything. So my neck is middling-short, is it?" I had always assumed, without giving the matter too much thought I admit, that it was

How to Miss Birds

more or less standard. What rules do you go by in classifying necks anyway, I wondered.

The next day was a dismal repetition of the others. Again I ignominiously missed eight pointed birds in the wide open, and bagged two unannounced swampers that went rocketing through the tupelos. Surely, I said, there ought to be somebody—. And there apparently was. A policeman tipped me off to a man across the river who Really Knew Guns. From A to Z. So across the river I hied myself.

Quite a ballistician and collector this fellow proved to be. He had more guns than Carter had oats. And I soon saw that he meant to outdo all his rivals in thoroughness of approach. Sundry parts of my anatomy were minutely measured, unguessed reflexes pried into, and my personal habits given a judicial airing. Again I stood before a mirror and shot myself nicely between the eyes. I had gotten used to committing suicide by this time and hope I acquitted myself better.

"Ah!" the man who Really Knew Guns finally announced, clucking like old Archimedes when he first discovered something else besides water in his bathtub. "We have hit the nail on the head!"

"On the head?" I repeated, for hope springeth eternal in the breast of the slumper.

"Beyond peradventure, my friend. Your gun hasn't got enough drop. You have a middling-long neck, you know, and with insufficient drop you would naturally—"

"Then the thing for me to do—"

"Is to leave your gun with me a few days. You see, I happen to be something of a gunsmith, and we have here in our own little home—"

Oh Grandmother, what makes your *eyes* so big! Come into my parlor, said the spider to the fly. With profuse thanks I picked up my gun, my slump, my neck and left.

"Damn!" I said on the way home. My neck was too short last night, and too long tonight. Versatile cuss, at least. I couldn't think of any use I had put it to overnight that might have stretched it. I had always gotten along with my neck

O.K. In fact, it had been the only part of me that hadn't ever had anything wrong with it. In a general way I suppose I was proud of it, although the matter had never been brought specifically to my attention. Now I was becoming neck-conscious. Anyway I was glad that I had been re-classified. Going around with a sub-standard neck is not the best thing for a man's morale.

A few days later I had an idea that approached brilliance. Maybe my trouble wasn't physical after all. Maybe it was a psychosis, a neurosis or some junk like that. My next door neighbor was a professor of psychology. In fact, the old codger had written a book or two. Besides, he wouldn't have the face to charge me anything. My lawnmower had been over there going on four months.

The professor listened with his best bedside manner, fondling his Phi Beta Kappa key the while. When my tale was told, he said:

"The psychology of the slump is quite intriguing. As I was saying to Professor Jenks only yesterday, my ping pong has undergone a most inexplicable decline during the past fortnight. Psychologically it is most interesting, but—"

"To get back to guns," I brought him back to earth.

"To be sure. Offhand, I'd say you merely have an inferiority complex."

That sounded plausible enough, especially the inferior part. About the complex I wasn't so sure.

"What can I do about this complex?" I pursued.

"Don't worry. Those things cure themselves, sooner or later. When you start hitting birds again, I dare say your complex will disappear. Now about my ping pong slump—"

"Maybe you are trying too hard," I said, and pushed my lawnmower back home.

During the next week I hunted nearly every day, absorbed advice like a sponge, and missed everything that got up in front of me. Except, of course, a few wild shenanigans that bounced up unexpectedly. You may wonder how I found time to do so much finding and missing. Well, hang it, they were

How to Miss Birds

mostly the same birds! It's surprising how a few coveys will last if you just shoot *at* them.

One night I sidled up to a soda counter for another bromo to assuage my miseries. There sat a fat bus driver licking a banana split.

"Hear your shooting is off," he opined.

"Yeah. I hear the same thing," I concurred.

"Maybe you got my old trouble. Had to give up hunting on account of it."

"What was that?" I dully wondered.

"Bifocals."

"Bifocals?" I perked up a bit.

"Yeah. Think right good now. Which part do you shoot through, your uppers or your lowers?"

After the fashion of bifocalers the world over, I bobbed my head up and down, picking out imaginary targets in the drugstore.

"Well," I answered, "when a bird leaves the ground I'm looking through my upper field of vision, which is correct."

"Okey doke. Now when that same bird rises into your shooting zone—?"

I flushed a bird from a case of cod liver oil on the floor and watched it ladder up the shelves, finally clearing a bottle of Lydia E. Pinkham's in the far corner.

"Great balls of fire!" I said. "Do you mean to tell me—"

"Exactly. Unless a man's got a didapper neck, he'll wear himself plumb out a-watching birds zigzag from his uppers to his lowers thataway. Yessir, them bifocals will sure Gawd ruin a man's shooting."

The sweet plausibleness of the idea overcame me, and my spirits soared into the empyrean. I had been knocking at the doors of experts in vain, yet this observing man-of-the-people had infallibly diagnosed my trouble. A tide of brotherly love welled up in me and I set the bus driver up to two more banana splits. I came home and aimed my gun all over the place to confirm the great discovery. Then I took Alice out and treated her to a four-buck lobster dinner. Life was suddenly sweet again.

The next day I had a pair of old-fashioned single-lenses made, using only my distance prescription. Now I could really see all over the world! Then I promised birds all over the neighborhood and jumped into my car. Those saucy covies that I had lulled into security were headed for a rude awakening!

But I came home that night feeling two grades lower than a corporal's orderly. My wonderful glasses made no difference whatever. I still missed shots a left-handed boy could have bagged with a set of dominos. I was beginning to rue the largess of that second banana split, and that Maine lobster I had squandered on Alice.

"By the way," remarked Alice, who is usually about two days late in her inspirations, "weren't those bifocals you discarded the same ones you shot so well with last season?"

"Aw, go to hell," I invited.

But she wouldn't even do that.

Now some of you will wonder how a man of my apparent intelligence could be such a sucker for advice. But a drowning man grabs at a straw. There are only three kinds of people who will believe absolutely anything you tell them: slumpers, boarding-school girls just turned 16, and voters on election day. Surely there must be somebody in the crowd who has had a kindred experience and can conjure up a little fellow-feeling!

I had now absorbed so much advice, both oral and written, that my shooting had become quite a ceremony. Also something of a memory test, since I had so many tips, admonitions, and scraps of advice to rehearse before slipping the safety catch. Whenever a dog pointed. I began automatically to check off the do's and don't's on my list. It was quite a memorandum that I had accumulated.

Having gone through my rehearsal with great fidelity and punctiliousness, I would step victoriously forward and miss with both barrels. The ordeal was then over, except for the

How to Miss Birds

post mortems, which usually lasted until the dogs pointed again. I had become such a fatalist that I missed before I shot, and found myself almost wishing that I didn't have to shoot at all. Heck, I said, I'd better quit before I become a darned blinker!

While all this slumping was taking place I hunted alone for two reasons: first, because my disgrace was bad enough without an audience; and secondly, because Dr. Jim Havers, my hunting companion for 20 years, was away during the first three weeks of the season. When Jim did get back I was so dejected that a proposed two-day hunt in the birdy low-country left me unmoved.

"Take somebody along who can shoot," I said, magnanimous in my grief. "Leave me alone with my miseries."

Never a loquacious fellow at best, Jim said nothing, just kept packing my things in his car. Two hours later Fleet and Tobey were pointing in a low-country peafield, and Jim beckoned me alongside.

"Wait until I get fixed," I pleaded.

Straightway I went into a rehearsal of the do's and don't's I had accumulated, anxiously ransacking my memory for additional scraps of advice that might save the day. I even shadow-boxed with my gun a few times to make sure of my timing and coordination. Then I stepped up and missed 18 birds with both barrels. It was quite a feat.

Jim didn't say anything because he was a gentleman. I didn't say anything because I didn't have anything to say. Like the boy the calf ran over. As I trudged along the uselessness of life hit me afresh, and I felt terribly alone in the world. After a while Jim lit his pipe and casually opened up.

"Tell me," he said, "have you been getting any advice about this slump? Talked with anybody, or read any books about shooting?"

"I've talked to everybody who would listen, and listened to everybody who would talk," I reassured him. "And I've read three books on shooting, including a piece I wrote myself some ten years ago. Thought it was pretty good too," I shamelessly admitted.

"In other words, you've become a walking encyclopedia on shooting, haven't you?"

Our dogs next pointed at the edge of a cypress pond, where the shooting would be fast and tricky. The covey, having been trailed a hundred yards, had scuttled under a brushpile, around which our dogs were expectantly frozen.

"Wait," I interrupted, "until I get fix—"

Suddenly Jim Havers ran amock. With a yell like that of an Indian brave being bereft of his family jewels, he bounded forward and came crashing down atop the brushpile. The birds underneath took off as if the Devil had a mortgage on their tails and went swooshing through the treetops. It was the best close-up of jet-propulsion I had ever seen.

"Of all the damned fool things! I told you I wasn't ready!" I exploded.

"You're not going to be hereafter either. I'll see to that. Now pick up your two birds, you shingle-butted old idiot!" grinned Jim, unscrambling himself from the brushpile.

"You mean I got a double? Why, I don't even remember—"

"That's why you got them. I didn't even shoot," he said, breaking his gun as evidence.

"But what prompted you to do a fool thing like that?"

"Everybody gets into a slump now and then—except the fellow who stays in one," he explained. "The best thing to do with a slump is to let it alone, if it's an honest-to-goodness slump. It will cure itself sooner or later. But you, being a superior sort of idiot, decided to hurry yours up. The result was an overdose of advice. When a man has been doing something reasonably well, it doesn't pay him to become too analytical about how he does it. You've just been thinking too much before you shot."

"Could that be the reason I miss the easy, deliberate shots and get those that catch me offguard?" I asked hopefully.

"Exactly. Now quit thinking and go to shooting. To make

How to Miss Birds

sure you do, I'm going to jump slam-bang onto every bird that's pointed this morning."

He did just that, the butt-headed and benevolent cuss, and I shot as in my palmiest pre-slump days. By noon his jumping antics were no longer necessary. I mentally did the jumping myself, walking up briskly and shooting fast, *before I had time to think.*

By nightfall we both had a jacketful of birds, and as we cruised slowly homeward we agreed that this old world, in spite of the ills that beset it, was still a pretty good place for two half-cracked birdhunters to be in.

"You know," Jim philosophized between puffs, "sometimes thinking is the worst thing a man can do."

When a Lady Undresses

It was a dismal afternoon. It had been misting for two days, a warm October mist, and the earth was sodden and fogbound. The weather was preordained for grading themes, the poorest pastime the mind of mortal man ever conjured up. Our radio announced the humidity was 99. It could go on and attain perfection if it would be any happier, I perversely reflected. I was standing at the window, absently watching a bedraggled sparrow trying to lift a scrap of ribbon from the driveway, when the telephone rang.

"What are you doing, Doc?" It was the quiet voice of Tip Hazzard.

"Nothing in particular. Just moping around and contemplating self-destruction if this weather keeps up. I'd planned to go fishing, but of course—"

"Can you run with me out to the pond awhile? I left something out there that I need right bad."

"You surely picked a cheerful day to do your forgetting," I grumped.

When a Lady Undresses

"Didn't I. And bring your rod along. Just in case."

When we reached the pond it was still misting. The sky was overcast and lowering. Patches of fog lay low over the water, rising here and there in slow swirls.

"You sit in front," suggested Tip. "I'll paddle across to where I left it. And take your rod and that pink-bellied top-water. Just in case."

"What did you leave that's got to be recovered in such headlong haste? And when, pray, did you leave it?"

"Laros catch meddlers! Get in," he tersely ordered.

The boat seat was puddling wet, and there was no cushion. I plopped my reluctant rump down suddenly to get it over with—and felt sort of self-conscious and ashamed for several minutes thereafter. The boat tipped a small water-soaked gum. An overloaded branch disburdened itself and sent the cold water cascading down my backbone as I humped over my tackle box. Rather be at home fussing over nouns and pronouns or squabbling with Alice, I dejectedly decided.

"Let it drop on that low cypress stump," Tip said, easing up on his paddle.

"Do what?"

"On that cypress stump, 80 feet to your left. And flip it gently into the water. If old Grampa can do it!" he grinned amiably.

"A grandpapa can do anything a papa can do. Especially out-of-doors," I countered.

I dropped the top-water soundlessly on the sodden stump, flipped it into the water, and let it execute a few trial didos. A patch of fog drifted between me and the capering plug. There was a resounding smack. No, not really a smack at all. I've just been reading too many books. That's not the way a really big bass strikes.

Your three- or four-pound sophomores smack resoundingly. But your real fish, your juggernauts, your deans and full professors sort of roll ponderously and engulf your lure. I sensed rather than saw a heavy swirl, and set the hook with a spirited yank. It became immediately apparent that something feet out there in the fog, something massive and powerfully set in its ways, had no interest whatever in going with me home.

Now I would like to say that I played the quarry with great dexterity and skill, adroitly depressing and elevating the rod tip in anticipation of its every maneuver, artfully pitting brain against brawn, and that after a gallant battle of 34 minutes, during which I remained as composed as a horse opera cardsharp holding four aces, I boated a 12-pounder and had it mounted for the delectation of posterity.

That's what I'd like to say. But it would be a masterpiece of prevarication. In fact, it would be a monumental lie. Now I am not saying what it would be if *you* told it. You are the custodian of your own conscience. I'm just saying it's a lie when I tell it.

I've never hung a 10-pounder yet without being scared to death until I had him in the boat, with my scrawny buttocks astraddle his floundering carcass. I might as well be honest about it. In my long and sinful life I have had many a 10- or 12-pounder *play me,* but I'll just be damned if I have ever intentionally played *him*! It is too late in life—and I am too well known—to start being a hero now.

Anyway, I vigorously addressed myself to the task of abridging the distance between the fish and me. A few minutes later —not many—Tip leaned over the gunwale, thrust a hand into a cavernous jaw, and hoisted our passenger aboard. It was a nice bass, not a belt-holder exactly, but a right considerable fish. About an associate professor, I'd rate him, who might have become a dean had he looked after his p's and q's and gone to church regularly.

"How much will he go?" I asked.

Tip hefted him a speculative heft or two. "In the discriminating phraseology of you outdoor writers, he is somewhere between a lunker, a behemoth and a leviathan. Which would put him in the neighborhood of eight pounds."

"Now you get up here and make a few passes at 'em," I offered.

When a Lady Undresses

"No. We've worn our welcome out for the present. After that fracas your bass raised, the customers in this corner will be a wee skittish. We'd better sashay down to the ledge and come back here later."

"By the way," I remembered, "what was it you left here and came back to get? Something you needed badly, you said."

"Could have been the one you just landed, but it felt more like his uncle. I'm always needing a fish like that."

"Do you mean that you were here fishing this morning in this soupy weather, and that you lost a big bass? Why, you double-dealing, two-timing—"

"In that brush pile," Tip nodded eloquently.

"But fish aren't supposed to bite in this weather. It's about the worst day in the year, and you know it," I complained.

"Ain't it though! I've been waiting weeks for it. Just about made to order," he rhapsodized.

"What do you mean?"

"Although this place is heavily fished, a respectable bass is seldom taken, and the pond is generally regarded as fishless. Yet you and I know that there are big bass here aplenty. They just don't bite on the beautiful sunny days that people fish for them. A fisherman is a self-centered sort of person anyway. When he says it's a beautiful day to go fishing, he means from *his* point of view, not from the fish's point of view. Now do you admit that a fish has a point of view?" he challenged.

"I'll admit anything if you'll just keep talking. And hand me the other paddle. It's a quarter of a mile to the ledge."

"This water is exceptionally clear," Tip resumed. "You can see a plug three or four feet deep. To the fish it must be something like a mirror, especially on sunny days when the surface is calm. They can see a moving boat a hundred yards away, can see the motion of your arm when you are casting, a plug arcing through the air. Haven't you ever seen the startled jump of a fish before your plug hit? Yes, these clearwater bass become boat-wise and man-wary."

"Keep preaching on that same text," I encouraged. "My attention is what you might call rapt. In the meanwhile, let's put more elbow grease into our paddles. That ledge—"

"Clear water, when sunlit and still, allows the customer too close an examination of your merchandise," he continued. "A cagey bass can detect phony offerings and synthetic glamour. But on a dark, foggy day like this, when the water is rain-splattered, Mr. Big's eyesight is not so good. He is off guard and unsuspicious. You can sell him a wooden nutmeg, if it has a ribbon around it."

"You mean he figures that nobody would be damned fool enough to be fishing in such abominable weather, and therefore lets his guard down? Well, there's an old codger on the Waccamaw who fishes only on Tuesdays. Says fish are less suspicious then. Gives them Monday to recover from their week-end disillusionment."

"Can't say I subscribe to the Tuesday theory," Tip smiled indulgently, "but the first rule of fishing is *not to let the fish know they are being fished for*. They are naturally somewhat off guard in weather like this because they don't figure anybody has designs on them. When a fine lady is undressing on a beautiful summer night, she is careful about pulling down her shades. But if the night is black and stormy—. Get my point?"

"Get it, but don't like it. Your figure of speech is ungentlemanly. I reject any suggestion of similarity between a micklemouthed, pot-bellied bass and a lissome lady in her negligee on a moonlight night," I gallantly defended.

"Of course," continued Tip, unimpressed by my chivalry, "there might be another factor involved. Bass are of all fish the most scatterbrained and unpredictable. It may be that the unregenerate sons of Belial feed in weather like this just because they like to. Anyway, a fact is a fact, and it is a mistake to get too analytical about something that already suits you. Besides, there's the ledge ahead, and if you will pass the word on to your paddle—"

The black pool undercutting the base of the ledge was a

When a Lady Undresses

favorite place for the old alumni to hold their class reunions. More than once we had seen the bay-windowed gents lolling in their arm-chairs, but we had never been able to sell them any nutmegs.

Tip dropped his top-water soundlessly on the wet rock, deftly flipped it into the water, and put Little Egypt through a few provocative gyrations. Tip could make the little strumpet show her panties as coyly as an ingénue. A four-pounder smacked lustily, came up to see how things looked on topside once or twice, and was added to our passenger list.

"Lunker class," commented Tip. "You know, there was a heavy-bodied swirl before that fish hit. Made by something else. Maybe Junior there beat his old man to the draw. We ought to play a return engagement here about dark. But it's your turn now, so hand me the paddle. I'll take you to the cypress log at the tip of the island."

"What about a few more passes around the ledge?" I suggested.

"Help yourself, but it's probably useless. They know they're being fished for."

It didn't take long to convince me his diagnosis was right, and we headed for the tiny island, our boat ghosting silently through the deepening fog. When Tip and I are fishing from a small boat, only one of us casts at a time. There are never two lures in the water. Tip has a theory that it's one of the things one man can do best, that one caster will take twice as many fish as two. It's a pretty sound theory, I suppose. Too many cooks spoil the broth. So we regularly take turn-about with rod and paddle.

At the tip of the island a bass *whooshed* at my top-water so hard the hooks jangled, and Little Egypt tightened up her garters. Two feet nearer he *whooshed* and missed again. Whew! I whewed. Would he hit a third time? If this sort of thing kept up long, the strongest characters would crumble. Little Egypt lay on her back and panted for a moment, then switched her hips seductively and started crawling toward me. *Whoosh!* And this time the pitcher had gone to the well too often. A three-pounder joined his disillusioned brethren in the boat.

"A spirited young cuss, wasn't he?" admired Tip. "Now if you'll give me another whack at that precious brush pile—"

Fifteen minutes later Tip humped motionless in the prow, idly balancing his rod and biding his time. The brush pile outlined itself in the fog ahead, and I eased off. With a flick of his wrist, Tip sent a long cast arcing through the air. Deftly pinching the line with his thumb, he feathered the plug down within a scant foot of the brush pile.

There it lay motionless and inert for a minute. For two minutes. For three—and then the battered old jade that Tip wouldn't swap for a horse and buggy impudently switched her hips, leered brazenly over her shoulder, and started down the street. There was a ponderous roll, a heavy *thwump*, and Tip stood up and addressed himself to the business at hand.

"Pretty fancy old rooster I got here," he said. "Seems to have notions of his own. Keep easing the boat away from that blessed brush pile."

A pretty fancy old rooster he was, around nine pounds I estimated as I lifted him into the boat. Maybe a shade better.

"Let me see that gent's mouth," said Tip.

Prying the jaws apart, he studied them minutely for a moment. "I'm not asking anybody to believe it, but just for the sake of science, this is the same fish I hooked and lost here this morning. I had him alongside the boat and noticed precisely how he was hooked."

"I've a notion that happens oftener than people think," I corroborated.

"Somehow I can't get that ledge off my mind. We've got time to make it by dark if we lean against the whiffletrees. Let's go," suggested Tip.

The mist had now become a steady drizzle, falling in a monotonous patter on the water. Apparently it had set in for the night. Darkness was settling like a visible cloak upon the water, and the blackest of black nights would soon en-

When a Lady Undresses

velop the pond. By the time we reached the ledge, the rock was almost indistinguishable in the gathering gloom.

My first cast overreached itself and had to be snatched free from debris alongside the rock. My second brushed lightly against the rock and pluffed precisely into the pool, and my fisherman's instinct told me that I had the old master of ceremonies himself on 90 feet of line. Have you ever had an argument with a big bass in the dark? If you have, you know the wave of helplessness that washes over you.

But Mr. Big and I were adjusting our differences pretty well. Stubbornly he headed for the log jam on my left, for the rocky ledge ahead, for the stump-studded shore line, but was effectually turned each time as Tip expertly maneuvered the boat. Then as if suddenly resigned and docile, he allowed himself to be brought alongside the boat. But as Tip carefully fingered for his mouth, he zoomed under the boat like a Missouri mule with the bit in its teeth.

My line slackened so suddenly I almost toppled backward. I reeled in the limp line and fingered the break. He had absconded with 15 feet of good nylon.

"That line hung something in the boat. I heard it *zing*!" thought Tip. From his tackle box he produced a pencil flashlight. "There it is—a jagged nail that some bream fisherman drove in the boat. There's a scrap of line still around it."

I wasn't happy about it, of course, but I wasn't altogether unhappy either. The fish I remember most vividly are those I didn't quite bring home. We had fish aplenty anyway. If a fellow killed every bird he shot at, or landed every fish that bit—

A hundred yards across the pond there was a mighty *suwash! suwash!* The abdominous old glutton didn't like that hot tamale he had bitten into and was trying to spit it out. In a day or so I'd likely find my beloved top-water floating.

"I wanted to see you land that golly-whopper," consoled Tip, then added cryptically, "but I can't imagine anything duller than getting what you want."

Back at the landing, we put the car lights on and admired

our string in the drenching downpour—a nine-pounder, an eight, a four and a three, about all a man wanted to tote. With the rain sluicing over our faces, we grinned like pranking schoolboys in an attic.

"How is your corporosity sagaciating, Grandpa?" Tip asked. "And how do you like fishing in the rain?"

That corporosity business produced a wide grin. When I was a country boy in Virginia 35 years ago it was the way one dude greeted another. Ultra-slick stuff, we considered it.

"My corporosity is O.K.," I replied. "And as for the weather, it's been the worst of days, and the best of days. I am as wet as a pair of flannel drawers in a washtub. Water is running out my ears, squidging out my shoe tops, sluicing down my back and spouting off my tail bone. And I never felt better in my life."

"Will it give you a cold?" asked Tip.

"No, and that's an oddity that might interest the medical profession. I never catch cold from getting wet *if I have had a good time getting wet*. It's a gospel fact."

Since that initial experience, I have repeatedly verified the soundness of what might be called foul-weather fishing. And I have asked other bass fishermen about it. Billy Fisher, one of the most astute anglers of my acquaintance despite his total blindness, kept a minute record of the exact weather conditions under which he caught fish for 15 years. This 15-year record furnished the raw material for several surmises, Billy says, and one scientific fact: that, especially in clear-water ponds, bass feed actively during a warm rain. The next best time, his log shows, is when a warm breeze is ruffling the surface of the water.

There are some rains that are uncongenial, however. I have never induced bass to strike *immediately* after a flooding downpour that sends the water roaring over spillways. A few days should be allowed for the water to become homogenized and return to normal temperature. I don't relish an electric storm either. It is unsafe, and I think profitless, to cast for bass when the earth is quaking and the skies are

When a Lady Undresses

rent overhead. Fish go down and bide the passing of the storm.

A kind of rain I do like is the brisk, quick-passing storm in the spring—the April showers that bring May flowers. Right after such a rain, the fish will follow you home—almost. But the best fishing rain in the whole repertoire of the master showman, J. Pluvius, is the Devil-is-beating-his-wife variety. All of us have witnessed this phenomenon: the spirited shower that streams down through the bright sunshine. "The Lord is using his sprinkling pot," my lovely mother used to say.

There comes a time in every man's life when he is either going to go fishing or do something worse. It is a sort of safety valve that keeps him from exploding. So I often go regardless of weather or what the fish's point of view might be.

But sometimes on beautiful sunny days, when almost every other car that passes my house bears the indubitable stamp of *pisces*, I sit at home in strange contentment. I grade my papers, work on income tax returns, and sing Oh-do-you-know-the-muffin-man with my three-year-old granddaughter —and dream of the dismal, fogbound days that Indian summer is sure to bring.

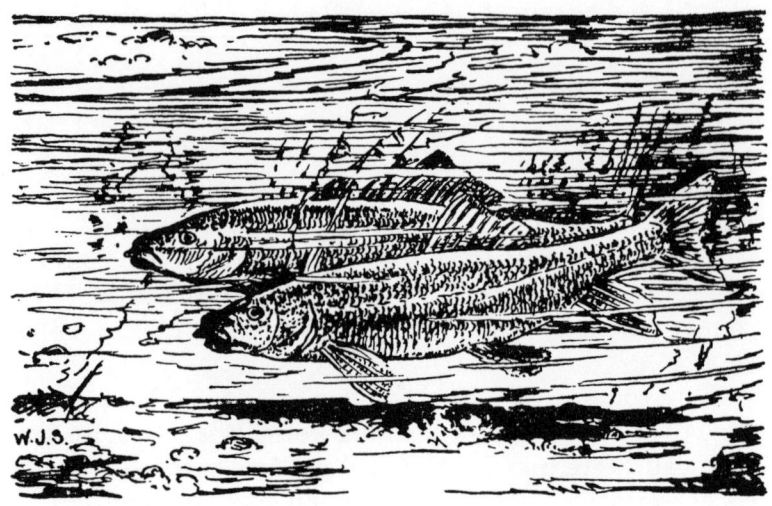

You Can't Go Back Again

Last spring, while minnow fishing for bass, I looked at the big sucker on my hook and grinned reminiscently.

It was a nice day for daydreaming. There was a midsummer mellowness in the air, and all about me the lushness of a prodigal June. Pulling a battered hat over my eyes, I lay half-dozing in the sun like a lazy lizard. Over my head a squirrel peevishly scolded a trespassing jay bird. A hickory nut ricocheted down the tree, thumping solidly from limb to limb. It was the kind of day that takes one back. Again I lifted the big sucker speculatively.

"Yessir, I would have done it as sure as shooting," I said.

And I would have. If I had caught a sucker that big when I was a branch-fishing boy in Virginia, I would have scampered home and had my prize in the frying pan within 10 minutes. Yessir, I would have been content to rest on my laurels with one like that.

Every country boy is entitled to a creek. If no creek is

You Can't Go Back Again

handy, maybe a meandering branch will do for awhile. But it must have a few holes that he can't see the bottom of. That is an absolute requisite, and there is no getting around it.

Mine was a creek by courtesy. I could jump across it anywhere without ripping my pants in the seat, which was the standard way of judging a jump in those days. But it was the best creek I could afford, and to a nine-year-old it was a thing of perennial mystery and enchantment. His journeyings up and down its lazy length are still vivid after the wear of 40 years.

For in my branch there were eels aplenty, an occasional sucker and fallfish in the spring, and little perch that shone like a queen's jewel in the sun. And there were horny-headed chubs galore. Ah, there was a fish for you! The spunky little hornyhead was preordained by Providence for a country boy to catch.

It is the black bass of the branches, the sparkling gamester of the foam-flecked eddies. And the fanciest biter that ever set a boy's nerves atingle and his imagination afire. What could put a tiny cork through such antics and didos as this agile dancing master! What would charge a cricket with such verve and derring-do!

Nor were they so small as one might think. Why, I used to bring them home all of seven inches long! And there was one memorable day when I hooked a nine-inch leviathan and pridefully carved my initials on a big sycamore to signalize the event. Why this urge to authorship I know not, since there were no other boys in the neighborhood to peruse my handiwork, and since there was no possibility of my ever forgetting it anyway.

I am quite sure, too, that the hornyhead is the most savory little pan fish in the wide, wide world. Since cutting my apron strings from the little branch years and years ago, I have sampled all manner of pan fish that were far-famed for their palatability, fish that epicures and gourmets argue endlessly about, but upon my word as a gentleman, the hornyhead of my boyhood was without a peer.

Of course, some of their unrivaled flavor might have been due to their freshness, for they were usually dropped into a pan with sizzling butter almost before they had stopped wriggling. And some of their savoriness might have been due to the heartiness of a country boy's appetite. For is it not written that hunger is the best *hors d'oeuvre?*

Mine was an easily discouraged little branch. In dry weather, you could see the bottom almost anywhere. Obviously there was no point in fishing where you could see what was biting. Also what *wasn't* biting. So I would go above and muddy the water, then return to my hole and fish contentedly. As long as I couldn't see the bottom, there was at least a possibility of getting a bite. Of course, *you* never did anything as silly as that.

After attaining to man's estate, I was saddened to learn that muddying-the-water is a practice to which adults are also addicted. I shall never forget hearing a great scholar say to his eager young students: "Gentlemen, whenever I appear to be deep, you may be quite sure that I am merely muddy."

When I was 11, a hired man on our farm gave me a recipe for catching everything in a hole at one fell swoop. Like most great ideas, it was simple.

"Jus' take an earthen jug, fill it with water and lime, and plug it up tight. Then mosey up to the hole, drop it in, and run like who-laid-the-rail," he advised.

The next day I dropped my lime-filled jug into the Round Hole, scampered up the hill, and cowered behind a log. With palms jammed against my ears, I waited for an earth-rocking explosion. The longest minute in history passed. Cautiously peeping over the log, I saw that which froze the very marrow in my bones. A calf had ambled up and was contentedly drinking over the death-laden spot.

I had grisly visions of trying to explain away a whole calf. But after a tentative sip or two, the little trespasser sauntered away and my heart began to beat again. The explosion never

You Can't Go Back Again

came. I must have put slaked lime into my atom bomb. But for weeks thereafter I skirted Round Hole at a respectful distance in fear of a belated cataclysm.

In the spring suckers would migrate upstream, threading their way even to the upper reaches of my branch. One illustrious day in May I landed a 14-inch behemoth, and was so surcharged with excitement that I ran all the way home. My stormy entrance into the kitchen caused the light-rolls to fall, and an indignant sister dusted the seat of my pants. But that was a small scimption.

I toted that sucker all over the neighborhood for people to see. In fact, I wore my prize smack out showing it off and let it spoil on my hands. It was the champion catch of my boyhood, the high-water mark of my prowess. All suckers looked small to me thereafter.

Suckers bit phlegmatically and tediously at best. They were diffident fish, not liking to eat in the presence of people. The best way to catch them, I discovered, was to go off and forget about your hook. When I grew tired of sucker fishing, I would squat by a likely run and waylay a gleaming migrant as it thrashed its way upstream, switching it into submission with willow branches.

Our farm was in the dark tobacco section of Virginia, and I was initiated into the mysteries of tobacco-suckering at a tender age. It was fun at first because my father bragged of my adeptness. I felt that I had to manhood grown. But day after day in a grueling July sun made me rue my aspirations toward manhood.

When the "heat monkeys" danced before my eyes and the unsuckered rows stretched dishearteningly ahead, I would sometimes run forward a hundred yards, hastily sucker a few plants, and run back so I could enjoy thinking about the "skip" ahead. I was not above this pleasant self-deception in my corn-thinning either. Of course, you never did anything as hair-brained as this when you were a boy.

At discreet intervals, I would sneak downhill to the branch and fish a few minutes. Had it not been for such precious interludes, I would have died of old age at nine. But sometimes my father, chancing to pass the tobacco field, would miss my bobbing head between the rows and issue an imperious summons for my return. Invariably my dereliction was discovered at the most inopportune moment—just when I was about to get a bite.

After as long an interval of silence as considerations of prudence warranted, I would holler "I'm a-coming!" and put on my hat. Then a furious spell of nibbling was sure to set in, and I would tensely await the final downward plop till the last second of safety. Those stolen moments were perhaps the sweetest and the most anguishing of my life.

But I haunted the branch only during the hours of daylight. Nothing could have induced me to venture near at night because of a vague and marrow-chilling fear. It was the fear of "lamp-eels." Now I had never seen a lamp-eel. I had never seen anybody who had seen one. But I had heard that they roamed the creek banks at night, seeking whom they might devour like the fabled dragons of old.

Their eyes gleamed eerily in the blackness, their bite was the most deadly thing known. They were the *bête noire* of my boyhood, the raw material of many a nightmare. Not until I had left the little branch far behind did I learn that the lamp-eel was a figment of somebody's imagination, for the lamprey, which presumably inspired the direful stories, is altogether harmless.

Perhaps the crowning disappointment of my boyhood was my failure to drain Cave Hole. Here the current of my branch angled sharply, undermining a clump of sycamores and leaving a dark and mystic pool which my imagination peopled with all manner of alien dwellers. It was here that I always got strange bites and always got my hook hung. It was here that I caught the giant eel that almost outmanned me. And it was here that I had the unforgettable encounter with the biggest fish any boy in this world ever saw.

I had hooked the sullen monster under the bank and tugged it to the surface, where it lay for a moment rigid and

You Can't Go Back Again

unresisting. Its slate-colored back protruded from the water, and its incredible length stretched half-across the pool. It was bigger than I had ever dreamed a fish could be. And there it lay almost within reach of my very hands. Then there was a sudden downward draft, my line snapped, and the juggernaut plowed heavily under the bank. For some time I stood limp and nerveless, staring ruefully at the broken line, gazing fascinatedly into the depths of the pool. Then I galloped all the way home.

I told the hired man. He smiled. I told my older brothers. They smiled. I told my father, who chided me for stretching my blankets. Throughout the household, my epic story fell on incredulous ears. Everybody discounted it as merely the figment of my imagination.

That night I lay for hours bewailing my witlessness, conjuring up all sorts of expedients now that it was too late. Why hadn't I used the stouter line in my pocket? Why hadn't I maneuvered the fish into shallow water? Why hadn't I jumped spraddle-legged into the water and bodaciously grabbed it? Why hadn't I—? But self-reproach was of no avail now.

Very well, I said grimly. I would convince the skeptics yet. I would spend the whole of next day fishing in Cave Hole—the whole of next week and the whole of next month if necessary. But would the big fish be likely to bite again, with the hook imbedded in its mouth? And if it rained and got the branch up—

With the great clarity that accompanies inspiration, I hit upon a plan for encompassing the downfall of my adversary and putting my detractors to shame. It would involve a little engineering and maybe a certain amount of work, but what could be neater or surer? I went to sleep congratulating myself.

The following morning I sneaked down to the branch with an ax, a shovel, and a grubbing hoe. Carefully I checked the feasibility of my plan. Yes, I would cut a diversion ditch from above Cave Hole into the branch below, run the entire flow through my ditch, and thus block off the hole altogether. Then I could dip the water out at my leisure, and Mr. Sassy would fall into my hands like an overripe plum.

I fell to work with great gusto. The ditch would not have to be more than 18 feet long. Anybody could dig a ditch like that. But I soon discovered that what looked like soft, yielding earth was a remorseless network of roots and rocks. After three hours of backbreaking work, I sat down and put on my thinking cap. Maybe I could inveigle the hired man into lending me a hand. Swiftly I inventoried the inducements I might offer. Then I trudged across the field to try a little bargaining.

Walking barefooted in the cooling furrow, I offered the hired man successively my pocketknife and my snakeskin belt; my trained rooster, Johnny Jump-Up by name; my three blue Andalusian hens; and finally, in a burst of reckless prodigality, the bull calf my grandfather had given me. "I ain't got no time for such foolishment," he said, and kept plowing.

I went back and addressed myself to my engineering project with do-or-die determination. But three hours later I sorrowfully surveyed my progress and found it negligible indeed. Tossing aside the broken shovel, I slumped to the ground and sobbed miserably, the most defeated and heart-sick boy in the world.

"God, can't you help me just a *little?*" I pleaded. "Don't you see what a fix I'm in? If you'll stick by me now, I'll start all over and . . ." But I couldn't get up a trade with God either.

During that night a heavy storm descended, swept away all vestiges of my handiwork, and presumably the behemoth of Cave Hole. The mystery was never solved. After 40 years, I'd still give right much to know what the strange monster was and how it got into my branch.

Life was simple in those days. In the morning, you stepped into your pants and you were ready for the day's business. At night, you stepped out of your pants and you were ready

You Can't Go Back Again

for the night's business. You slept in your shirt. Pajamas hadn't been invented, not for country boys anyway. Nor such refinements as neckties, music lessons and toothbrushes.

But life was not altogether an unalloyed pleasure. There was the nightly ordeal by water, for instance. Before jumping into bed, I must go into the kitchen and scrub the day's accumulation from my feet. It was gall and wormwood to me. Besides, it was such an extravagance. Hadn't I been wading in the branch all day? But it was a ritual that was rigidly observed, one that I always delayed to the last bitter moment, and one that I was rarely ingenious enough to circumvent.

How I loved to curl up across the foot of my mother's bed and doze while the family talked around the big fireplace! It was perhaps the most untroubled sleep I have ever known. But all too soon I would hear the uncompromising voice of my father: "Get up and wash your feet!"

Then sometimes the gentle and understanding voice of my mother: "Homer, the poor boy is so tired tonight. He has been fishing hard all day long. Let's not wake him."

I would lie there all unheeding and doing my best to look pitiful, hoping my mother's intercession would avail. Sometimes it would. My father would pick me inertly up, deposit me on the trundle bed, and cover me up. And how I would lie there in the dark and chuckle over the success of my theatrics!

After I had grown up and left home, I often thought of this oft-enacted lie with a twinge of conscience. I finally decided to confess my 'possum-playing to my father, who later became proud of me and would have enjoyed the joke hugely. But alas, I waited too long.

The trundle bed was quite a contrivance, and a masterpiece of household economy. During the day you trundled it under your parents' bed and everything was shipshape and tidy. At night you trundled it out again, and there was a wide low bed that you wouldn't roll off. Admirably simple, really. And how it enabled a household to stretch its guest accommodations! Its reintroduction might accomplish wonders toward solving the housing shortage.

The trundle bed fell into desuetude along with the old-fashioned parlor, another institution that had much to recommend it. With the austere portraits of countless uncles and aunts looking down, the sedate old horsehair sofa, and the innocent stereopticon on the table, the parlor was a much safer place to court in than a night club or a rumble seat.

Our parlor was a sort of *sanctum sanctorum* forbidden to small boys except on rare occasions, and then on the most punctilious behavior. It was always immaculate and untouchable. You instinctively tiptoed when you got inside.

My favorite employment of a Sunday afternoon was looking through the stereopticon at such slides as Consider-the-lilies-of-the-field-how-they-grow-They-toil-not-neither-do-they-spin-Yet-I-say-unto-you-that-Solomon-in-all-his-glory-was-not-arrayed-like-one-of-these. This inscription was meaningless but awfully impressive, and I tried in vain to extract some moral lesson from it.

When I was 12 we left the farm, and the subsequent course of my life took me far from the little branch. My love of fishing grew keener with the passing years, led me into strange and untraversed places, and brought me a rather full and adventurous life. But I never forgot the branch.

Last summer, after the lapse of nearly 40 packed years, I found myself on the old Virginia homestead again. This is fine, I said. I was young, and now I am old. I will revisit the wonderful branch of my boyhood. I will recapture the ineffable flavor of long ago. I will take a frying pan along and a hook for hornyheads, and make of it a sentimental journey. And I will go alone. The pleasure is not one to be shared with another.

With a pocketful of worms and a neat cane under my arm, I ambled jauntily down the familiar slope. There stood the welcoming sycamores as of old. And just below them . . . I stopped in befuddlement and stared about me. Where was my branch?

You Can't Go Back Again

At my feet was a straight ditch, in which a beaten stream flowed dully. Gone were the well-remembered pools, the foam-flecked eddies, and the noisy little cascades that had made up my branch. In their place was an efficient ditch, in which there were no signs of fish. It was a nice job of engineering, no doubt, but it wasn't my branch. I was suddenly a stranger among strangers, standing embarrassed in the presence of my own boyhood.

Packing up my things, I trudged sorrowfully up the hill as one disinherited. And not once did I look back. Somehow I had suddenly grown old.

My friends and brothers, you can't go back again!

The Earthworm Cometh

I was lying contentedly in my barrel-stave hammock perusing the *Sayings of Epictetus,* hoping therefrom to pick up a scrap of culture to show off in class, when Alice ambled up with a jar of wigglers from her camellia bed. A wiggler is prime panfish bait anyway, but a wiggler extracted from a camellia bed, either because of its pampered existence or the acidity of the soil, is the most fetching and flavorsome of all earthworms. My resolutions toward self-improvement straightway went a-glimmering and I went a-bluegilling.

It has been that way all my life. Whenever I set about improving my mind, somebody chanced along with a fishingpole or a bird-dog, and the book was closed for that day. As a result I am more at home outside of houses than inside, and my scholarly attainments have remained modest indeed.

Fishing worms turn into lightning-bugs during the summer, a black snake draped across a railfence will invariably make it rain, and a snapping turtle will hold you until it

The Earthworm Cometh

thunders. If you didn't believe these things when you were young, and if you haven't a sneaking suspicion that they might still be true, you have never been a country boy. For these were universally accepted facts, evidence whereof was not lacking. In the summertime when fishing worms were scarcest, lightning bugs were most plentiful. Ergo, they turned. Who could refuse such logic as that?

However blissfully unscientific some of our ideas were, we were right about one thing: a fat juicy worm was "de bonus good" for branch and creek-fishing. Indeed, it never occurred to us that fishing worms had any other function, that the Lord had anything else in mind when he fashioned them. The term *earthworm* we had never heard, and the more sophisticated *angleworm* did not swim into my ken until I had my own buggy-whip and started parting my hair in the middle.

Now, after thirty-five years of experimenting with nearly every kind of finny temptation nature could conjure up or the cunning of man devise, I have returned to my boyhood conviction: the common, unfurbished, unheralded, and unconcerned earthworm is the finest all-round fish bait in the whole wide world.

Certain distinctions this lowly earthling has. It is beyond peradventure the most widely used of all freshwater lures, providing more pleasure to more people than any other. More fish are taken on the earthworm than on any other single bait known, either natural or artificial. In fact, it is possible that more fish, *in number alone,* are taken on earthworms than on all other baits and lures combined. I can't prove this, of course, but neither can you disprove it. It is not a matter that lends itself readily to statistics.

Furthermore, the earthworm is the most widely distributed, the most easily obtainable, and the least expensive of all freshwater lures. And certainly it is the most *versatile* one in the whole book. I do hereby guarantee that an ordinary ungarnished earthworm will catch more different kinds of fish than any other bait God or tackle manufacturers ever devised!

It is *par excellence* the bait for the all-round fisherman, taking everything from a horny-headed chub, a three-ounce pumpkinseed, a rock bass, bluegill, sucker, eel, bullhead and channel cat, and a big- or small-mouthed bass to a ten pound carp or what-have-you. Yet in the hands of an expert angler it will encompass the downfall of the wariest gamester known, often when more sophisticated lures fail. Shucks, right now I can't think of any kind of freshwater fish I *haven't* taken on earthworms. Let's be honest now. Can you?

Yet the earthworm is one of the least known and most misjudged entries in nature's card index. It does not turn into a lightning bug or *anything else,*—just burrows deeper into the ground during dry spells in search of moisture. It is distributed practically throughout the world, and has been used as fish bait so long that the memory of man runneth not to the contrary. More than a thousand species are on record. In some tropical countries earthworms attain a length of four feet—big enough to put a man on a hook! How I should like to see the face of my indomitable Alice when she spied a four-footer slithering around in the bait-compartment of our refrigerator!

The earthworm is neither a *he* nor a *she,* nor yet exactly an *it*. A true hermaphrodite, it possesses both male and female organs in the same body. (By the way, when I was a boy I pronounced the word *morphidite*. Did you?) An earthworm can thus strike up an acquaintance, fall in love, and breed with whatever it meets down in the subway. All is grist that comes to his mill, and he is sure to meet the right people wherever he goes. Offhand, this hermaphroditism would appear to be quite a convenience and a great simplifier of courtship, obviating the necessity of delicate negotiations and protracted romances.

Not only is the earthworm hermaphroditic, but it is also sexually ambidextrous, being able to breed with either end. When he feels the old biological urge, he simply ascertains

The Earthworm Cometh

which end of his date is nearest, shifts gears, and goes into production. This provision in his constitution also has much to recommend it, since he might find philandering a bit awkward in the narrow hallways of his domicile.

In pairing, two worms come together with the head of one directed toward the tail of the other, or vice versa. The resultant egg-bearing cocoons are "a product of the glandular epithelium of the clitellum," which sounds like a hell of a courtship. The eggs hatch directly into worms and remain worms until they shuffle off their mortal coils or are abducted by some enterprising angler.

Fisherfolk sometimes seek to enhance the earthworm's effectiveness by anointing its carcass with sundry tinctures, lotions, potions, and essences of this-and-that. The finished product often smells like an apothecary's second-assistant. Here and there I have encountered anglers who had implicit faith in their particular magic potions. Ordinary unglamourized worms they hold in high disdain.

"I'd as lief go without a hook as without this here tickler of Annie's oil," a gangling mountaineer told me up on Troublesome creek. Then he meticulously placed a single drop on his bait, tossed it into a riffle below a niggerhead rock, and plucked out a 13-inch trout. "See thar, stranger? It's hard to beat old Annie," he bragged. In a burst of generosity he offered to part with his wonder-working elixir for $1.25. When I demurred, he offered to throw in a flask of peach brandy, on which basis the deal was quickly consummated. I bought the dog for his collar.

Oil of anise—Annie's oil as it is known in the vernacular—is an established favorite. Other alleged enticements are compounded from the oils of wintergreen, thyme, sweet orange, rose geranium, eucalyptus, peppermint, lavender, sassafras, and bergamot. A druggist of my acquaintance dotes on benzedrine, a powerful drug used as an excitant in cases of nervous exhaustion. But as a pick-up for his worms rather than himself. Very earnestly he explained his technique to me.

"I dissolve the tablets in water and immerse an inert worm in it for a few seconds. He comes out fighting like a wildcat in a gunny sack and offers to whip anybody in the whole saloon. When he sobers up and slows down, I dip him in again. Boy, when that worm starts cavorting around in the water, every fish within twenty feet begins to bristle up!"

Most of these magic potions are sticky and cloyingly sweet, but some are as fetid as asafetida. Down on the Ashepoo last spring a tipsy swamper spilled a bottle of his own compounding into my tackle box. For weeks thereafter everything in it smelled like the executive committee of a pole cats' convention.

Personally, I will take my earthworms straight and unsanctified, just as Dame Nature manufactures them. I see little sense in gilding the lily. As far as I know, the sundry brews designed to enhance a worm's personality have about as much to recommend them as the famed love philtres of the 18th century, which were guaranteed to make a voluptuous blonde fall in love with an octogenarian afflicted with rickets, nocturnal frequency, and ingrowing toenails.

I will take my earthworms naked and undandified, without their rouge and lipstick, without their *Evening in Paris* and their *Chanel No. 5*. It is my private conviction that (1) when the Lord made a worm he probably knew what he was doing, and (2) a worm is most effective when it looks, acts, and *smells* most like a worm. I have long ago learned that what counts is how a bait is handled, that as much depends on the angler as on the angleworm.

But if my tolerant neighbor wants to send his worms to a beauty-parlor and have them all primped up, that's his indefeasible right under the constitution. And he may not be altogether silly. For who can testify in matters of taste? If there is one thing that life teaches it is this: the other fellow *could* be right. Almost daily science discovers that some hoary superstition or folk-notion has a foundation in fact.

In a sense, whatever a man believes is true. If faith can move mountains, it maybe can catch fish. For there is another

The Earthworm Cometh

thing I have observed through the years: if a man has faith in a particular lure, he will naturally fish harder and more confidently—and naturally catch more fish.

Do you spit on your hook for luck? To spit or not to spit, that is the question. For there be in this great country of ours stalwart and straight-ticket citizens aplenty who invariably expectorate on their worms before casting them into the water.

"Does spitting on your hook do any good?" I asked a grizzled wood-chopper in the Nantahala hills. "Hit mout do some good, and agin hit moutn't," he replied. "But hit sho Gawd don't cost nothin' to try. *Spit is powerful cheap.*"

A great fraud was my Uncle Abernathy, who lived at our house when I was a boy. But I didn't discover his duplicity until after he was dead, and I am sorry in a way that I ever did. Uncle Ab was a great fisherman, by common acknowledgment the champion of the neighborhood. He fished differently for different things, but in his varying methods there was a common denominator observable to even a barefooted boy with a perpetually "stumped" toe: he invariably anointed his worms with the contents of a mysterious vial he carried in his pocket.

I can see Uncle Ab now, punctiliously placing a single drop on each worm, and looking awfully wise and furtive about it. Gladly would I have traded the philosopher's stone for that magic formula. As it was, my only resource was to bargain for a few precious drops now and then in exchange for my errand-running. Reckon I would have thinned corn or milked the cows or picked up cider apples a solid month for a full bottle, because I never failed to catch fish when I used it. Yessir, it was the greatest invention a body ever heard of.

When Uncle Ab passed on to his dubious reward, I grieved that his secret formula had not been preserved for posterity, especially me. But my grandmother soon disillusioned me: the magic fluid was nothing more esoteric than bluing water. Hastily I compounded a whole quart of bluing water and hied myself to the creek, but for some reason I could never quite figure out, I had little luck with it thereafter. There is a lesson of some sort here. I don't know precisely what it is, but there is a lesson nevertheless.

The precious old swindler did give me a scrap of philosophy I shall not soon forget. "Never take enough bait when you go fishing. Fish always bite best when bait is scarcest," he solemnly adjured me. How many times have I confirmed the profound wisdom of his utterance!

Earthworms have different savors and flavors whether they are glamourized or not, for a worm partakes of the soil as a fish partakes of water. Both smack of the medium in which they live, move, and have their being. Both fish and fishermen seem to have discovered these differences, one species enjoying high favor in one locality, another in another. 'Tis a poor fisherman who hasn't discovered the uses and virtues of his own worms. With several hundred species to select from, everybody should be accommodated in one way or another.

There's a knack to putting a worm on a hook, though your technique may differ from mine. When I was a creek-fishing boy, my brothers and I fished with a single worm tediously threaded on the hook. And what pains we took to keep the point concealed! My older brother was continually upbraiding me for my remissness in this particular. At intervals he would order my hook produced for inspection and invariably say: "No wonder you're not getting a bite. Your point is showing!"

That was the most damning thing you could say about a fellow, and in a way it has haunted me through life. As a whole, life has been good and I have gotten more than I deserved, but now and then when I have missed a cherished goal or failed where I very much wanted to succeed, I have heard a chuckling echo from a long-departed brother: "No wonder . . . Your point was showing!"

In time I outgrew the worm-threading practice of boyhood. One worm no longer satisfies me. Now I have become old

The Earthworm Cometh

and gluttonous and must have several—what my prosaic companions call a *hunk*. "Damned if you didn't put on fifteen cents worth!" a friend complained when he passed me his hook to bait. Three or four worms may tantalize a fish where one fails. You have got to make it worth his while—like the Scotchman who dropped the second quarter into the water because one wasn't worth going in for.

And I have long ago confirmed the astuteness of the Compleat Angler: "Put him on as if you loved him—*that he may stay alive the longer.*" Therefore I stick the point through his well-balanced middle, thus impaling one after another, so they can squirm and writhe and wriggle as freely as they please.

There is a popular assumption that "anybody can fish with a fishing worm." Nothing is more fallacious. Worm-fishing is something of an art, one calling for both experience and expertness. During my life I have been called about everything except an artist, but may I describe a technique that I have found highly successful?

The first principle in all fishing is simple: *never let the fish know he is being fished for.* Therefore I dress inconspicuously, remain as invisible as possible, and move warily lest the quarry suspect my sinister presence. Using a long light flyrod with a six-pound camouflaged leader, I cast the squirming "hunk" into likely spots from 20 to 40 feet away. The hook is small and long-shanked to accommodate more worms and facilitate removal from the fish's mouth. No cork or float whatever.

The second principle in fishing is also simple: make the fish think your bait is alive, healthy, and digestible—*and behaving naturally.* The bass or bream lurking under that overhang must say to himself: no worm in that place and acting like that could possibly have anything tied to him. In still water I want no sinker whatever, because the writhing mass of worms must work its way gently downward, squirming unhappily as it descends, *precisely as if it had fallen into the water and were manna from high heaven.* A fish likes to think he is a lucky fellow and is getting a bargain.

In accordance with the third principle in worm-fishing, I seldom permit my bait to remain long in one spot. After it has gravitated slowly to the bottom, I twitch the line gently between my fingers, then let the bait settle down again. I do this to re-activate my worms and simulate life-likeness, for as far as I know there is no fish in the world that prefers a dead worm to a live one. This maneuver I leisurely repeat until a fish strikes or the lure is retrieved for another cast.

Many people freeze into immobility when a fish makes an experimental pass at a bait. But is this the normal way for a nipped worm to behave? Its very submissiveness may excite suspicion, because normal prey lights a rag when something makes a pass at it. When a fish nibbles indecisively or shows only a lackadaisical interest, I start withdrawing my lure with tantalizing twitches to make him think he is about to lose it.

For a fish and a man are rather much alike: they both want whatever they can't get, and they want whatever they're chasing to run! They are alike in another respect too: there are only two kinds of fish and two kinds of men: the *caught* and the *uncaught.*

Quail Hunting in the Old Dominion

I have learned to love the ragged pea fields, the inhospitable bays, and the spacious pinelands that make up the birdy low country of South Carolina. I had as lief do my quail hunting there as in any other segment of Bob's habitat.

But the last autumn was one of the wettest on record. By Thanksgiving much of the low country was inundated. The fields became sucking bogs, and every depression a shimmering lake. A bird hunter needed hip boots, pontoons, or webbed feet. For three weeks I sloshed around behind my dogs. Day after day I trudged home covered with black muck and soaked to my umbilicus. It was too much. Much too much.

"I'm no durned duck," I said with considerable vehemence, and headed for my old homestead in Virginia. My 10-day sojourn in the ancient Commonwealth proved an altogether pleasant one. It enabled me to renew old friendships, to rediscover some embarrassing facts about Virginia quail, and to make the acquaintance of a superb little hunter, a dog so good that I had to hark back a decade to the incomparable Daphne for a basis of comparison.

Lady was a little English setter weighing not more than 30 pounds. She was a shy sprite, with pensive eyes and a forlorn look, asking of the big world only a small part. When her robustious yardmates jockeyed each other around the feed trough, Lady would sit sedately in a corner, with a soft petition in her eyes. "If you *should* have a little piece left over . . ."

But her self-effacing and spiritless air belied her real nature. In the field Lady was a flashing little dynamo, and the very paragon of quaily virtues. Her speed and stamina were almost incredible. And her judgment and sweet precision stole my heart the first day and kept it enthralled thereafter. I spent 10 days trying to find the rent in her armor. I never found it, for with Lady bird-finding was a passion as well as a profession.

Lady's master, Will Carrington, was a tall, graying and mild-mannered Virginia gentleman, an elegant quail shot and a peerless trainer. He could train a dog with less exertion, and with less expense to the English language, than any other man I have ever known. I verily believe he could take a full-blooded July hound and turn out a passable bird dog in six weeks! And he was as unassuming as the little dog that shyly worshiped him.

During the first morning, we stopped the car at the edge of a rolling lespedeza field. Most dogs would have pottered around a moment and selected a spot to jettison their cargoes, as has been the habit of hunting dogs from time immemorial. But not so with Lady. She was instantly gone.

"Where is your dog?" I asked.

He nodded toward a distant rise.

"Over by that rock pile. She's got company already."

Scanning the reaches of the field, I espied a black-and-white statuette 300 yards away.

"Whew! That little doggie must be jet-propelled. Let's go over and see what sort of company she's keeping."

Quail Hunting in the Old Dominion

"No hurry," said Will. "Let's lock the car and light our pipes before we start."

Leisurely we sauntered across the field, chatting idly as we walked. As we drew near the skulking covey, Will spoke to the little setter for the first time.

"We are ready, Lady."

A bevy of rocketing brownies whizzed toward the woods. Two birds were downed in the field. A third was winged and sideslipped down in the woods. Without a word of instruction, Lady sprinted forward and pridefully delivered the dead birds to her master, to whom all good things belonged. Nor did she ruffle the satin of their breasts in so doing.

"Another fell over there," Will said quietly, flicking a hand toward the woods.

Lady raced away. Will gave no further directions, nor did he presume to go over and intermeddle in the little setter's affairs. In a few moments she came switching through the tall lespedeza with the disabled bird.

It was a sparkling performance, and I expected to see Will show his approbation by patting her head or fondling a ragged ear. Instead, I saw Lady lift a shaggy little foot, which her tall master leaned over and took in his big hand. Then Lady streaked away as if inspired.

It was an amusing and fleeting little byplay that I almost missed. No word had been spoken, no articulate sign of approval. This simple recognition from her master was all the accolade her eager heart required. It was a medal on her chest.

"Spoiled brat," grinned Will. "Artful little jade."

"An elegant little lady," I defended, "and I wish I had her."

"Let's sit on the rock pile and give our legs a breather," suggested Will. "We've got a long day ahead. The time to rest is before you get tired."

"But this must be a 30-acre field. Shouldn't we hunt it?"

"We are," he said succinctly.

Standing atop the rock pile, I watched the black-and-white

form flash around the edges of the field with the speed of a disembodied shadow.

"What is she doing?" asked Will.

"She's circling the whole field now. Sort of reading the headlines to see whether any birds have fed in from the woods," I broadcast between puffs of my pipe. "Now she's splitting the field wide open. Sort of reading the classified ads to see whether some enterprising family has flown in to breakfast. Now she has taken a taxi and is heading back to the office for another assignment."

And there she was, lolling her red tongue and saying: "The folks are not at home yet. What next, Cap'n?"

"She's faster than a cockroach on roller skates," I said.

"Pretty fair little dog, I reckon," modestly appraised Will. "Especially for a lazy man. That woods covey had around 18 birds in it. Let's follow them and try a few singles."

The woods were dry and leafy, with a scattering of noisy brush piles here and there. Now, I said, if Lady doesn't want to run her skiff too close to shore, she had better ginger-foot it through these woods. But her slackening speed was hardly perceptible.

"Won't she overrun her birds in those clattering leaves?" I anxiously asked.

"She's got nose enough to back up her speed," replied Will, which was his nearest approach to praise during the 10 days we hunted together.

Two hundred yards away Lady came to a peremptory halt 10 feet from a small brush pile.

"I've got this one locked up in the pantry," she said.

Within 15 minutes she had found half a dozen widely scattered singles, and we had downed three. Then Will said: "Enough for this time, Lady. We might want to visit these folks again sometimes."

A mile away, we stopped at the edge of another big lespedeza field, and Lady streaked away.

"We'll sit this one out," suggested Will, parking himself on

Quail Hunting in the Old Dominion

a fender of the car. "Let Lady do the work. She's got four legs and I've got only two."

A moment later I saw Lady pause at the far end of the field, only her head visible above the rank lespedeza.

"Has she got company again?" I asked.

"No. Just standing by for orders," he said, and waved an arm toward the right. Lady vanished over the hill. "There's a smaller field down in the hollow," he explained.

Throughout our hunt, this procedure was regularly followed. When Lady had finished an isolated field and found no ore worth working, she would promptly return to Will, who implicitly trusted her verdict. When there was another likely field nearby, she would ask for orders before returning.

Regardless of the distance, a wave of her master's arm was instantly sufficient. Not once during our entire hunt did he find it necessary to shout at Lady. Will was not one to tear a passion into tatters, nor she one to require it. Such orders as he gave were quiet and unobtrusive, usually a casual flick of a hand or a curt monosyllable.

"I never saw a dog that required less conversation," I complimented.

"She's knocking on somebody's door over there in the hollow," replied Will.

She was pointing at the edge of a jungle of bristling cedars. The covey had evidently scurried from the field into their sanctuary, and what a formidable sanctuary it was!

"I'll stand back and let you take this rise," generously offered Will.

I looked appraisingly at the wall of cedars. I saw no possible way a bird could fly that I could hit it. Under the circumstances, I could be as chivalrous as anybody else.

"I'll be damned if you do!" I answered.

Will was chuckling mightily at my embarrassment.

"What is the best tactic to follow here?" I asked.

"Let Lady put them up. Maybe we can annex a few singles up in the woods."

In the woods Lady plied her trade with her usual deftness.

And it was here that she cut a cunning caper that won for her a private niche in my affections. She pointed behind a small brush pile, and Will walked up behind her. But before she could put up her skulker, another bird bounced up in the woods ahead. Will shot, and a winged bird fell 30 feet away and lay fluttering in the leaves.

Lady was still statuesquely planted by the brush pile, not in the least perturbed by the shooting. But she heard the wounded bird kicking in the leaves, and apparently foresaw the possibility of its scrambling under a pile of logs near by. She was in something of a quandary. Warily backing away, she circled her brush pile at a discreet distance, retrieved the wounded bird in the leaves, then quickly resumed her original point. Will downed that one too, which she also retrieved.

"One of the most remarkable things I have ever seen a dog do," I said. "She ought to have an honorary degree for that."

"What was remarkable about that?" Will discounted. "She was afraid the wounded bird in the leaves would escape. She figured the one in the brush pile would keep. It was just putting first things first."

But I noticed that when the starry-eyed little setter proffered her paw, Will shook it right cordially. Then she demurely lifted a shaggy foot for me.

"I am right honored, Lady," I said. "In fact, I never saw a glamour gal I had rather shake hands with."

"Pampered show-off," grinned Will. "Begone with you!"

During our last day afield, Lady gave us another neat performance. In the center of a large lespedeza field, she paused a moment to read the society column. A few minutes later she had picked up a stray visiting card and was asking for an interview.

"This is a tremendous covey, with quite a reputation," said Will. "I haven't tried them myself, but other hunters say they are the worst ground-runners in the county. Nobody can get a shot at them."

Lady confidently planted herself, advanced, and pointed

Quail Hunting in the Old Dominion

again, a maneuver that was rapidly repeated three times within 75 yards. This covey evidently deserved its reputation. For 200 yards this successive pointing and repointing continued. A dozen times I prepared to shoot, a dozen times I weakly lowered my gun.

"They figure a good run is better than a bad stand," commented Will.

"My blood pressure is 'way up in G. Right now I couldn't hit a barn door with a bull. I mean . . ."

A scant 50 yards ahead I espied a veritable jungle of honeysuckle. If that scuttling battalion could make it to the honeysuckle . . . Lady evidently sensed the situation, too.

"I declare, I never saw such inhospitable folks!" she said. "They just don't want any visitors at all. Maybe if a fellow would try the back door . . ."

Quickly backtracking, she circumspectly skirted the decamping covey and planted herself between them and the honeysuckle. The maneuver stopped the scuttlers dead in their tracks. When they got up, we dropped four bouncing birds. But truth to tell, Will got three of the four. He always outshot me. With his light 16-gauge double, he had a way of making the trickiest shot look easy. Yet he was as modest about his shooting as he was about his little dog's performance.

Whenever I miss a shot, I am apt to expatiate at some length on the difficultness thereof. And when I make a good shot, I am not particularly averse to advertising the fact. There is nothing in the world I like better than hearing somebody else brag about me, for with all my faults I love *me* still! We admire in others the qualities which we ourselves lack. I am a great lover of modesty in others because I am notably lacking in this ingredient myself.

Whenever Will made a brilliant shot at a bird slithering through the woods or rocketing through the treetops, I would venture a word of praise. But he would grin depreciatingly and say: "The shot just happened to get there at the same time the bird did." Or mayhap he would make some vague allusion to luck, or insist that he was shooting over his head. Verily, modesty is the first requisite in a shooting companion.

Virginia quail, especially those from the upland areas, are big and fast. They are probably the finest specimens I have found during my 30-year sojourn in the precincts and purlieus of the old Confederacy. Although a gallant gamester wherever he is found, Bob is not at his best in the southern tip of his range. A five-ounce Florida bird is a good average. But as the gunner travels northward and into the invigorating uplands of Tennessee and Virginia, he finds quail that are noticeably bigger and faster, and incidentally more palatable.

Our Virginia birds averaged around seven ounces. During a single afternoon Will bagged four that weighed exactly two pounds. A half-pound quail is a heck of a quail. And are these plump Republicans from the Virginia foothills fast! Several years ago a President of the United States came down into the picturesque Valley of Virginia to shoot quail. After repeated attempts to bag a bolting Bob, he grinned wryly and asked: "Do they really fly that fast?"

Now and then Will and I ran afoul of crafty old wood coveys that got away too fast for either of us to shoot. Those lusty bushwhackers surely didn't need any starting blocks! All I could see was a brown smudge slithering through the trees. The whir of their twin propellers left my ears ringing. After one such debacle, Will remarked: "They were in somewhat of a hurry, weren't they?"

"Somewhat, hell!" I replied. "That's the greatest understatement in history."

I found myself in sympathy with the baseball player who turned sadly away from the batter's plate and delivered himself of that epic and melancholy dictum: "You can't hit 'em if you can't see 'em!"

I once read the statement: "Quail do not fly fast. Their apparent speed is an illusion created by the whir of their wings." If the fellow who wrote that would hunt these fugitive foot-hillers awhile, he would expunge his statement from

Quail Hunting in the Old Dominion

the records. It is true that the disconcerting clamor of his take-off is Bob's ace in the hole. It has possibly played a part in the survival of the species. It is also true that quail seem to fly fast mainly because they *do*. As a quaking youngster told me last season: "They don't fly as fast as I think they do, but I still think they do. I am always scared when they get up, and the scareder I am, the faster they fly."

During my sojourn in the Old Dominion, I was constantly breaking the tenth commandment. I did not covet my neighbor's house, nor his manservant, nor his maidservant, nor yet his ass, but I did have an entrancing vision of the incomparable Lady flashing through the spacious pinelands of low-country South Carolina. And on the last day I put Will's affection for the little setter to the sovereign test.

"I'll give you 20 acres of land for her," I offered.

"Any buildings on it?" he grinned.

When Fish Don't Bite

During nearly four decades of fishing, I have tried probably as many different lures as any other impecunious schoolteacher. A body can hardly move around in my ramshackle habitation, however svelte his figure and lissome his tread, without bumping into evidence that an experimental type of brain resides there.

And anybody whose fecund fancy can conjure up something new, something that might conceivably interest a fish, will always find me an eager customer.

Yet there are times when the most plausible improvisations of the tackle makers fail me, conditions under which fish will not respond to orthodox methods. Like tired businessmen, fish become jaded and require an occasional *hors d'oeuvre*. There are times too when a man feels an urge to experiment, an urge to pit his native resourcefulness against the cunning of the quarry, when he says to himself: "If I were suddenly bereft of my precious tackle box and shorn of the accoutrements of civilization, could I still catch fish?"

When Fish Don't Bite

Being one of the lower-bracket gentry, I have no exclusive places to fish in. I have to compete with a teeming citizenry in heavily fished waters, taking potluck along with my sweating brethren and not complaining too much about it. The fish in these meccas are daily offered an assortment of temptation. In the grim and unwearying quest, few lures or baits are left untried.

The other afternoon I saw 25 casters working over a 50-acre pond. It was worse than a sheriff's posse chasing a one-legged rapist at a carnival. The wily rustybacks in that pond can look up and instantly give you the name and serial number of the plug some hopeful Homo sapiens is dragging over their heads. The merry-go-round probably affords these old wiseacres considerable amusement.

"Whoso would catch fish must be a nonconformist," I sagely paraphrased. "Those puissant lads have already offered those bass everything in my repertoire. I've got to figure out some new temptations for these jaded night-clubbers."

Whereupon I scratched my sparsely hirsuted noggin and came up with an idea. "Fish are becoming more practical," I reasoned. "Whether they bite or not, they've got to *eat*. I'll make this an experimental season."

I decided to take up bass catering first, since down in my bailiwick the large-mouth is yearly growing more fastidious in his tastes and more uncooperative in his habits. In the deep South there are perhaps a hundred thousand small ponds that are overgrown with moss and weeds, a big percentage of them so clogged-up as to make artificial lure fishing well-nigh impossible. But however unfishable and uninhabitable they look, they all have a redoubtable battalion of cavernous-mawed behemoths.

In these local ponds, most of them heavily fished by the cane pole gentry, the good—and the gullible—die young. The survivors grow big because they grow smart. These juggernauts are a band of ravening wolves, devouring whatever stock you may put in, keeping the ponds woefully out of balance and unproductive, and defying all efforts to encompass their downfall.

What is the principal item on the large-mouth's bill of fare? Live minnows, of course. In the choked-up ponds hereabout, the sucker is apt to constitute his *pièce de résistance*. The bigger the sucker the better. If you don't catch a bass, you can just go home and eat your bait. A 10-pound bass can't live on tidbits, although some tyro providentially catches one on an earthworm now and then.

So I went a-suckering in tired ponds that had long ago acquired the degree of A.F.O.—all fished out. I got some valuable tips from a few old-fashioned bass-masters such as Charlie Adams, perhaps the most skillful angler of my acquaintance, and Gene Reynolds, dean of the 10-pounders. We finally worked out a technique that yielded a respectable quota of Goliaths from almost every pond we laid siege to, although the ponds were generally regarded as barren and sterile.

We fish our suckers shallow, not more than 18 or 20 inches, because they are friskier near the surface, more visible to marauding bass, and our hooks are less subject to fouling on submerged debris. To insure the right depth, we often use a sliding cork with button backstop. With a long sidewise sweep of the arm, I can cast a big sucker 40 or 50 feet away. But Charlie and Gene disdain reels for this kind of fishing, using long slender canes instead. With a 17-foot cane and line of similar length, they can deposit their suckers in a precise spot, which I cannot always do with so unwieldy a bulk.

A 10-pound bass is not a very trusting soul. He got that big by being suspicious. As my paddler says, "He ain't trust nobody for nothin'." You have got to convince him that the big sucker cavorting seductively above his head is a free agent and not somebody's private chattel.

You've got to make yourself inconspicuous when you go a-courting a 10-pounder. It takes time to lull a paunchy old cynic into a sense of security. He may spend hours appraising a frisking sucker before ordering it for lunch. When a big

When Fish Don't Bite

bass eventually makes up his mind and engulfs your minnow, you must wait a short forever before setting the hook. As Charlie Adams says: "You've got to sit there like patience on a monument, while your heart trip-hammers against your ribs and climbs into your throat. Just before it cuts your breath off, pull."

I have prescribed big suckers for this kind of bassing, but some friends favor the large silver roach, depending on which species constitutes the bass forage in a particular pond. In a sucker-infested pond, suckers seem more effective. In water overrun with silvers, some anglers prefer the silver as bait, on the theory that it is easier to cater to an existing taste than to cultivate a new one.

Sucker-fishing has a few drawbacks, however. It requires a certain serenity of disposition, and a deal of time and patience. Indeed, it requires a sovereign contempt for the fugaciousness of time. If you are a big executive and your time is worth so much a minute, you had better forego so time-consuming an enterprise.

If the board of directors can't meet without you and you are perpetually consulting your watch, skip it. If you are henpecked and worried about a spouse who is nursing her wrath to keep it warm, skip it. But if you have the requisite time and patience, and stick to it long enough, you may peradventure hang a bass so big you'll not have to stretch your blankets in the telling thereof.

Bass was not the only species on which I tried the give-them-something-they-can-wrap-their-gastric-juices-around theory. I experimented also with that legendary and mettlesome little gamester of the deep South, the bluegill sunfish. And his first cousin once removed, the red-breasted sunfish. The redbreast, or robin, is not to be confused with the ordinary bream, which is the name we call the sunfish down here. To describe it merely as "one of the bluegills" or "a long-eared sunfish" is to be guilty of what a Frenchman would call lese majesty and a southerner treason.

The redbreast is distinguished from the bluegill by its long ears, its larger mouth, its predilection for fast water, and its gorgeous coloration. It is perhaps the most brilliantly hued of all fresh-water game fish. It is also distinguished by the greater verve and spirit with which it attacks, and by the matchless flavor of its flesh.

A 16-ounce redbreast on a fly rod is beyond peradventure the gamest pound in history. And Southerners may not agree in politics, but they are "plumb unanimous" in the opinion that the red-breasted bream is the most savory pan fish with which a benevolent Providence ever blessed a favored commonwealth.

Since bream are primarily insect feeders, I decided to offer them an heroic assortment of creeping and crawling temptations, including flavored earthworms, the pupae of drone honeybees and wasps, corn worms, cockroaches, June bugs, cicadas, wood sawyers, crickets, grasshoppers, tobacco worms, tiny frogs, catalpa and oak caterpillars, and several unidentified nymphs and beetles. In short, anything that an aging but agile old pedagogue could contrive to lay hands on.

My house became a teeming insectarium, a habitation of creepers and crawlers. Alice walked around on stilts for six weeks. I discovered that something would bite almost anything I could catch, which convinced me afresh that fish enjoy eating and that they have versatile appetites. But I ultimately narrowed my entomological pets down to half a dozen, and with these I caught more and finer bream than I had taken during a single season in 20 years.

The earthworm has been standard bream bait for time out of memory. Indeed, throughout this *e pluribus unum* of ours, more fish are caught on the lowly earthworm than on any other lure—living, artificial, or embalmed. It is the most versatile, and the most unappreciated, of all natural baits.

Dictionaries are strangely reticent about its value to the angler. One informs me that it is "a burrowing terrestrial worm useful in enriching the soil," and that Charles Darwin wrote a famous book about it. Another informs me that there are 1,000 species, and that in some tropical countries they attain

When Fish Don't Bite

a length of four feet. Still another gravely advises that the earthworm is a hermaphrodite, a fact which I don't give a damn about, but I suppose it is a considerable convenience to them. The earthworm is one citizen that can properly be referred to as *he, she* or *it*.

I grew up in the country and never heard the term earthworm until I went off to college. They were just fishing worms, a use for which they were obviously destined. But I did discover that earthworms have distinctive flavors, and that some species rate higher on a fish's bill of fare than others. Sunfish in particular have a weakness for the sweet-scented, bluish species found only in swamps. So highly regarded are these that "blue bait" has become almost a household word in the bream country of the South. Along our highways, "blue bait for sale" posters outnumber barbecue signs and shaving-soap rhymes. Wayfarers and pilgrims are often puzzled by these roadside proclamations. A few days ago a New Englander asked me: "What in the name of Martha's Vineyard is blue bait? I counted 150 signs between Columbia and Moncks Corner."

Crickets are also highly esteemed, not only for sunfish but for pan fish in general. Judged by the spirit and avidity with which a bluegill goes after it, a cricket on the hook must be a delectable morsel indeed. Along the meandering coves of the sprawling Santee-Cooper reservoirs, the cricket business really booms in spring and early summer, the price ranging from 30 to 50 cents a dozen. But I pulled a fast one on these Carolina cricketeers. I drove up to my Virginia farm over a week end, and by the simple expedient of moving shocks of unthreshed wheat, captured more crickets than Carter had oats.

What can be said for the grasshopper? That although he is regarded as a plague in the West, he is considered excellent pan fish bait in the South. *If you can catch him!* I could take you to any number of inky pools in the Four Hole Swamp where a dozen big hoppers can be quickly translated into a dozen big warmouths or bream.

But grasshopper chasing is one of the most disillusioning and heartbreaking pursuits I ever engaged in. I've chased them across a 40-acre field in tantalizing 10-foot hops. Invariably just as you are ready to pounce on one, he blithely and saucily leaps away, and you start stalking again. 'Tis a pastime somewhat uncongenial to a man of my age and station, one at which I am neither graceful nor effective, but a friend of mine stoutly assures me that grasshopper-chasing is a sure cure for neuritis and kindred ills.

Young wasps too are almost unsurpassed as sunfish bait, especially in the pupal stage, just before emerging from their cells. There are bream connoisseurs aplenty who will pay a fat fee for a plump nest, swearing that the wasp is unrivaled as a bluegill delicacy. But reducing such a nest to safe possession is attended by certain difficulties which I need hardly amplify. I shall not soon forget what happened to my mother-in-law when I deposited a big nest in the trunk of my car to ripen, and forgot about it. It stirred up sort of an international incident in our household.

For years I regarded the pupae of drone honeybees as sunfish bait unbeatable, counting on the succulent amber-colored morsels to fill my basket when all other enticements failed. They are at their best when they reach the purple-headed stage, just before emerging from their hexagonal cells, and are incomparably better than the pupae of working bees, which are undersized and too soft to remain on the hook.

For 20 years I asked little more of this mundane sphere than a light cane, a square of drone comb in my pocket, and a black creek winding its way through the swamp. They were the very ingredients of self-sufficiency and sweet content. And I never lacked for my precious drones, since I have ten colonies of bees in my front yard.

The lure of the drone is not restricted to bream. Crappies and bass also have a sweet tooth for such dainties, and anything may happen to a bee-fisherman. Last May Dr. Earl Copenhaver, my crony and companion for two decades, caught an

When Fish Don't Bite

eight-pound largemouth on a fly rod while drone-fishing for sunfish. He has had a one-track mind ever since.

I still consider the drone excellent pan fish bait. In fact, I verily believe that you can get more bites per minute with drones than with anything else under the sun. But however good crickets, grasshoppers, wasps, bees and their ilk may be, there is one objection they all have in common: they are too attractive to small fry and too conducive to hook-robbing. You are eternally baiting your hook and jerking your arm off—*unless only big sunfish are present.* Furthermore, crickets, grasshoppers, wasps and bees are often difficult to come by and are procurable for limited seasons only.

All factors considered, therefore, the sunfish bait nonpareil is the catalpa caterpillar. To big bluegills, this horrendous critter is manna from high heaven. Only a mature bream or redbreast will attack a full-grown catalpa. Perhaps its size and ferocious aspect are too much for weanlings and hook-robbers. And its carcass is tough and resistant. I have taken as many as five big bluegills on a single worm.

The catalpa tree abounds throughout the bream country. It is a conspicuous feature of the Dixiecrat landscape, and caterpillars are ordinarily procurable in the South from May to October. Many ardent breamers pride themselves on their private groves, which are veritable bait factories. The catalpa worm has another advantage too: it may be refrigerated (I simply use my wife's refrigerator) and kept in a torpid state for weeks, provided it is not subjected to freezing temperatures. When released and exposed to the sun, it soon begins to crawl around and is as good as new. I have 100 horrific, handsome specimens in bank at present.

And none of this tedious and nauseous business of turning catalpa caterpillars inside out is necessary. Just stick a hook through the middle of a big one, cast him out to the edge of the pads, and let him waft gently and naturally downward. If there is a big, bad, bald bream within 10 feet—

Much of the effectiveness of insect-fishing depends on the method employed. Regardless of the insect, the technique is uniform: using an invisible leader and unweighted line, let the lure flutter or wiggle its way gently downward—*precisely as if it had fallen into the water*. Natural bait should be offered naturally.

When your way of life falls into the sere and yellow leaf, when your sterling qualities as husband and father go unappreciated by the family, cultivate your insect neighbors. It will enable you, after a fashion, to take your living from the land. And, brother, *catching* your bait is guaranteed to keep you spry!

My Husband Is Slightly Off

I read the other day that the institution of matrimony was invented for the convenience of women.

After living with a man on rather intimate terms for 29 years, I should like to offer a few crumbs of evidence to the contrary. In moments of quiet desperation, I sometimes wonder for exactly whose benefit it was invented. At other times, I am quite sure that the institution of matrimony was set up for the sole convenience of husbands who hunt and fish.

My husband, who is something of a wit, has a way of saying: "Alice and I get along beautifully. She does what she wants to do, and *I* do what she wants to do." He is not above depicting me as a household tyrant, a latter-day Xanthippe, and a female Attila. He imputes the most outlandish things to me. By the time I hear about them they are scattered over the country.

Nor does he scruple to vilify me in print at so many cents a word, as witnesseth the inscription in his latest book: "Affectionately dedicated to my Alice, without whose many suggestions *it would have been finished in half the time.*" I had no inkling of this piece of villainy until it was too late to do anything about it. Tell me, can a woman sue her husband for defamation of character or something?

Whenever I open our refrigerator, I am confronted by assorted jars of huge caterpillars—the precious catalpa worms which he uses in sunfish fishing. They are sacrosanct and inviolable, and he raises pluperfect Cain if anybody touches them. If left outside, they metamorphose and become valueless; if placed too near the freezing compartment, they kick the bucket.

They must be kept in a torpid state for weeks, so that when taken out they revive and crawl around. I am not too squeamish about such things, but the precise spot where the temperature suits them best happens to be right next to my butter. He refers to our refrigerator as his bait bank, and speaks of making and withdrawing deposits. And when the refrigerator gets out of whack and starts defrosting of its own accord—

My alleged helpmate has theory trouble now and then, and embarks on sprees of experimenting. A few months ago he evolved what he fondly calls his gastric-juices theory, and I call the squirming hypothesis, the nub of which is that fish have made such rapid intellectual strides that they no longer fall for artificials that merely *look* edible, and should therefore be offered things that are *really* edible.

Since the advent of this momentous theory, which must be as ancient as the hills, our house has become a convention hall for odd little characters that creep-and-crawl and flit-and-flutter about. My life has become a succession of shocks, and I live in a constant state of wonder-what-in-hell-will-happen-next.

Yesterday morning I overslept, hastily jammed my foot into a shoe and laced it up—and instantly slumped to the floor in wild panic. Something was squishing and squirming between my toes. What the shoe-doffing record of the United States

My Husband Is Slightly Off

and Canada is I don't know, but I am satisfied that I either broke or fractured it. But it developed that my panic was altogether unfounded.

It was nothing more than an unhappy little frog that had escaped from a bait cage and sought sanctuary in my shoe. My husband regarded the proceedings with scholarly complacency, gently upbraiding me for spoiling a bait. Yet people gravely address him as "Doctor" or "Professor," and he gravely bows in return. I tell you, this higher education business is the bunk.

What he solemnly calls his "library" looks like an apothecary shop that has been closed for about six months. The shelves are lined with cages of weird little invertebrates that ooze along in varying degrees of contentment. Other vessels are full of flitters and flutters in different stages of transmogrification and sometimes putrefaction, since he sometimes forgets where he puts them.

He is waiting for his assorted captives to "ripen" into bream bait. Judging by the conglomerate odor which assails my nostrils, his definition of "ripe" must be pretty advanced. In fact, my whole house has been smelling funny for months. Nor are his entomological experiments confined to the library.

Last week, while scrummaging around in the pantry, I bumped the lid from an innocent-looking crock. Immediately a legion of odd little characters spiraled up, filled the pantry, and overflowed into the kitchen. I evacuated the premises with great celerity.

And yesterday I opened a jar in my bedroom and a huge grasshopper popped into my bosom, wiggled his way southward with great dexterity, and began to execute the Charleston on my diaphragm. It was a new experience for me, and probably a new one for the grasshopper. I don't know which of us was the more perturbed by the predicament. Had the incident happened in church, it might have embarrassed a lot of fine people.

I have developed an uneasiness about poking my fingers

into nooks and crannies lest some unregistered little house guest misconstrue my intentions, and I have become wary about removing the top from anything in the house lest it prove another Pandora's box.

My husband is at times highly contagious. While prowling through the swamps, he gets his carcass and his clothing infested with chiggers, or red bugs. Then he hangs his clothes in the closet with mine, or manlike, strews them about the premises, and I go on a scratching jamboree.

Now I enjoy scratching when I itch. Come to think of it, there are few greater pleasures than scratching. It is the cheapest of all luxuries. But there are times and places when it is not considered aristocratic to scratch. A man can do it and remain respectable, but a woman can't. It is one of the unfair things about life, this double standard.

Whenever I sleep with my husband, I always wake up with chiggers. For some damnable and inexplicable reason, they seem to prefer me to him, and I don't mean that to sound conceited. They use him more or less as a means of transportation. I think that's why he lures me into his bed after a fishing or hunting trip in the swamps.

A few years ago I returned unexpectedly from a sweltering August trip, rushed upstairs to take a bath, and found Jonah's whale swimming around nonchalantly in our bathtub. My husband had caught a 10-pound bass, brought it back alive, and deposited it in the bathtub. Then he had turned the spigot on to keep his prize alive while he went out to corral his friends.

For two days I waited for the abdominous old hippo to be gathered to Abraham's bosom, for the procession of curious-looking people to stop coming and going. Some of the people who trooped in looked as if they could read; others looked as if they might be able to write, but they were definitely not University folk. My husband has queer friends, and vice versa, if you know what I mean.

When I finally suggested the appropriateness of my taking

My Husband Is Slightly Off

a bath, he eyed the tub narrowly, glanced mathematically at my hips, and said:

"Honey, ain't that tub big enough for both of y'all?"

Yet they tell me that my dim-witted spouse is listed in *Who's Who*. The title of that book ought to be *Who's What*.

They say cleanliness is next to godliness. In our house it's next to impossible. I sometimes find hundreds of live minnows disporting themselves in our bathtub. When my husband and his graceless cronies are planning a weekend trip to the Santee-Cooper, they sort of accumulate minnows through the week, dump them into the tub, and keep the water running constantly until they are ready to go. Reckon I'll come home some day to find a walrus in the living room and a hippocampus in the kitchen sink. Yet all some women have to worry about is the ring their husbands leave in the bathtub.

One night last summer I was awakened by the sensation of something crawling up my backbone. "Pure imagination," I said, and lay heroically still. "Now most people would raise a hullabaloo. But I am an intelligent woman. After all, an I.Q. is bound to mean something. I shall be strong and go back to sleep."

Suddenly something nipped decisively at my shoulder blade. I somersaulted out of bed and switched on the light—to find a three-inch caterpillar scowling balefully at me. Awakened by the fracas, my husband opened one glazed eye and maundered sleepily: "Had the cage in the sun parlor where your things were drying. Be a good girl and put 'im back, darling."

His flies and bristling plugs are forever sticking to my personal effects. I find them embedded in quilts, carpets, window curtains, and even my own clothing. Last Easter I paraded down Main Street with a bass plug dangling and jangling from that precise part of my anatomy which is prominent enough already. The incident seemed to tickle the risibilities of my husband, who labeled me Ding Bat the rest of the summer.

When he goes out to feed his bird dogs, whatever he lays his hands on is a proper utensil. I go out once a week to retrieve my pie pans, skillets, and whatnot. Here lately he has been using my best dinner plates, the ones with the red apples on them. No amount of protesting does any good. So a week ago I began setting the plates aside and feeding *him* out of them. He doesn't know it, the poor sap, and what he doesn't know won't hurt him. By the way, the doctrine that what your husband doesn't know won't hurt him is the most useful weapon an abused woman has at her disposal.

Whenever one of his puppies gets into the house, as straight as a martin to its gourd he heads for my living-room rug and proceeds to irrigate it. Those pups will stay outdoors for hours in perfect self containment, scamper indoors through the first unguarded crack, and instantly make for the aforesaid rug. It seems to have some strange fascination for them. Will someone who knows about rugs and puppies explain this phenomenon to me?

My husband is forever trying out something that somebody tells him about. Last year he had a spell of drinking goat's milk. Somebody told him that it would supplement his gastric juices or something. My own gastric juices are not complaining, and I'm not particular about having 'em supplemented, but for six weeks I was never quite sure what I was drinking. Everything in the refrigerator got to smelling goaty. And goat is like garlic: there is no such thing as a little of it.

One day last spring I came home to discover a clump of catalpa bushes growing in the middle of my roses. The catalpa is a fast-growing and heavy-foliaged nuisance, on the leaves of which caterpillars thrive. Then my husband scoured the countryside and brought back patches of caterpillar eggs. Two weeks later every bush was crawling with ravenous and bilious-looking worms. My husband draped himself across the back steps, regarded the half-ravaged trees with proprietary pride, and smiled benevolently at the world.

"Aren't they beautiful? They are my bait factories. Much

My Husband Is Slightly Off

more convenient to raise worms than to buy 'em. Also more economical. The bushes set your roses off too, don't they? But be careful with that spray. They might be allergic to it."

In the fishpond beneath my window are half a dozen huge bullfrogs. On damp nights the earth fairly quakes with their bellowing. But this devil's orchestra is sweeter than a dulcimer to my husband's ears. He says it soothes his overwrought nerves, and makes him think he's sleeping in the swamp. But their clamorous courtship keeps me as wide-eyed as an owl.

Their resounding "knee-deeps" come at the exact interval that is psychologically calculated to prolong wakefulness. Just as I am dropping into sweet oblivion, they bring me back to raucous reality. I start over again, hoping to make it before the next quaking overture, but invariably they beat me to it.

Between the baying of his dogs and the bellowing of his frogs, relations with our neighbors are constantly strained. I remonstrate and preach respectability to him, but he remains shameless and unrepentant.

"What will the neighbors think?" I ask.

"Shucks, you can't pull that on me. The neighbors think I'm half-cracked anyway, and you know it. Nobody is surprised by anything I do. That's the advantage of being considered half-cracked. Besides, our neighbors are too refined. Don't belong in this part of town. I don't like people who are too damned respectable anyway."

Wherein he spake a parable. His reputation for eccentricity is such that nobody is ever surprised by anything he does. It enables him to get by with murder. Whenever new people move into our block, he straightway shocks them by some piece of outlandish behavior, and they are prepared for anything thereafter. Come to think of it, a reputation for being queer does have its advantages.

Why do I stay with my husband? I have been asking myself that for lo, these many years! The answer is just plain *inertia*, which may be defined as the state of staying where you are because it's too much trouble to go somewhere else, the state of suffering the ills you have rather than flying to others you wot not of. I already wot of troubles aplenty, but there may be others I wot not of.

Yessir, inertia is the greatest friend the institution of matrimony has, the greatest homemaker and preserver of hearthstones. It is the tie that binds. Inertia keeps more couples together than any other one thing. When you have lived in the same house with the same man for 29 years, it's just too much trouble to pull up stakes.

Yes, my husband does a lot of witless things and has a lot of vices, but so far as I know, they are all of the outdoor type. In general, I favor outdoor vices rather than indoor. And I really don't object too much to his hunting and fishing.

I mostly pretend to object for psychological reasons. A man is so constituted that it is not good for him to get what he wants too easily. There must be enough resistance to whet his appetite. So on general principles, whenever my husband mentions a hunting or fishing trip, I think up excellent reasons why he shouldn't go, knowing full well that he is going anyway. If I appeared too eager, he'd get suspicious and stay at home, the sap!

As long as it's a bass rather than a blonde, a bream rather than a brunette—as long as he comes home with scales and feathers in his pockets rather than bobby pins, I'm really not complaining too loud.

I'm Betting on Bob

You don't have to be a good shot to get quail. Expert marksmanship is really not necessary. A man can become a good quail shot without becoming a good marksman if he does the thing right—if he will add an ounce of brains to the ounce of shot in his gun.

Long ago I recognized the fact that I would never become a really good shot. My vision is not what it might be. I lack the coordination and nerveless composure that a top-notcher must have. And I have too much imagination, I reckon, ever to become very good.

How, I said, can a fellow who is only a fair-to-middling shot become a good game-getter? Well, I decided, by taking thought. I didn't add one cubit to my stature by so doing, but I did add birds to my bag. I made myself something of a game strategist. Since I've admitted I'm only a fair shot, maybe you'll forgive me for calling myself a strategist. Got to have one leg to stand on, you know.

As a result of my thought-taking, I have become a better-than-fair game-getter. In fact, I often outshoot better shots, and bag more birds than hunting companions who are crack marksmen.

Quail hunting is the hardest sort of wing-shooting if you do it wrong; one of the easiest if you do it right. As I have often said, it is like golf: fun that people make work out of, an easy game that people make hard. And the secret of quail shooting—the sum and substance of the bird hunter's strategy—is figuring with Bob instead of against him.

Quail hunters are hard on themselves. Many of the hard shots they get are of their own making. They really are. Due more to the dumbness of the shooter than the smartness of the shootee. The unwary gunner invites trouble by putting himself at a disadvantage and giving the breaks to Bob, a fidgety fellow who doesn't need them, thank you. Too many hunters do their thinking after the covey gets up.

"What do you think about," I asked a young fellow, "when you walk into a point?"

"Think hell!" he laughed. "It's too late to think. I'm just hopin' and prayin'."

"Do a little thinkin' before you step into 'em, and you won't have to do so much prayin' later," added an old-timer.

And that's gospel. What the average bird hunter needs is a little preventive medicine. A good prognosis will save many a bitter diagnosis, in hunting as in other things.

The first principle in this business of figuring with Bob is to catch the same train he does. Get behind the covey. This is common sense of the commonest sort, and its practicality should instantly appeal to anybody—except an overanxious hunter. Let's take a laboratory case.

Your dogs are on point in that clump of ragweed. If you are quail-wise, you don't rush heedlessly in, hell-bent for election, and start shootin' and hopin'. You do a little thought-taking, surveying first the immediate lie of the birds, then the more distant features of the landscape, to ascertain the proba-

I'm Betting on Bob

ble line of flight. And in many cases, this is a definitely ascertainable fact.

If the covey is an old acquaintance of yours, a casual glance will reassure you on this point. Every covey—you can depend on it—has a haven of refuge to which it scurries in time of danger. Its flight habits are almost invariable as long as the landscape remains unchanged. This sweet constancy is one of the things that makes quail hunting the matchless pastime which it is.

Flight habits, indeed, become almost hereditary in certain coveys. Birds that I have hunted for twenty years, here in my home state, betake themselves to the same harborage when harassed. There's a homestead covey that I have been shooting as far back as I can remember. Ever since I was a boy in corduroy breeches and brogues, they have always made for an overgrown Negro graveyard. They did it again yesterday.

If a man has shot a covey before, there is little excuse for his not knowing how the birds are going to behave. And even in new territory it is comparatively easy to spot their flight. The recipe is simple: just pick out the place where it would be most impossible for you to shoot them—the place you'd fly to if you were a bird yourself. If you know the abc's of quail nature, your deduction will be better than a bet.

Now, your dogs are still pointing—if they are any good—and you have more or less satisfied yourself as to the covey's line of flight. It is, then, a relatively simple matter to maneuver yourself into position so that you will be behind them when they take off. If the cover is sparse, skirt the skulking covey widely, keeping your gun in readiness for a premature flush.

If all goes well, you have assured yourself a straightaway shot, not at one target, but a dozen. Not at a single that flares crazily over your head, a spinning jenny that hasn't bought his ticket, or a ragged flanking contingent. You get the whole cake rather than the scraps. And there's little excuse for missing.

They are apt to fly straight when flushed from behind, because Bob is a practical mathematician; he reckons a straight line to be the shortest distance between where he is and where he'd like to be. The necessity for estimating lead, therefore, arises less frequently than it otherwise would.

Such positioning of the gunner, in fact, eliminates many of the difficult angle shots, since capering birds caper because they have to, or because something—often the thoughtless hunter—interposes itself between them and their destination. The gunner is also in much better position to watch the singles. They go down in a more restricted area, with enough in one place to make hunting worth while.

Everything I have said about jockeying for position before a covey rise applies also to a pointed single, especially if the single is in the open. But wherever it is, there is always one way he is more likely to fly than any other. Take a minute to figure it out, and let your *gun* be thinking of that likeliest line of flight before you kick the bird out.

You might as well get behind them whenever you can and get whatever advantage there is, because anything else you do is likely to be love's labor lost. And worse. A partridge is going where he's going, and there is little you can do about it. To get between him and home-sweet-home in the fond hope of influencing his line of retreat is sending yourself an engraved invitation to trouble. 'Tis a boyhood folly, to be put aside with mumps and falling-in-love-with-teacher.

The opportunity the quail hunter has to maneuver for position while the quarry obligingly waits is another thing that makes bird hunting a unique and peerless pastime. What other kind of wing-shooting, pray, gives a gunner time to call a meeting of the ways and means committee?

When hunting birds whose haunts and habits are familiar, you can often avoid the necessity of such maneuvering by hunting *toward* the customary haven, so that both you and the dogs are naturally behind the covey when it rises. Sometimes it is just as convenient to hunt a field from one direction as another. It is an expedient that I often resort to, even when it necessitates a little extra walking.

And when I locate a new covey whose line of retreat I

I'm Betting on Bob

am unable to anticipate, I can at least get on the same side as the dogs. When the dangers that beset a covey are concentrated, the birds are likely to take off less frantically, to break up less, and to fly straighter. Also, your dogs are not endangered by an accidental discharge or an erratic pellet. After all, it is but an elementary—and inexpensive—precaution and one which every hunter should take.

There is another trick that pays dividends too, especially on windy days, when birds are fluttery and apprehensive. A little reflection will tell anyone what old hands know—that it is best to hunt against the wind whenever practicable. When you approach a covey with the wind, the body scent is swept ahead, so that the most irreproachable dogs may over-run their birds and flush them. In hunting against the wind, the scent is wafted towards the dogs and they have ample warning of the skulking covey. This is not a hypothesis, but a common-sense fact that you can demonstrate for yourself. Time and again it has meant more birds in my bag.

What is the most difficult shot in quail hunting? I'm sure I don't know. One man's meat is another's poison. I seldom connect with a bird I've seen on the ground first, which, praise Allah, seldom happens. And a bird flying straight toward me always gets my whatever-it-is.

Some of the reputedly hardest shots are hard because of poor timing on the gunner's part. For instance, the customer that pirouettes dizzily around your head is the nemesis of many a man. Yet the recipe for such a customer is simple: don't make up your mind until he makes up his. Wait until he decides where he's going and gives the conductor his ticket. When he quits his acrobatics and straightens out, he'll probably still be within range. Most of our missing is due to shooting too soon, anyway.

A bird that bounces unannounced from the edge of a woods and pitches over the trees is another elusive shot. It is well-nigh impossible to hit such a skyrocketing target at close range with any consistency. But timing counts again. Wait until your bird gets to the top of the ladder and levels off, and you've got an almost stationary target. Drop him while he's shifting gears. It's like hitting a tin can in the air: wait until it reaches the top of its arc and stops. Learning to shoot birds is learning to wait.

Knowing your dogs is, of course, a fundamental part of hunting. Not merely knowing them as dogs, but as individuals. For dogs are as individualized as the men who hunt them. Except within rough limits, there is no such thing as standard behavior.

One dog will pass unawares a trail an hour old. Another will give it a cursory sniff and decide it's yesterday's newspaper. Another still will seize upon it avidly, follow it painstakingly, and ultimately lead you to a covey that was congratulating itself.

One dog will "die standing up" ten yards from a covey. Another will think his performance sloppy unless he nails it at ten feet. One, a general practitioner, is content merely to locate his birds. Another, a specialist, will give you a bill of particulars by pointing his muzzle at the precise spot. "That's where they're at, Boss. Jes' follow my nose!"

If you are a good diagnostician and can read the signs, you will not only get more birds, but have a lot more fun in the bargain. To a man who knows his dogs, "every little movement has a meaning of its own," as the song hit ran. That telltale mannerism, unobserved by strangers, is an open book to you. But you've got to love a dog to understand him. And sometimes you've got to be charitable.

I have a waggish Llewellin who loves to point a rabbit now and then. She's a grand old dame, and I never reprimand her, because she never fails to semaphore me with her tail: "You needn't rush. This is off the record." I love the old thing for her foibles and harmless conceits. As my hunting companion remarked: "It don't cost nothin' and she enjoys it. And you needn't worry about a grandma's morality."

If you hunt quail nowadays, you can't afford to miss any tricks. Bob has become smart, and you've got to hunt him smart to make any headway. Knowing where to hunt, when

I'm Betting on Bob

to hunt, and how to hunt is becoming more important than shooting straight. "You gotta be more 'n a hunter," a Georgia guide gravely told me. "You gotta be a politician."

Time was—but everybody is tired of hearing that, and nobody ever believed it anyway. It was, though, but it ain't. Bob is no longer plentiful, and what there is left of him has a strong interest in self-preservation. There's a lot about his politics that I haven't learned. There's also a lot that I have. Heck, I've been long enough learning. A man doesn't live with one woman for twenty-five years without finding out something about her.

I bagged 100 quail last season—in spite of my undistinguished shooting—because I learned to figure with Bob instead of against him. But I have not learned to outfigure him. Nor has anybody else. Whoever says he has is a bald-headed, flat-footed, pigeon-toed liar—unless he weighs more than 158 pounds!

Don't worry if you have birdless days. We all do. Don't worry if your dogs have off days. They all do. Don't worry if you sometimes get so you couldn't hit a bull in the posterior extremity with a horticultural implement. Don't we all? And don't mind it if a covey rise flusters you. It rattles everybody who hunts for fun. And Heaven help the fellow who doesn't!

A Bird Hunter Must Walk

Even my worst enemies admit that I am a good walker. It is one of the few things they are unanimous about. They will tell you that I am an undistinguished shot, that I am addicted to sleeping in church, and that my language is not always as chaste as driven snow. Then they will all say in unison: "But how that moth-eaten old biped can walk!"

And that is a source of considerable pride to a 45-year-old chap who has been a heart suspect for twenty years, and who is regarded as a third-rate investment by all insurance companies. I do have a good pair of legs. Somewhat skinny and unromantic perhaps, but eminently practical.

If I were not a good walker I would be in a sad way, because quail hunting is pre-eminently a walking business. Is there any other sort of hunting that requires so much of it? Just to keep you grouse and turkey hunters from ganging up on me, may I restate my case this way: I maintain that more people walk more miles while quail hunting than while hunting anything else.

A Bird Hunter Must Walk

Bobwhite, or *Colinus virginianus* as the Ph.D.'s call him, is getting to be a pretty shady citizen. He has abandoned his open-field tactics and taken to all manner of ruses. The old boy has become a swindler and trickster of the first water, and a denizen of the deep tangled wildwood. If you want to find him, you must go where he is, not where he ought to be; and I lay that down as an unassailable fact.

Now I confess that I hate to walk just for the sake of walking. I can truthfully say that I never have taken a walk in my life. And I especially abominate city walking. Fifteen blocks of it would put me in the hospital. Yet I can return from a fifteen-mile bird hunt feeling fresher than a daisy. Maybe it's the van Winkle in me. Old Rip was not lazy, you remember. Nobody who hunted and fished as indefatigably as he did could be called that. Rip just had an "insuperable aversion to all kinds of profitable labor."

At any rate, no one could walk as much as I do without discovering a few things about walking. If you are a bird hunter you may have discovered them for yourself; but if you'll listen to me now I'll listen to you some other time—and right patiently, too.

Let's start with the very foundation of good walking, and of course I mean the feet. That's the part we do our walking with, the part subjected to the most punishment during a long, arduous hike. Watch your feet, brother, if you expect to return from an all-day hunt in any sort of fettle.

A prudent hunter always takes an extra pair of shoes and breeches, and a change of socks. Bird hunting nowadays will take a fellow into the darnedest places. In spite of all the assurances he has given his doting spouse, he is liable to have wet feet when he starts homeward.

Now you may hunt in wet shoes and clothing, and suffer no ill effects *as long as you keep walking*. I have yet to catch cold or suffer any discomfort from hunting while wet, even after wading knee-deep through the inundated bays of the Carolina low country. Yes, it's all right so long as you keep moving. But when you stop walking and dawdle about, or get into a car with feet and clothing wet, you are philandering with danger. You are sending an R.S.V.P. invitation to colds, pleurisy, pneumonia, and various other miseries that will make you sorry you didn't have better sense.

Invariably I have paid the piper when compelled to keep wet clothing on *after* the hunt. Haven't you had the same experience, or are you one of those shaggy-chested, red-corpuscled birds who can take it—for a while? As for me, maybe I'm just not rugged. Or maybe experience has knocked a little sense into my noggin. Anyway, I always have the proper accessories in my car or at my return point, and I change into them immediately when I quit walking. I'd hate like the dickens to be laid up for a week in the bird season!

Whether your feet are wet or not, a change of shoes can be extremely restful. On an all-day hunt I start with boots and woolen socks. I am feeling more or less vigorous in the forenoon and can stand the gaff. But around noon I change to lighter equipment if possible, replacing the boots with well-worn shoes, or even a friendly pair of low shoes and light canvas leggings.

Such a change tends to offset fatigue. Regardless of how much I've walked, the lighter equipment makes me feel like a barefoot boy in the spring, when he doffs his "prison cells of pride," as Whittier called them.

No two pairs of shoes fit alike. That fresh pair you put on around noon will fit you in different places. Your foot appreciates the change instantly. Changing shoes redistributes the stresses and strains, and often prevents a horny induration of the epidermis, which is what my dictionary calls a corn. I'm not podiatrist enough to explain just how such a change helps, but I know it does. I imagine it is comparable to the pleasure a woman derives from doffing her party girdle when she gets home. But now I'm getting on alien ground.

If you haven't an extra pair of shoes, even a change of socks will be a big help. You will wonder how such a little change can make so much difference in walking comfort. Have you

A Bird Hunter Must Walk

ever tried this recipe for jaded feet—just a change to fresh socks?

Several years ago, in the course of a long hard hunt, a new boot began to rub my heel. The hunting was good, and at first I was hardly aware of discomfort. You can stand a lot of pain when you are having a good time. Besides, I didn't have an emergency pair of shoes in the car, and there was little I could do about it. That night when I removed the boot a strip of skin came off with it. The net result was an infection that kept me from hunting for two weeks.

Had I been able to change shoes, the trouble might have been averted. But from that blistered heel I did derive a scrap of wisdom: never, never embark on a long hunt in a pair of boots or shoes that have not been thoroughly broken in. How many of you bird hunters can verify this?

A hunting companion had a similar experience with a protruding nail in his boot. Having no extra footgear in his car, and no means of removing the nail, he kept limping and cussing. A disabling infection resulted.

Have you ever waxed blasphemous over a nagging nail that was too bad to let you walk with comfort, and not bad enough to make you take the boot off and do something about it? You just cuss the thing—and keep hobbling. Strong characters have been known to tolerate such torture the livelong day.

In dry weather, when you are reasonably certain of not encountering water, an excellent equipment is a pair of flexible low-quarters or friendly old shoes, and light leggings. Thus outfitted, you really can stride along. But to prevent slipping, any hunting shoe or boot should have a rubber or a composition sole, or else short cleats. While hunting in new leather soles, I once slipped down a bank covered with pine straw—slipped so hard I broke my specs and jarred my very ancestors. Now when I use leather bottoms I screw three or four short golf cleats into them.

Such a nonskid surface gives me confidence in climbing hills, walking over ice-coated ground, and jumping ditches.

In ditch jumping, you must jump with a will, and he who hesitates is lost. It is not a matter to be undertaken half heartedly. Cleats are also a great help in preventing fatigue. Try them sometime. But if your wife gives you Hail Columbia for treading on her floors, don't try to involve me as an accessory before the fact! Cleats, though, aren't the only solution. There are nonskid soles and other devices. Maybe you have hit upon one that has proved satisfactory.

If something goes amiss with your feet, whatever it is and wherever you are, stop instantly and correct it. Otherwise it will surely lead to trouble—probably before the day is over. Some time ago, while ten miles from my car, I became aware of the fact that my boots were too short, that my toes were painfully cramped. Now, a too-short shoe is an abomination. I took my boots off and tried to stretch them, but couldn't. Walking became more and more painful and I was soon limping on both feet, which is twice as bad as limping on one. I had paid ten bucks of school-teacher money for those boots, but ten miles was ten miles. Besides, I had planned to hunt all the following week, and wanted to risk no disablement. So I decided to operate.

First, I considered ripping out the toes. No, I reflected, that would let the briers and thorns in, and mayhap a damaging sliver of wood. So I sat down and methodically cut a hole in the back of each boot—so that my heels could protrude. When I put the boots on again, what a great and gladsome difference!

How sweetly unconscious walking can be when everything fits! What agonizing exertion when you are tormented by pinching footwear! And what can give a poor mortal such blissful relief as easing off a pestering shoe? Ever take yours off in church, or at a movie? Ah-h-h! How grateful and happy your embattled tootsies felt!

But to get back to the story of my own boot troubles, my rough surgery did little harm after all. A good shoemaker sewed soft leather over the holes so that my heels could protrude just a little—but that little meant the difference between comfort and downright suffering.

A Bird Hunter Must Walk

Never walk in a shoe that is too short. It will double up your toes, make them painful and touchy for days, and even put you out of circulation for a while. A toe injury can be extremely painful. Once I broke a big toe, suffered acute walking discomfort for weeks, and got no sympathy from anybody. In fact, everybody else thought it was funny. I never before realized how indispensable one toe is.

I have found that some of my shoes got shorter as I wore them. Maybe it was because they were continually subjected to water and heat and consequently shrank; or perhaps an arch gradually weakened and let my foot down. Anyway the aftermath was a crippling leg-cramp. Has this sort of thing ever happened to you?

So to be on the safe side, when you buy hunting shoes be sure you have plenty of room—say about half an inch clearance for your longest toe. A hunting shoe should be not only long enough, but big enough in every way. If I have any contribution to make to posterity anent shoes, it is this: Buy a shoe that is big enough—big enough when it has dried out, big enough when you have that extra sock on, big enough even if your arches should let you down.

Why does man, who has been called the masterpiece of evolution, the crowning glory of civilization, the smartest of the bipeds, the paragon of animals—why does he buy shoes that hurt his feet? Vanity of vanities, saith the preacher, all is vanity. Sometimes it seems that *Homo sapiens* should be abbreviated to *Homo sap;* there might be some excuse for a woman to be vain about her feet, but mister, who the heck would ever think of *your* nether extremities as being romantic?

Have you ever noticed the shoes Uncle Sam puts his nephews in? They're all oversize. At first the boys exercise their immemorial prerogative of griping; but talk with those same boys after a 25-mile hike with full pack. They'll grudgingly admit that those oversize shoes are good walkers. From what I hear, most of the lads in uniform have had less foot trouble from walking than they had in civilian life, in spite of the many hardships they undergo.

There is a saying that all policemen have big feet, and actually that's a compliment. They are big men, as a rule, and they have to do a lot of walking. The important thing to bear in mind is that they are smart enough to buy shoes that are large enough. Take a lesson from men who know their feet!

When you try on a hunting boot, stand up and let your foot flow down into the leather under your weight. Also, put on that extra sock first. Don't guess, or merely try to make allowance. Try on *both* boots. Remember, your feet have separate personalities. One can't speak for the other.

With these admonitions in mind, keep trying until you find shoes which you think fit you perfectly—then put them back and get a pair at least half a size larger. Brother, if you ever regret it, you can charge them to me. I've got so much charged to me now that a few boots won't matter. In the long run, your feet will thank me, whether you do or not.

Also keep in mind this simple truth: the way you feel at night will depend largely upon how your feet have fared during the day.

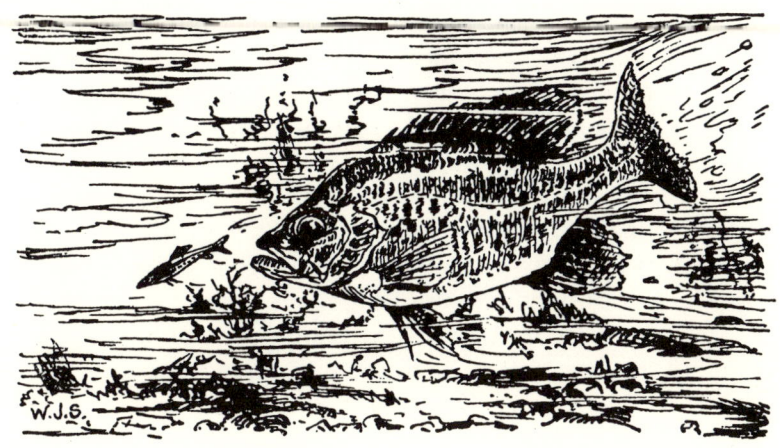

Minnows for Sale

A few days ago I saw a retired schoolmaster fishing for bass in an overgrown millpond. His chair was tilted comfortably against the cooling trunk of a sweet gum, an opened book lay on his lap, and a look of sweet benignity on his face. As I drifted by, his big demijohn cork plopped noisily and plummeted downward.

"Pardon me, but aren't you getting a bite?" I ventured.

"No. Just the minnow I'm using. See?"

And he levered up a seven-inch sucker in confirmation.

"Goodness! Will they tackle a king-sized minnow like that?"

"Well, if a bass takes the sucker, I'll go home and eat the bass. If not, I'll go home and eat the sucker. One way or another," he chuckled judicially, "I always take fish home."

Here was an arrangement that had something to recommend it, leaving little to the element of chance, or to caprice of wind and weather.

"Another advantage of fishing with a big minnow is that I don't have too many interruptions," he resumed. "Can get more reading done. When a man's reading Aristotle—"

But I was more interested right then in *Huro salmoides* than in Aristotle. I always figured that if I didn't bother Aristotle, Aristotle wouldn't bother me. Besides, the placid old schoolmaster caught more potbellied behemoths from the pond than anybody else in the neighborhood. Here was a local authority worth respecting.

"Your position on Aristotle is undoubtedly sound," I magnanimously conceded. And blithely skipping some 23 centuries, I added: "Are live minnows the best bait for this pond, sir?"

"I couldn't say unqualifiedly that minnows are best, but I will say this: when bass will take anything else, they will take minnows. And they will sometimes take minnows when they *won't* take anything else. Even under the most adverse conditions, when all other enticements fail, I can still waylay a reluctant few with frisky minnows. Yes, sir, a minnow bucket is always good creel insurance."

"Do you minnow-fish exclusively?" I asked.

"Oh, no. I do a deal of casting, too. But when I have got to have a fish or two regardless, I always count on minnows."

I find myself in accord with the unruffled philosopher of the millpond. Indeed, I am brash enough to go further. In Virginia, the Carolinas and Georgia, more crappies and bass are taken on live minnows than on all other lures, both animate and inanimate, combined.

The same thing may be applicable to other localities as well. You will have to testify as to the gustatory preferences of crappies and bass in your own purlieus. I am restricting myself to my own neck of the woods lest I be indicted for taking up too much territory.

I do not mean that Rebel bass and crappies are less gullible or more discriminating than their northern and western cousins, nor that Rebel anglers are more primitive in their methods. After all, live minnows are the natural vic-

Minnows for Sale

tuals of bass and crappies, in spite of the omnivorousness of both species. They head the daily bill of fare. As my blackwater paddler remarked: "These here fish was raised on minnows, and they seldom git above their raisin'."

I am not exclusively or even generally a minnow fisherman. For 35 years I have been offering bass and crappies all manner of thingamabobs which I hoped they would consider edible substitutes. I am continually experimenting with this and that, continually inviting insolvency by acquiring every specious device designed for the seduction of the species. In short, I am just as big a sucker as you are. But when the most enravishing prima donnas of my tackle box fail and I have got to have a fish or two, I resort to the plebeian practice of minnowing.

As an example of the popularity of minnow-fishing in the unreconstructed and unrepentant South, let's have a look at South Carolina. Within easy fishing distance of Columbia are such reservoirs as Lake Murray, with its 500 miles of shore line; the Santee-Cooper lakes with their 166 thousand acres teeming with crappies and bass; uncounted sand-hill ponds with their quotas of bulging carnivores; and such legendary game-fish streams as the Edisto, Pee Dee, Cooper, Ashepoo, Combahee, Black and Waccamaw rivers. No wonder fishing is not a pastime but a passion with South Carolinians!

Within a radius of 20 miles of where my posterior extremity is at present deposited, there are at least 200 places where you can buy minnows—if they haven't sold out. Along the lazy, meandering Santee-Cooper shore line there are uncounted thousands of minnow-dispensing establishments. Highway and sidestreet signs with such legends as *Minnows for Sale* and *Blue Bait*—the fragrant blue angleworms of the swamp—are as ubiquitous as plug mules and pickaninnies.

An enterprising dealer in Columbia sold 5 thousand minnows in a single day. A statistically-minded friend figures that as many as 100 thousand are sold in this immediate area on spring week ends when the weather is propitious. And this is hardly a drop in the bucket. The number distributed by the enterprising entrepreneurs up and down the shore line of the Santee-Cooper is beyond decent conjecture.

Yet at times it is virtually impossible to buy minnows. Unless we reserve them in advance, we sometimes drive considerable distances to eke out a week-end bucketful. Last spring the local supply was completely exhausted. Harassed dealers resorted to importing bait.

Run-of-mine minnows sell here for around 75 cents a dozen. For five- or six-inch suckers you will pay $1.50 per. Minnow-merchandising is a pretty big business. Most of the minnow seining is done at night. The lowly seiner's main qualifications seem to be an immunity to mosquitos and cotton-mouth moccasins, a contempt for personal comfort, an enviable ability to dispense with sleep, and a wife he had just as lief spend the night without.

But a lucrative business it is. One minnow seiner with two husky sons told me that he made $5,000 last year; yet his shanty leaks so badly that the whole family has to pile into their new Buick whenever it rains. But verily, whatever its emoluments, 'tis a business of which I had rather be on the consuming than the producing end.

What kind of minnow is best? That depends somewhat on the type of fishing, the season of the year, and the particular body of water one has designs on. The shiner, roach, hickory shad, sucker, mullet and madtom (not all of these will mean the identical species in other regions) all have their uses and their advocates. Perhaps nine tenths of the minnows used in this section are shiners—genus *Notropis*—but "shiner" here is a generic term that also may include small hickory shad, some of the roaches and mullets, and, unfortunately, carp. In other words, almost any variety of small silvery fish.

For crappie fishing small shiners are best, although Mister Goggle-Eye can engulf a surprisingly large minnow when he has a mind to. The crappie is the cottontail of the finny fins. The best place to fish is the precise spot where you are most likely to get your hook hung. Down on the Santee-Cooper there is a saying: "Under every log there are three crappies

Minnows for Sale

and one bass waiting for somebody's minnow." And there are millions of stumps, submerged brush piles and half-drowned logs that were anchored to the bottom before the water was impounded.

Crappies are highly gregarious and feed ravenously when they feed at all. No fish in the world will outbite them when they take a notion. Being less temperamental than bass, they are the stand-by of the average fisherman, redeeming for him many a bad day. While parked over a brush pile in Murray last fall, a companion and I caught 20 handsome specimens within 30 minutes, and with only a dozen minnows, by the simple expedient of squeezing our shiners out of the boated crappies and dropping them back into the water again. Crappies will take dead minnows readily if the water is choppy, or if the bait is moved up and down to simulate life.

Throwing crappie lines over the gunwale and letting the boat drift lazily is another method highly regarded by some, and an excellent way to locate schools. Big, shimmering crappies may be taken rapidly in the hydroelectric reservoirs of the South, at almost any time of the year, if one knows how and where to fish.

The crappie is at its biggest and best in these reservoirs. In them it frequently attains a weight of three, sometimes five pounds. A big crappie never ceases to amaze me by its bigness. A five-pounder is about the biggest fish for its size in the world.

Your Yankee books all say that crappies may be readily taken on small spinners and other fly-rod lures, but this information doesn't seem to have gotten down to the Southern crappie yet. We seldom take them on a fly rod with any sort of lure. Ninety-nine out of every hundred are caught on live minnows, although they occasionally succumb to the blandishments of small trolled plugs.

In some waters the sucker is the most effective minnow, particularly in ponds where the sucker is the principal forage for bass. And when one is fishing for really big bass, the big sucker is the best bait in the world. Nine tenths of the big-mouth leviathans I have seen—from nine to 15 pounds—were taken on big suckers.

If you told me I *had* to catch a big bass, I'd buy a dozen big suckers, get a leave of absence for about three days, and kiss Alice good-by. And I'd probably report the mission completed when I got back. I said probably. I often see pictures of giant bigmouths with favorite plugs in their cavernous jaws, or with some embattled citizen standing proudly by disporting the alleged rod-and-reel. Sometimes the pictures are honest. But if the bass weighs much over eight pounds and was caught in Virginia, the Carolinas or Georgia, I'd risk a certain amount that it was really taken on a big, fat sucker. Of course, it may be that I am just a cynic. I'm not talking about the one *you* caught, anyway.

The hickory or gizzard shad is also highly esteemed as bass bait, especially in large new reservoirs where it abounds. I have seldom found the shad in small ponds or in old waters. The big hydro-electric basins of the South, particularly in their virginal years, are a shad paradise. They multiply and grow incredibly fast, furnishing the *pièce de résistance* of the first largemouth crop. And how bass do fatten and batten on them!

Everything considered, the hickory shad has no superior as a forage fish for bass, however offensive its greasy carcass may be to the gastronomic sensibilities of you and me. In such basins as Murray and the Santee-Cooper, whenever you see a school of shad cut the water in a frantic somersault, you may be quite sure that a committee of largemouth bass is busy collecting taxes.

In some sections of the South, the mud kitten or madtom is *par excellence* the bass bait. If you are fishing the Shenandoah, the Potomac or the upper reaches of the James in Virginia, "minnows" will always mean madtoms, which are cast downstream and retrieved slowly up through the ripples and falls. As a matter of fact, madtoms are good bass minnows anywhere, but because of their venom-laden spines and quickness on the draw, many people are disinclined to try them. A

Minnows for Sale

madtom is the only thing with fins that I am honestly afraid of, the result of painful boyhood memories.

In recommending minnows, I am not suggesting that you renounce your rods and tackle box. I am just saying that when fish are not biting at all, when they are so lackadaisical that your most glamorous offerings and your most energetic efforts fail altogether, you may still coax a few into the frying pan with live minnows. I have found a sprightly minnow to be a pretty sure fillip for a jaded appetite. I know, of course, many lure fishermen will not agree with me. But I am citing my own experience, in my own part of the country.

When fish are feeding actively, you will probably catch more by casting or trolling than by live-baiting because you cover more territory, you speak to a bigger audience. But there are times when all fathomable factors are wrong and fish won't bite at all. There are also times when fathomable factors are right and fish won't bite at all. Almost every body of water has its own idiosyncrasies. It is seldom safe to dogmatize.

Generally speaking, fish show a pronounced disinclination to feed before or after a major weather or temperature change. They have a strange prescience in weather matters. I have always observed, for instance, that bass seldom feed after a downpour heavy enough to affect the temperature of the water. And in extremely hot weather, when water bears the accumulated fevers of a long summer, fish betake themselves to the cooling depths and become phlegmatic, feeding only sporadically.

Last summer I spent a livelong day on the Santee, under a searing August sun, trying every item in my bulging tackle box—of both fly and plug variety—with commendable zeal and impartiality. By late afternoon I had not caught enough to convince my skeptical wife that I had been fishing at all. En route to the landing, I pulled alongside a friend with a handsome string astern.

"How come?" I asked.

"You haven't done any good?"

"Alice will swear I've been out with that blonde again," I shook my head dismally.

"Fish are down deep. To catch 'em, you've got to go down where they are. You can't reach 'em by casting. Here, take these minnows and drop 'em down 20 feet."

"Twenty feet? Why, that's as tall as a—"

"Twenty feet. And drop 'em down fast. They'll curl up their toes if you let 'em dally around the surface too long."

I dropped a hefty minnow down into the abysmal depths. It never got to the bottom because a three-pound crappie intercepted it. Other nice crappies followed, and I took enough fish home to salvage my pride, and dispel all skepticism on the part of my loving spouse. So I am in favor of minnows when the chips are down. As a weather-beaten old bass fisherman said to me: *"A minnow is the only thing in the world you can catch a fish with when he doesn't want to bite."*

There are times, I am sure, when even the most inveterate rodsman feels an urge for a spell of cane-fishing. Perhaps we think thus to snatch a fragrant page from boyhood. Or maybe there is something dark and primordial about it. At any rate, there are times when I've just got to see a cork go down. Are you that way too?

Cane-fishing, especially with live minnows, has its peculiar satisfactions. When you are casting, you know instantly whether the quarry is hooked. Not so with live-minnowing. When your capering cork suddenly plummets down, there follows a period of delicious uncertainty that brings a tingle to the most calloused spine. Shall I pull now, or shall I bide a wee? It's like waiting for a clock to strike in the dark, or for the fellow next door to drop that other shoe.

Beside, cane-fishing can be "mighty tranquilizin'," as the old schoolmaster remarked. You can read poetry if you like, or commune with Aristotle if you like the cut of his jib. You can get more worrying done while cane-fishing than any other way. You can drink in the blended colors of a waning after-

Minnows for Sale

noon, chat amiably with a companion, or ponder life's imponderables. You can sit and think. Or just sit.

"There are three classes of people who enjoy cane-fishing," I said to a whimsical companion. "The very young, the very old, and the—"

"And the pure in heart," he supplied with an engaging grin.

Maybe it wasn't what I had in mind, but I let it pass.

"I Went to See a Man About a Dog"

"It is cheaper to buy a good bird dog than to train one," I am continually hearing. And it might well be. But the oft-repeated statement rests on the tacit assumption that a good dog stays good, that a well-trained dog is more or less unruinable, and that the mere acquisition thereof is a passport to hunting happiness.

But as many a buyer can ruefully testify, parting with a liberal amount of specie doesn't necessarily bring sweet contentment to the parter. Dog buying is at best a precarious investment. A canceled check and a pedigree do not guarantee that one will continue to have and to hold a good bird dog. For unless you are one of the Lord's anointed, various unbeautiful things may happen to that paragon of virtues to which you have just acquired title.

The unvarnished truth is that a trained dog is a *perishable* commodity. Few things are so subject to deterioration. It is almost as hard—and it takes almost as good a hunter—to *keep*

"I Went to See a Man About a Dog"

a dog good as to make one good. Eternal vigilance is the price of a good bird dog, regardless of who you are, or where and how virtuously you live.

What are some of the untoward things that might happen to a good dog? I don't mean such physical mishaps as his coming into fatal juxtaposition with a speeding auto, his being picked up by some larcenous gent, or his succumbing to any of the multitudinous ills to which canine flesh is heir.

I mean rather the insidious and unphysical things, for which the owner may be unwittingly responsible, that may overtake a well-trained dog. How, in other words, can an inexperienced hunter ruin a good hunting dog without being aware of it?

"You've probably seen many a good dog go bad," I said to a crack trainer. "What are some of the chief factors in dog deterioration, especially the controllable human factors?"

"I'm glad you are giving trainers their day in court," he laughed. "A dog is seldom better than the man who hunts him. Not for long, anyway. Half the dogs we train and sell are ruined by the men who buy them."

"That's a pretty heavy impeachment of dog buyers," I defended.

"Oh, I don't mean they are an ungentlemanly lot. There's a special friendliness about people who love dogs. If I'm ever tried for my sins, I hope they'll have a lot of them on the jury. The kind of mishandling I have in mind is never deliberate. It is the result of inexperience or thoughtlessness, but the consequences are just as serious. A lot of dog buyers just have more money than they have sense. I don't like to sell a dog until I have hunted with the buyer. His style of hunting determines the sort of dog he needs. One man's aristocrat is another man's cur, you might say."

"Can you be more specific, and cite a few cases?" I suggested.

"Well, retrieving, for instance, which is more important than it used to be because more birds fall in inaccessible or unfindable places. Good retrieving often makes the difference between a good hunt and a passable one. Last season I sold a sharp retriever. Not a seasoned performer, mind you, but an intelligent youngster who took pride in his work. A few weeks later, Mike had quit retrieving entirely."

"Why?" I asked.

"His owner had unintentionally made him bird-shy."

"How did it happen?"

"As well as I can reconstruct it, his inexperienced and over-anxious owner shot a bird to pieces. Mike picked up the mangled carcass, savored it a moment, and gulped it down. The wrathful owner, thinking to check a bad habit forehandedly, whaled the stuffings out of the pup. And Mike just did a little dog arithmetic and played safe thereafter."

"What would prompt a trained dog to do that?" I asked.

"In Mike's case, it was simple. His owner had been feeding him an unbalanced ration—too many carbohydrates and not enough proteins—and Mike was meat-starved. I took him home and straightened him out, suggested a meatier diet during hunting season, and Mike and his boss finally became bosom cronies. When you bring a meat-starved dog and a mutilated bird together, it's powerful easy to fall from grace.

"But any number of factors might prompt a dog to crush or swallow an occasional bird. He might deliberately do it to get even with his master for some grievance. Maybe he resents the attentions shown a yard mate, or something like that. Some dogs are extremely jealous. Two retrievers will get to arguing about who's going to carry the mail, and one will settle the argument in the most direct way. And sometimes a dog will eat a bird just because he's a dog. They have their moments of weakness, like the people who hunt them. Even an old dog will sometimes get tired of wearing his halo and step completley out of character. An observing gunner learns his dog's weaknesses and favors them."

"Do you mean that young Mike should not have been disciplined?"

"Certainly he should have been disciplined, but not *over-disciplined*. Dogs differ greatly in the amount of punishment

"I Went to See a Man About a Dog"

they need, or *can take*. A word of disapproval here may have as much effect as a whacking there. *Never give a dog more than that particular dog needs.* It's the inevitability of punishment, rather than the severity, that counts anyway. When too harsh, it may backfire and overreach itself. Through temper or inexperience, a dog owner may overcorrect one fault and replace it with a worse one. A cure sometimes cures too much.

"For instance, there are more fool recipes for insuring tender-mouthed retrieving than you can shake a stick at. One fellow follows his neighbor's advice and lustily twists his pup's ears when he misbehaves. Then he wonders why the pup quits behaving altogether, if you know what I mean. Another hears of a highly ingenious remedy that never fails, so he stuffs the carcass of a bird with needles or pins and gleefully tosses it out to be retrieved. Another fills the carcass with cayenne pepper and invites his trusting pup to fetch. And they think it singular that their dogs sometimes acquire a lifelong distaste for birds!

"Now the hunters who ruined these dogs were most of them nice people. They probably paid their taxes, joined the Kiwanis Club, and remembered their wives' anniversaries. They were just inexperienced or thoughtless, and never dreamed of the probable wreckage they had caused."

This trainer's observations on retrieving, for which his dogs are noted, struck me as being altogether sensible and fair. But the best retriever specialist I ever knew was an old schoolmaster of a bygone day, whose thoroughness and quiet persuasiveness I shall not soon forget. Now most hunters are too impatient to teach retrieving. They are in such a blistering haste to be gone that they are content with a desultory quest. Sort of a lick and a promise when a bird is downed. And their dogs soon become infected with their masters' impatience and lose the habit of thoroughness.

But the old schoolmaster was a perfectionist, and a man of infinite patience. Well do I remember chancing upon him one autumn afternoon when he was training a starry-eyed little setter. The bevy had long ago rocketed away. Indeed, another party of hunters were already bombarding the dispersed members in a neighboring field, but the schoolmaster and his frisking protege were still sifting and resifting every scrap of evidence, and prying into every likely nook and corner. This they quietly continued until the lost was found.

"I'm more interested in training Princess than in pocketing a few birds," he explained, "so we are following the parable of the ninety-and-nine. In dog training, thoroughness must be your aim, sir. Thoroughness and obedience. Your word must be law and order. You mustn't ever tell a dog to do anything he shouldn't do—and see that he does it. For that reason, sir, you must always be right. Now the bedrock of habit formation is this: *Never allow an exception to occur.* Can you remember that, sir?"

"Yes, sir," I answered.

"I want Princess here to be a faultless retriever. It's retrieving that makes partridge hunting a gentleman's diversion. I'm training Princess for my grandson, and she must be as proficient in all departments as possible. That dog—and this watch—are about the only legacies I can leave him. And it would hurt me powerfully, sir, to think that I had left my grandson a dog that might embarrass him."

Thirty years and more have passed since the grand old schoolmaster paid the debt of nature and left a beloved grandson a matchless hunting dog. Grandson and dog too have long since gone the way of all flesh, but still the lesson lives in the passionate heart of one who loves, but has never quite achieved, perfection in anything he tried.

Dogs are often damaged by indiscriminate lending. A borrower, however fine a citizen he might be, can grievously mishandle a dog without intending to do so. I have in mind two beautiful prospects that were made gun-shy last season when strangers began cannonading over their sensitive heads. The youngsters had no center of gravity—such as the presence of their master—to allay their fears and restore their faith in mankind.

"I Went to See a Man About a Dog"

The damage is seldom so serious. But unseasoned dogs, however well trained, may acquire hurtful habits which pass unobserved and unchecked by a borrower. They may take unaccustomed liberties with a stranger, and go in for some de luxe backsliding in the owner's absence. Weeks of patient work may be undone in a single afternoon. So, generally speaking, lending your dog to a neighbor is bad business, and of course you must understand your neighbor's reluctance to lend his. There are naturally a few exceptions.

Some dogs are as impersonal as an umbrella and will hunt for anybody. "They never meet no strangers," as they say in Georgia. Others are as individual and personal as a fountain pen or a pair of garters, one-man dogs that should never be lent to anybody. Indeed, only a small proportion of dogs can be safely lent, and only a small proportion of hunters can safely borrow.

"Only two kinds of dogs are lendable," a hunting companion remarked, "those that are so good—or so sorry—as to be unhurtable."

"Lend your automobile, your grand piano, and your cooking stove," another advised, "but never your bird dog."

And a quiet Virginia gentleman who has been hunting birds for half a century chuckled: "Son, always keep one fine-looking dog to lend out—and be sure he ain't worth a damn!"

In commenting on what might be called the ruinability of dogs, I wish to except old and thoroughly seasoned hunters. Ordinarily the more mature a dog is the less he will suffer from being mishandled. His habits are more fixed, his responses more stable and predictable, and he is less likely to deviate from the conventional pattern of behavior. Therefore, *give a boy an old dog to hunt*. They won't hurt each other. The same advice applies to all inexperienced gunners, who might well ponder Franklin's counsel anent the wisdom of a man's choosing elderly ladies to do his consorting with!

"If I could just send my dogs to the country during the summer!" I often hear. But the country, with all its virtues, can be a great begetter of bad habits. Letting a dog roam the countryside untrammeled is not only an invitation to all sorts of physical mishaps, but may completely undermine his training. A foot-loose dog is not only a menace to bird rearing, but a wide-open candidate for such pernicious habits as chicken and rabbit chasing and bird bolting.

An unchaperoned dog may drift into the insidious habit of self-hunting, which is the worst species of backsliding known, and a vice which quite overtops anything else in the book. Thereafter he is wrapped up in his own business, and to heck with you. If you happen to be near enough to shoot his birds, he has no particular objection. If you happen to be a mile away, he has no objection either. Instead of hunting for you, you are hunting for him—literally most of the time. There are a dozen ways in which even a trained dog may go to seed when given a passport to half the county.

"How to ruin a dog? Talk him to death while he's trying to hunt!" contributed another trainer. "Many hunters are forever giving their dogs instructions, delivering lectures and preaching sermons, telling them where and how to hunt. In other words, telling a dog how to run his own business! One of my customers ruins every dog I sell him because he thinks he has more sense than the dog."

"Many like that?" I asked.

"You'd be surprised at the number. They are trying to be helpful, of course, but they are not doing their dogs any good. You can hear them half a mile away, like a portable radio. And most of them are great whistle blowers. I sometimes think a whistle has hindered more dogs than it has helped—especially a whistle in the wrong mouth. The best dog trainers I ever watched were the least noisy.

"To much butting in befuddles a dog, especially when he gets instructions which run counter to his nose and judgment. He loses his spirit and initiative, just piddles around to give the appearance of hunting. Leaf-raking, we called it in the old WPA days. A dog's instincts are refined out of him. He quits thinking and soon forgets *how* to think. He becomes

"I Went to See a Man About a Dog"

man-conscious instead of bird-conscious, and pleasing his master is more important than finding birds. Now, if a dog has a nose, let him use it. If he hasn't, trade him off for a wheelbarrow or something useful."

I myself have seen dogs injured by an overdose of advice, by too much solicitude on the part of the owner. That's one way to make a blinker, than which few things are than whicher. Three seasons back I hunted a spirited young pointer just after a plantation owner had bought him. No man could ask a finer gun dog. Last season I was again a guest on the plantation, and I was shocked to discover that Rollicking Bob had become, of all things, an incorrigible blinker.

How had it happened? A caretaker on the place gave me the inside story. The plantation owner, an elegant gentleman but inexperienced gunner, was immoderately proud of the young pointer and sought to make him as perfect as possible. Whenever Bob pointed, his master would begin cautioning him, keeping up a volley of advice and admonition while he maneuvered for shooting position. When on rare occasions the dog misjudged the precise location of the quarry, or a bevy flushed prematurely of its own accord, the owner would severely reprimand the dog.

Breamers Stop at Nothing

When I came to South Carolina 24 years ago, there were three things I swore never to do: eat grits, drink okra soup, and turn catalpa worms inside out. As regards the first two, I have remained stanch and uncompromised. I am still a virgin Virginian. But as regards the third—

Well, here I squat above a spillway, with my legs dangling over a tiny maelstrom 10 feet below. And I am straining my bifocals and trying to persuade a three-inch caterpillar that he looks handsomer with pajamas on the outside of his pants. Which shows how the strongest characters will degenerate in time.

Regardless of how adroitly it is done, catalpa-turning is not recommended for aristocrats, or for prudish souls with over-nice stomachs. The catalpa caterpillar is a juicy and overco-operative critter. When turned or squashed in the fingers, it exudes a greenish and bilious-looking substance that leaves an ineradicable black stain on hands and fingernails. A glance

Breamers Stop at Nothing

at a man's hands will tell you instantly whether he is an addict. It is the badge of the brotherhood of turners.

But there are times, especially in June and July, when the saucy redbreast sunfish, which we call the red-breasted bream down here, will disdain all other enticements. During March, April and May, he is not so fastidious. A big green catalpa, whether turned or unturned, is a banquet in itself. Inside-out business is gilding the lily then. But in late season the prized redbreast can be consistently seduced only by a freshly turned catalpa.

Squatting beside me are two other bream fishermen engaged in a similar enterprise, and apparently meeting with dubious success. They are both doctors, and their fumbling endeavors in this new field of surgery tickle me no end.

"How are you doing it, Henry?" one asks the other.

"With a matchstick," the other replies. "A fellow told me to push the stick through the worm lengthwise, then slide 'im off onto the hook."

"How does it work?"

"Nothing to write home about. They turn all right, but won't slip off onto the hook. I've been arguing with one customer here for five minutes. How are you doing it?"

"With a nail. A fellow gave me the same directions, with a nail. Sounds plausible, but ain't worth a tinker's. Besides, a damned caterpillar just squirted in my eye and it stings. Wish I had brought my surgical instruments along."

"What we really need is a first-class chiropractor," clucked the other doctor. "Wouldn't a job like this be duck soup for a chiropractor!"

"What method are you using, Professor?" They both turned to me.

"Gentlemen, your operative technique is wrong," I solemnly counseled. "You are endeavoring to turn them inside out. That is a mistake. Turn them *outside in*. It is somewhat disillusioning to hear two more or less reputable physicians confess their ineptitude at such a simple procedure. When I think of the confidence your patients repose in you, and your intimate knowledge of anatomy—"

"We don't turn our patients inside out, thank you. Now quit stalling, Prof, and show us how to do it."

"How much is it worth to you?" I bargained. "When I consult a doctor, I get a bill for professional services. If each of you will knock off a five-spot from what I owe you—"

"Go ahead, Shylock. No chance of collecting your bill anyway. I've already told my secretary to deduct it from my income tax as a bad debt."

"Then if you sons of Hippocrates will come closer, we'll conduct a clinic in worm-turning. First, remove the head. If you are a stanch States'-Rightist, bite it off. If you are a sissified Junior Leaguer, pinch it off like this. Then take a small, long-shanked hook—say a Carlisle No. 8—and place the rounded bottom of the hook—not the point—into the tail of the patient and press gently, slipping his petticoat up the shank with thumb and forefinger. Like this.

"Now your caterpillar is upside down, inside out, and outside in, and he doesn't know his what from a hole in the ground. In other words, he's in a hell of a shape. Now jab the point of your hook against your thumb to clear it. Like this," and I displayed a black-dotted and well-punctuated thumb as evidence of my skill. "Then you flip this anatomical anomaly into the current 30 feet away and—"

My rigmarole ended abruptly as the line cut a fast monogram across the frothing pool, into a foam-capped eddy, and back through the swirling current again. Quite a dancing master he is. Cocky as a bantam rooster. But a moment later a 16-ounce gamester flashes in the sun beside me.

Tricked out in the scarlet finery of spring, the redbreast sunfish is perhaps the most gorgeously hued of the freshwater game fishes. Its brilliance is always startling, like a resplendent jewel instantly drawn from its case.

And there are two other distinctions I ungrudgingly accord the red-breasted bream: the pluckiest and most flavorsome of all the pan fishes.

Breamers Stop at Nothing

Whenever I am fishing for bream in still water, I use a three-ounce glass fly rod, a leader almost invisibly small, and neither float nor sinker. I want the lure to waft downward with disarming gentleness, precisely as if it had fallen from an over-hanging tree. In fast water I make two adjustments: sufficient sinker to carry the hook down under the cypress knees and swirling "hammocks," and a leader *stronger than my hook,* so the hook will straighten out to disengage itself when hung.

Otherwise I would be continually replacing tackle, for the handsome reds and the big copper-headed bream (bluegill) hang out in the identical places a hook is most likely to get snagged. A slender hook thus straightened may be readily pressed back into shape between thumb and forefinger. When a body is deep in the mazes of a cypress swamp, a tiny hook can be a precious possession.

The catalpa caterpillar has certain unique advantages as pan fish bait. First, it is not commonly molested by hook-robbers and undersized feeders, as are crickets, earthworms, May flies, wax worms, honeybee and wasp pupae, and other small insects. When you get a strike, the probabilities favor a nice fish. Secondly, the catalpa is so tough-skinned that it will cast almost as well as an artificial fly.

And thirdly, it is so durable and water-resistant that several fish may be successively taken on the same bait. I have taken as many as four without rebaiting.

The necessity of identifying the red-breasted bream, and distinguishing it from the copper-headed or bald bream, would hardly occur to even a tyro in the Deep South. So traditional are these rival species, and so immemorial the arguments as to their relative merits, that any 12-year-old boy from the Carolina low country can write you an "A" theme on either—and probably take you where you can catch a mess.

But for the benefit of those who have never angled in the unreconstructed kingdom, it might not be amiss to say that although the red-breasted bream (*Lepomis auritis* Linnaeus) and the copper-headed bream (*Lepomis macrochirus* Rafinesque) are both sunfishes, they differ in color, body conformation, habits and habitat.

The redbreast is instantly recognized by its flaming breast and sides, and by its extremely long ears, contrasting sharply with the somber hues and the short ears of the copperhead, which may flaunt a bar of burnished copper across its forehead. The redbreast is also the larger-mouthed and gamier of the two. It shows a marked predilection for rivers and creeks, while the copperhead bream attains its maximum size in ponds and lakes. And the redbreast is regarded as the more palatable, although it is hard to distinguish between two such incomparable table delicacies.

In size, they are similar. The largest redbreast I took this spring ran 21 ounces, the largest copperhead 24. It is always a mistake to weigh a fish, particularly a bluegill, which is undoubtedly the most eye-deceiving and overestimated fish in the world.

When you take a 10-ounce bluegill, you swear that it weighs 14. When you take a 12-ounce specimen, you swear that it weighs a pound.

Our low-country creeks and spillways are famed for their fishing. A serpentine black-water creek that steals its way through a brooding cypress swamp is to me a thing of dark enchantment, a mystic and primeval region where the strangest things happen naturally. And nowhere else on the habitable globe, I think, will one find such an amazing variety of game fish in comparable water.

Although I have fished these swamp creeks for years, I am perennially surprised by the size of the fish that sometimes thread their way up the log-jammed and tortuous channels. In a creek that a boy could jump without splitting his britches, an astute angler might hook a ponderous bowfin, a lithe chain pickerel, or a tackle-wrecking bass.

I have yet to return from an extended swamp foray without fish, and a tale or two to tell. But creek fishing is not without danger and discomfort, especially in late summer.

Breamers Stop at Nothing

For then the swamp is so infested with mosquitoes, horse flies, deer flies, chigoes and snakes that only a hardy or misguided wayfarer will venture far into its singing recesses.

I am not particularly snake-conscious, proceeding on the theory that a snake is as uncomfortable in my presence as I am in his. But only a witless wight will go blundering through a semitropical swamp in late summer with his eyes shut. There are rattlers and big cottonmouths aplenty, and in July and August the cottonmouths hang head-high from bushes and drop ponderously into the water as you pass.

I have had few upsetting encounters with snakes myself, but last summer I did get into one rather ticklish situation. A rusty cottonmouth blocked the narrow path ahead of me and refused to budge. There he lay hissing his displeasure and insisting on his privacy. Not a blessed stick or rock presented itself. That's one thing I dislike about this Carolina low country: no rocks. You can't for the life of you find one to flatten a chunk of lead, turn a tack-point in your shoe, or throw at a snake. Think I will bring some down here from my farm in Virginia. I am rock-rich up there.

Well, the big cottonmouth was still coiled and insisting on his rights under the constitution. I was confronted with what a diplomat would call an impasse and a taxpayer would call a hell of a fix. My little glass fly rod had a big catalpa dangling from the tip. Maybe I could tickle this peevish gent into vacating my parlor.

A moment later I rued my impulsiveness, for I had a heaving cottonmouth on a 50-dollar fly rod. It was a brand-new situation for me, and probably for him. I didn't know what to do, but he did. With one massive lunge, the gut leader snapped, and Mr. Cottonmouth suddenly remembered a business appointment and highballed it through the swamp, with a hook in his mouth and a green catalpa worm for a chin whisker.

There are people who can detect the presence of snakes by the sense of smell. I have no such gift. There are others who have a strange immunity to marauding insects. I have one swamping acquaintance who swears he has never been bitten by a mosquito, another who is blithely impervious to chigoes. The Lord failed to endow me with such talents.

Whenever I get chigoe-infested, I hit a beeline for 803 Sumter Street and diligently anoint myself with each of the seven brands of guaranteed insect lotion on my shelf. Alice regards such wholesale therapeutics with disfavor.

"That's the trouble with you," she lectures. "When you get sick, you use so many remedies you never know which cures you. When you get chigoes, you use so much different junk you never know which one does the work. Anybody with an ounce of gumption would use one at a time in the interest of science. A good education was sure wasted on you."

Our precious catalpa worms are sometimes hard to get. Incredibly plentiful at times, they are incredibly scarce at others. As a matter of fact, they seem to be scarcest when fish bite best, and most plentiful when fish bite least, but I reckon that's the way the world is run. The trees in my section normally produce four crops of caterpillars a year, with a three-week interval between egg-laying cycles.

During the dearth period between cycles, an ardent breamer will canvass a whole countryside for a hundred worms. One friend of mine drove 170 miles on a caterpillar quest. Another had a supply shipped by air from Alabama.

Caterpillar dealers can supply only a fraction of the demand, although many fishermen raise their own worms, or have sources of supply about which they are highly secretive. A man might tell you his wife's age, how he is going to vote, or how much money he owes the bank, but he will lie ingloriously to protect the source of his bait supply.

Catalpa worms, which are universally called "catawbas" down here, retail for three cents apiece in the spring, but during scarce periods a good bargainer can get almost any price he asks, especially around full moon in May, June and July. A full moon seems to affect breamers as well as bream. During May I saw a levelheaded banker pay $5 for a hundred caterpillars. During full moon in July, I heard a party of dis-

Breamers Stop at Nothing

traught breamers on the Santee-Cooper offer $1 a dozen for the horrendous critters that many benighted folks spray to get rid of.

The worms can be successfully refrigerated for two weeks, and thousands of breamers keep emergency supplies in their iceboxes, in spite of indignant squawks from their abused wives. After considerable experimenting, I have discovered a method of preserving the caterpillars almost indefinitely. But try to get me to tell you about it! My most coveted possession right now is the 15 cartons of caterpillars snugly reposing in my deep-freeze, each carton conspicuously labeled for Alice's benefit: "Worms: do not cook."

This spring an 80-year-old South Carolinian fell from a tree and broke his leg—while picking catalpa worms to go fishing. Catalpa trees are notoriously brittle-limbed. Worms were pretty scarce at the time, and after I had related the story to a group of bream fishermen on the Cumbahee, the comment of one clownish fellow broke up the party:

"Wonder if he got 'em all?"

"Every loyal South Carolinian has three ambitions," opines a waggish friend of mine. "He wants to re-fight the Battle of Gettysburg, run for governor on a States'-Right platform, and inherit a grove of catalpa trees. And he thinks maybe that Gettysburg affair might turn out different, now that we've got the atom bomb factory in Confederate territory!"

Good Bird Hunters Go to Heaven

Have you ever taken a friend hunting with you, then dropped him like a hot potato? Without drawing up a bill of particulars, you just made a mental note that said: never again! And have you ever spent a pleasant day with a hunting acquaintance and wondered why you were not invited again?

I have been in both positions—inviter and invitee—and I have speculated a little about the whys and the wherefores. Could it be a question of hunting manners?

There are some things a man can do best when alone, when any and all society is definitely unwelcome. But bird hunting seems not to be one of these. There is something about bird hunting that makes it peculiarly a social pastime, something about it that makes one man call another and say: "Hey, Bill, you old potlicker hound, how're you fixed for this afternoon?"

Seldom does one meet a solitary gunner, for companionship is surely half the hunt. The most gracious tribute one

Good Bird Hunters Go to Heaven

hunter can pay another is not to say that he is an accomplished shot, nor that his dogs are superbly trained, but that he is a fine companion in the field. Well might one ask himself, then, what sort of hunting companion am I?

Now, the components of good companionship are few. All one needs is a passing acquaintance with the rules of the game and a modicum of charity for his partner's idiosyncrasies. Compatibility is based on the little generosities which one friend shows another during the day, and for the most part these generosities are inexpensive.

A good hunting companion may find it necessary to engage in an innocent little fiction now and then. I do not mean that he is expected to tell a lie—perish the thought—but he might on occasion permit himself to fall into a sort of terminological inexactitude. I don't want any halos on a hunt.

After all, there are times when you've got to tell a lie to get the truth believed, as any married man can testify. There are also times when no gentleman will tell the truth. Now, don't hold up your hands in holy horror. What is courtesy, anyway? How much of it is little more than a beauteous and highly perfumed lie, the art of fibbing gracefully?

To get back to hunting, here is how our friend-making recipe works. When your companion makes a difficult shot, congratulate him. Help him admire himself. This doesn't cost anything. It doesn't hurt anybody, nor will it impair your chances of attaining the pearly gates. It is, in short, one of the cheapest ways of making a man feel good. And it will definitely improve the likelihood of your being invited on another hunt.

The exact phrasing of your felicitation may vary with the intimacy of your acquaintance and your intellectual attainments. If you belong to the intelligentsia, you might say: "A lovely performance, Henry, a lovely performance." But if you are a low-brow like me, you might say: "A damned good shot, old horse!" and let it go at that.

Brag about your companion when he makes a good shot. Maybe he'll be noble enough to brag about you when you make a good one. "An ideal hunting partner," a whimsical friend of mine remarked, "is one who makes it unnecessary for me to praise myself."

I have an acquaintance, incidentally a crack shot, who is employed as guide on a millionaire's quail plantation. "What is your main job?" I asked him. "My main job," he grinned, "is shooting at everything the boss shoots at—and persuading him that I missed." No wonder that fellow pulls down a good salary! I can think of several professions in which he would rise to the top.

Conversely, you must extenuate your companion's bad shots. If he misses a hard shot, you needn't bother. No extenuation is needed. He's got some sense himself. But if a fat partridge impudently lights on the barrel of his gun and he misses with everything in the foundry, that's the time a fellow needs a friend. Be one.

Try to say something that will restore your companion's self-respect, something reasonably honest. No masterpieces of mendacity, mind you, just face-saving little fictions. Did he step into a stump hole as he shot? Did the artful dodger duck behind a sassafras bush, slip through a hole in the shot pattern, or peradventure fly into the sun? Or maybe it was one of those tricky shots that few people appreciate the trickiness of.

Be charitable toward your companion's misses, and he will endorse your note, vote for you for sheriff, buy an insurance policy from your company, and let you sit up late with his pretty granddaughter. He will also invite you hunting again. Besides, when you miss one that a nine-year-old boy could have downed with a gravel-shooter, your companion might come gallantly to the rescue and explain away your embarrassment.

Good hunting manners also require you to be generous toward the other fellow's dog. The way to a man's heart may be through his stomach, but the shortest route to a bird hunter's heart is through his dog. You are not expected to connive at flagrant transgressions in the field, of course, but you *are* ex-

Good Bird Hunters Go to Heaven

pected to give your companion's dog the benefit of the doubt. Dogs are entitled to it oftener than they get it, anyway. There is such a thing as a dog's point of view, you know.

Love me, love my dog. The wisdom of the ages lies in that pithy saw. You can intimate that a man's uncle was a Republican, that his great-grandfather's conduct at the battle of Bull Run was pusillanimous, or that his half-brother has rickets and the seven years' itch, but never belittle his dog! Now, it's quite all right for him to belittle his own dog, and for you to belittle yours to your heart's content, but never vice versa, my wayfaring brother, never vice versa. Never lift ary finger agin his'n! That's the way feuds and political parties get started.

There's a funny thing about this business of explaining away a companion's embarrassment. It's all right for you to alibi his shooting, and for him to alibi yours, but it is bad manners for a man to furnish his own alibis. It is one of the things that a man can't do for himself. One of the surest ways a hunter can make his presence unwelcome is to insist on giving his companions voluble reasons for every shot he misses. Nobody is interested in such post-mortems.

"Why did you miss that rabbit?" I chided an ebony game-toter.

"De mainest reason was dat de rabbit and de shot didn't cohabit de same place at de same time," he replied, which is about as profound as anybody can get on the subject.

Some men are so constituted that they've got to blame something other than themselves for whatever goes wrong. Whenever they miss, it's their guns, their shells, their dogs, or something safely inanimate. Missing a shot is no disgrace. Only liars and writers hit everything they shoot at. If a man can't miss gracefully, he has no business hunting.

The same thing is true about being charitable to a companion's dog. I can excuse a miscue on the part of yours, and you can excuse a miscue on the part of mine, but a man must never whitewash his own dogs or gloss over their faults. That is distinctly not cricket. The only thing as abominable as a spoiled dog is an overindulged brat who can do no wrong in the eyes of its doting mother.

The prime test of a good hunting trip, of course, is whether all parties thereto get back home without any holes in them. The first requirement of a good companion is that he be a safe person to hunt with. However gracious and charming a fellow might be, you'd just as lief not have him drawing a bead on your bald spot. Making widows of nice women is not exactly good manners.

Bird hunting has its hazards, especially singles shooting in heavy cover. A gunner can be so intent on overtaking the gyrating target that he is unconscious of such intervening objects as the back of a companion's head. Many a bird hunter owes his life to his agility in hitting pay dirt in the nick of time.

A feeling of insecurity is ruinous to one's shooting. It is impossible to shoot well when you are constantly wondering whether your heirs and assigns will arrive at an equitable settlement of your estate. It is impolite to shoot too close to a companion, even if you miss him!

When anybody makes my ears ring, I am a little dubious about him thereafter. I figure that if he came that close he might come closer. Might as well shoot me as scare me to death. I am more important than a bird or two, at least to myself, and I hope to my wife. And although Alice is an amiable old dame, I am in no particular hurry for her to start collecting my life insurance.

One of the best ways to gauge a man's character is to take him bird hunting. There his frailties and his virtues, his shortcomings and his longcomings, his meanness and his magnanimity are all sure to crop out. People are inclined to behave naturally outdoors, unnaturally indoors. So before you take a fellow into partnership, or let him marry your youngest daughter (if you have any say-so in the matter, which I doubt), take him hunting with you. Of course, it works both ways. The young swain may be sizing you up as a father-in-law.

Good Bird Hunters Go to Heaven

What are some of the human frailties that come to the surface in bird hunting? Well, there's the gent who, too embarrassed to admit missing, pretends to have downed a bird. He holds up the hunt thirty minutes while looking for one he missed by a mile and a quarter. A great actor, this citizen. With great assiduity he canvasses and recanvasses the terrain. He makes a wry face and bemoans his luck. "Dead bird! Dead bird!" he calls masterfully to his dog.

A companion soon suspects the bluff. A smart dog suspects it sooner still, but he knows on which side his bread is buttered and decides to humor the boss. What to do about this face-saving citizen? Nothing. He's harmless, and will outgrow this frailty in time. Just chuckle tolerantly, because you've probably done the same thing yourself!

But I know one old hunter who, sensing the bluff in a similar situation, decided to have a little innocent fun. Removing a dead bird from his jacket, he surreptitiously dropped it in front of the head-bent seeker. "Damned if I didn't hit one!" the searcher shouted in amazement, as a huge grin crinkled the face of the old-timer.

Speaking of hunting for dead birds, have you ever met the gent who is the very paragon of patience while looking for a bird he has downed, but who is always in a steaming hurry when you have one down? How *tempus* does *fugit* along when the shoe is on the other foot! This fellow is not such a bad egg, though—just mortal man without his diadem. He is merely exhibiting a human symptom that upstanding citizens like you and me might exhibit on occasion, but the trait is somewhat character-revealing, isn't it?

There is another type that cannot be let off so lightly. I refer to the bird-claimer, who follows the advice a perennial candidate for office once gave me: "In politics, son, claim everything in sight and holler fraud." When he and his partner step into a bevy, and a bird falls within thirty feet of where the claimer has aimed, he instantly and vociferously asserts title to everything on the ground.

He congratulates himself with great enthusiasm. Before

learning whether his companion has shot or not, he broadcasts: "Boy, did I mow 'em down that time! Caught 'em on a cross. Four birds with two shots!" and he gallops forward to gather in the sheaves. It does not occur to him—or does it?—that his companion might have had a finger in the pie.

This type of fellow is pretty numerous. And pretty obnoxious. Starting out as a pest, he winds up as a pestilence. What to do about him? Put strychnine in his coffee, making sure the dosage is lethal? Or quit shooting when he shoots and see what happens? Not much, probably. Let him hunt alone, so that he can stake out his claim to everything that falls. Whatever you do, don't let him marry your granddaughter. He'd be claiming everything you have, even before you kicked the bucket.

Of course, honest mistakes often occur. When two gunners shoot a covey rise together, one seldom hears the other's gun. Indeed, one seldom hears his own gun. A covey rise is right pressing business, and the whir of partridge wings is the loudest little noise in the world. I learned this indelibly at a tender age.

While walking ahead of two companions I stumbled into a big bevy that bunched and sailed straight away. Letting go with both barrels, I was amazed and overjoyed to see a hatful of birds fall. "I got four!" I jubilantly announced, wanting the whole world to witness this masterstroke. But even as I stood there exulting, one companion walked ahead and picked up two birds; then the other picked up the remaining two. A lone feather I garnered as recompense. I had heard neither companion shoot and was incredulous when I saw them coolly ejecting their empties.

There is another nuisance who should have a niche in the hall of infamy. A big-hearted character he is, with a great interest in teaching you how to shoot. "Now just take your own sweet time," he refrains before each rise. "The bird is all yours. Ignore my presence completely." Then he drops the bird before it's ten feet off the ground. Easy son-of-a-gun to ignore, isn't he? Why does he do this? Because he is a

Good Bird Hunters Go to Heaven

congenital, unredeemed and unmitigated hair-triggered hog. But his excuse? Well, dog-gone it, he just shot before he thought.

There is another type of companion whose intentions are good but whose presence is equally disconcerting to a beginner. "Now, when this bird gets up, take your own good time. I won't shoot unless you miss with both barrels," he generously reassures you. And he keeps his promise. He doesn't shoot until you have missed with both barrels, which you nearly always do under the circumstances, for the simple reason that you shoot too fast out of politeness.

After a time you fatalistically bang away to make your benefactor feel better. Your shooting becomes a perfunctory prelude to his. This is the worst conceivable way to teach a youngster to shoot. Don't ever try it. If you really want to help, lay down your gun and walk clean away. A boy is entitled to miss in privacy.

There is another pernicious character you have doubtless encountered in the field. I refer to the companion who always manages, regardless of where he is standing, to shoot at the same bird you shoot at—especially if the bird falls! He is notably "shut-mouth" about the coincidence unless something falls.

There can be twenty birds in the rise. You deliberately pick out two that are hurtling through the tree-tops on your side and neatly drop them. As you step forward to pick them up your companion says with disarming innocence: "Oh, excuse me. Did you shoot at those *too*?" I have been suspicious of this character for years, but it's hard to prove anything against him in court.

He is first cousin once-removed to another nuisance you might have met in the field. While the dogs are holding the bevy you and your companion map your strategy in gentlemanly fashion: he is to take the right segment, you the left. Then this scalawag almost invariably shoots on your side, apologizes lamely and picks up the birds. His excuse? The birds crossed over while he was following them.

Now, they probably didn't, but they could have, because the birds were not let in on the arrangement in advance and did not know what was expected of them. So we mustn't be too hard on this gent. Besides, have you ever noticed that you usually get better shots on the other fellow's side than on your own? Damned if his birds don't seem to fly slower and straighter than mine!

It's an axiom of bird shooting that companions must alternate on pointed singles. Of course, this does not hold on unadvertised singles that pop up without benefit of ceremony. Nor is this beautiful arrangement always feasible in woods shooting. But excusing the excusable, when such an agreement is made it should be scrupulously followed. Turnabout is not only fair play, but a great preserver of tempers and sweetener of dispositions. Every now and then, however, you run into a hunter who, after suggesting such a compact, repeatedly shoots your bird.

"I forgot it was your turn," he weakly apologizes. "You can take the next one." And you can—if you beat him to it!

"The real test of hunting manners comes at the end of the hunt," observed a spry old-timer who has been a fine partridge man for half a century. "It is the fairness and graciousness with which a man divides the day's bag with his companion. That, sir, is the real measure of a man's breeding."

That sentiment awakened a cherished recollection from my boyhood days. While hunting with an elderly gentleman I had disgraced myself by missing every shot I had. I was mortified by the prospect of returning home empty-handed and running the gantlet of my brothers' scorn. But when we separated at nightfall, my fine gentleman quietly stuffed eleven birds into my jacket and made a heart-sick country boy speechless with gratitude.

"Be sure to include that scoundrelly Buck I hunt with," a friend grinned. "Whenever we begin to divide our birds Buck always engages me in rapid-fire conversation, or distracts my attention in some way, and when I get home I find

Good Bird Hunters Go to Heaven

every chewed-up and over-shot bird in my half. Now, I ask you, is that etiquette?"

A graceless acquaintance of mine confided unblushingly: "I hunt with a preacher who is the very soul of honor and generosity. Whenever he divides our birds, I always come out at the big end of the horn; so I always insist on his dividing them. He appreciates my showing so much confidence in him, too. That's ethical, isn't it?"

Well, I reckon it is. The same sort of ethics that prompted me, as one of nine children, to pass around a platter of apples and courteously insist that each brother and sister help himself before I did. Figuring that each would be too polite to pick the biggest, I always saved my manners and wound up with the apple I had had my eyes on from the beginning.

Thus early in life I acquired a piece of useful information, namely and to wit: there is more than one way to skin a cat.

Bird Hunting— Muleback and Otherwise

He was a mountain of a mule. I'd hardly undertake to put him down in hands and stone, but I'd venture the opinion that he would hold up his end in any assemblage of mules you could bring together. And the nearer I approached, the bigger he got. There he was, saddled and bridled, looming like a gaunt mastodon before me. And there was Honey Chile standing by, and saying: "Us ready, Cap'n, soon as you gits aboard."

I found myself suddenly in sympathy with the armored knights of old who had to be lifted astride their steeds with a block and tackle when they had been unhorsed. My mule-climbing muscles had been neglected these 20 years. But handing Honey Chile my gun, I boldly grabbed the pommel of the saddle and swung aboard.

"Still right spry, aren't you?" my host grinned. "Last week a New York banker took one look and squalled for a stepladder."

Bird Hunting—Muleback and Otherwise

"Whew!" I said. "I feel like a maharajah atop his howdah or something. I can see three states from up here."

"Dat mule very becomin' to you, Cap'n," grinned Honey Chile.

"Thank you, Honey. What's his name?"

"Us call him Georgia Pine."

"Why Georgia Pine?"

"Kase he so tall and long-laigged."

My host, whom all the Negroes on the 3,000-acre plantation called simply De Boss, smiled appreciatively from the back of his mule. Honey Chile draped himself negligently over the back of his villainous-looking mount and whistled for the dogs, and thus our motley cavalcade headed for the birdy pinelands.

"That Honey Chile," I mused, "where in the world did he get a name like that?"

"Honey grew up as our kitchen boy, and he was such a cunning little fellow that my missus started calling him that. Everybody on the plantation has called him that ever since. About the only name he knows now, I reckon."

"That easy-swinging and lithe figure of his reminds me of something untamed, as if he were almost a part of the landscape. How tall is he?" I asked.

"Honey is around six feet four and weighs around 190, I reckon. His strength and agility are almost legendary in the neighborhood, but as a field hand he is altogether undistinguished. Instead of hoeing his cotton and corn, he is rummaging around the swamp 'possum hunting, 'coon hunting, or fishing—and usually with me. Missus says he has been ruined by associating with me too much. But he knows these 3,000 acres as he knows his own kitchen—every covey of birds, every duck and dove roost, every bream hole, and every deer crossing."

"Peculiar way he has of riding that venomous little mule, sidewise and without a saddle. Sort of half on and half off, with one long leg brushing the top of the broomstraw."

"That little mule—we call him Boll Weevil, by the way—

is the bellwether and boss of the 30-odd mules on the place, and the very apple of Honey's eye," De Boss said.

Up ahead I espied Honey's long, upraised arm.

"Us hab a p'int, gennermans!" he called.

My host and I alighted and loaded our guns. Honey Chile jounced up on Boll Weevil and took the reins of our mounts. The four dogs were frozen around a fern thicket at the edge of a bog. When the explosion came, every absconding Bob seemed to me to grab a ticket for a different destination. But De Boss dropped two, and I dropped one, apparently missing with my second barrel.

"Reckon we'll find any singles? They broke up so badly—"

"That's Honey's business, not mine," replied De Boss. "Where did they go, Honey?"

"T'ree o' dem down yander in dat honeysuckle, five in dem Chrismus berry-bushes, and de yudder eight in de bay. And dat second bird whar de Cap'n shot done fall daid by dat black gum snag. He a rooster bird."

"Do you mean to tell me that Honey—"

"I mean to tell you that Honey can see a stink sparrow 200 yards away," replied my host, "and that he has an uncanny gift for watching birds down and outfiguring wild things in general. That's why I put up with his shiftlessness in other respects. Why, when we are hunting together he often tells me whether the birds I've downed are cocks or hens before the dogs retrieve them."

I had brought along a dog of my own, just in case. My Buck was a lithe-limbed and bottomy fellow, and I had a rash idea of showing up De Boss's dogs. But Buck was an ignominious flop. It was his first experience with muleback hunting, and he was definitely not in favor of it. Keeping at a discreet distance from the mules, he stiff-legged along and eyed me malevolently. "If you want me to hunt, come on down here where you belong," he glowered.

As the day progressed, Buck became more resentful and churlish. Around noon he whipped the other four dogs and indignantly stalked off. When I got in at nightfall, he had

Bird Hunting—Muleback and Otherwise

fortified himself under my car and was daring any mule to come within a hundred yards and live. Some dogs just don't go in for horseback hunting.

Such was the beginning of my first hunt on muleback, and although it was many years ago now, many incidents of that day are still enshrined in my memory. Within recent years I have hunted on horseback or muleback often, perhaps five or six times each season, largely through the generosity of plantation-owning friends.

My old friend, De Boss, still invites me down once or twice a year, but always on condition that I hunt muleback, although he has half a dozen fine saddle horses in his stable. For that reason I look forward to an invitation from him with mixed emotions.

"Why can't we hunt afoot?" I sometimes ask.

"Because I want you to hunt like a gentleman at least one day a year," answers De Boss. "And because I like to see a dignified and pompous professor on a mule. Sort of humanizes the mule."

But I have a shrewd suspicion that De Boss is just getting revenge on me for making him memorize the whole of *The Ancient Mariner* when he was one of my freshmen at the University.

"As a matter of fact," he explained, "a mule is a better mount for this sort of hunting than a horse. A horse may have more education, but a mule has more sense. Ever hear of a mule eating himself to death, or working himself to death? He may not have any pride of ancestry, or hope of posterity, but he knows how to take care of himself. You can't get a mule to step into a stump hole, tackle a rickety bridge or anything chancy. Remember how old Georgia Pine used to stretch his long neck like a turtle, watching for stump holes and such? A mule won't rub your leg off against a tree or crack your noggin against an overhanging limb either. Horses are generally too skittish and high-strung."

Horseback and muleback hunting is quite popular in low-country South Carolina, a sprawling section almost as unfenced as the old West. Few outsiders know how free and untrammeled this unreconstructed kingdom is. Low-country plantations and preserves are large, each almost a tiny commonwealth in itself, and are somewhat suggestive of the feudal estates of old. I have hunted muleback the livelong day, traversing perhaps 20 miles, without encountering a single fence or similar barrier.

I have done a deal of horseback and muleback hunting in this section. I have also done a certain amount of buttocks-bouncing and rib-jouncing in stripped-down Fords, bird buggies, plantation carriages, and every other contrivance that the inventive genius of a lazy man could conjure up. I feel, therefore, that I can compare the relative merits of hunting mounted and hunting afoot with some degree of judicial detachment.

Horseback hunting has its points, to be sure. Nothing so restores a man's ego as being atop a mule or horse on a wide-spreading plantation, where he is for the time being monarch of all he surveys, with foot attendants to perform such democratic tasks as holding the horses, managing the dogs, and watching the singles. It makes you feel that you are one of the landed gentry, one of the upper-bracket boys for the frail duration of a day. So go de luxe now and then, just to see how the upper crust does it.

You will come in at night fresh and chipper, not too leg-weary and fagged to pull off a recalcitrant boot or pick beggar-lice from your shirt-tail. You will have walked perhaps one mile while shooting singles instead of the 15 or 20 your mount has walked. You won't have lacerated shins, briers in your eyebrows, or callouses on aching feet. Nor will your clothing be all chewed up and hanging in unpicturesque tatters.

There are other advantages too. The added elevation of horseback hunting is a distinct advantage in flat and comparatively open country, enabling the hunter to keep his dogs under almost constant surveillance. He can see which

Bird Hunting—Muleback and Otherwise

dog is making game, which one is malingering, which one bungled on that premature flush.

The added elevation may enable him to follow the errant singles to their ultimate destination. And of course the mounted hunter can cover vastly more territory, which may be a real advantage when coveys are few and far between. He doesn't consume so much time in getting from hither to thither—from where one covey was to where he hopes the next one will be.

But mounted hunting has its disadvantages too. Although the mounted hunter will cover more territory, he will not cover it so thoroughly as if he were afoot. He will consequently pass up some coveys that have ensconced themselves in pockets and crannies. He must, in other words, reconcile himself to the concomitants of an extensive rather than an intensive day afield.

Unless one's dogs are absolutely stanch, birds will flush prematurely while Sir Galahad is dismounting, waiting for his horse boy to come up, or kicking the kinks out of his legs. There is inevitably a lot of commotion in mounted hunting. Even when the dogs behave impeccably, there will be plenty of accidental flushes and untimely rises.

If one is hunting with inexperienced dogs whose habits are not fixed, all sorts of calamitous things may happen. If you are trying to train a timorous or impulsive youngster, stick to shanks' mare. Mounted hunting may be ruinous to young dogs. Your mounts will often walk into birds that your dogs have overlooked, and they will fly slowly and tantalizingly while you sit wistfully watching. In my whole experience, I have seen only two horses or mules over which one could shoot with a reasonable expectation of retaining his elevation.

Certain physical discomforts may attend mounted hunting too. Unless you have a good stirrup and saddle fit, you may acquire a saddle gall that will embarrass you for weeks thereafter. A saddle gall is an insidious thing. You don't know you're getting it until it's too late to do anything about it. I once rubbed off so much epidermis on a hard saddle that for two weeks I had to lecture from a strictly plantigrade position.

You may call me a city slicker and mollycoddle if you wish, but I always insert a sheepskin or pillow under that part of my anatomy which comes into juxtaposition with the saddle. I am peradventure not so well-upholstered as some people I can think of.

Other misadventures may befall you. Your horse may step into a blind ditch or stump hole and throw you into the middle of July. I once got my mules mixed and shot over the wrong one, winding up in a brier patch a considerable distance away with the saddle bags around my precious neck. Or you may draw a wayward jade or leather-mounted mule that will utterly disregard even your most muscular mandates. You will feel like a stepchild of destiny, ardently hoping that nothing immovable gets in your way.

According to tradition, the gentlmen of the old South invariably shot from their saddles, the dogs climbing up and delivering the birds to their unruffled masters. I once coaxed a big pointer into trying it. My mule emitted a snort that must have echoed over half of Georgia, and what happened to me is my own private affair.

Yes, I like both kinds of bird hunting—*all* kinds of bird hunting—but if I had my rathers, I'd rather hunt afoot. Truth to tell, I've never come in from a horse or muleback hunt without having enjoyed it, and without feeling *that I could have found more birds and got more shots had I been afoot.* I just naturally get more shots when I'm down on the ground where things are happening.

I confess, too, that I like the society of my dogs, a sentiment which I hope is mutual. You don't get much society atop a mule. I like to be down where I can deliver a timely admonition here, cluck a friendly encouragement there, and pluck a thorn, sandspur or cocklebur from the old maid's foot, even if it is but an imaginary one. And I admit that I

Bird Hunting—Muleback and Otherwise

feel a little guilty a-sitting up in the empyrean like a gentleman while my dogs are doing all the work.

Then, too, I like to walk. Just plain walking can be a luxury. Bird hunting is peculiarly a pastime to be undertaken afoot if one is to derive all the sensory pleasures therefrom. The smell of the bog at eventide, the overripe persimmon on the ground, the chameleon basking in the noonday sun, the lurking lark that made old Joe look silly for a second, the resilient sod under your feet and the gentle emanations of mother earth herself—these things I can't explain exactly, but I can feel them. And you earth-loving plodders feel them too, and will know exactly what I am talking about.

I want to continue walking. I want to walk as hard, as far, and as much as I can. I rejoice in these sinewy old legs of mine. All too soon the time will come when they won't cooperate. All too soon the time will come when the best of us will feel his once-stalwart pins yielding to the encroachments of age.

Yes, hunting from a mount has its merits. It's all right to try it, but not as a steady diet. Of course, if some of you plutocratic preserve owners are contemplating an invitation to the old pedagogue, well, that's an apple off another tree. I don't want to sound ungrateful. But after all, if a bird hunter is too damned lazy to walk . . .

Let 'em Fall in Love First

In the ante-bellum South it was taken for granted that a young gentleman would sow a few wild oats, and his escapades were looked upon rather indulgently by his elders. There was an abiding faith that blood would tell; that the roistering blade would ultimately turn out all right; that after the ebullience of youth had spent itself he would settle down, inherit his father's plantation and mint patch, and wind up in the legislature or peradventure the governor's chair. And the aforesaid young gentleman often did just that.

It occurs to me—and I hope my rebel progenitors will pardon the homely comparison—that this philosophy applies somewhat to the upbringing of dogs. It is true that many dogs are ruined by over-indulgence and laxity. But is it not also true that many a promising pup is ruined by the harshness of an over-zealous martinet?

Everybody knows it would be utter folly to abandon a puppy to his own whims, since every instinct of a dog urges

Let 'em Fall in Love First

him to hunt for himself and the devil take you. And a lawless dog is, of all useless things, the most useless. But isn't too much discipline as ruinous to a spirited and frolicsome tyke as too little? Isn't there such a thing as refining the hunting instincts and initiative out of a dog?

A neighbor of mine acquired a handsome pup and announced his intention of bringing up a perfect dog. It was just a matter of discipline, he said, of concentrating on the subject when he was young and impressionable. He was going to make him a finished performer, right there in the backyard, so that when the hunting season opened—

My neighbor went to work on that pup with infinite patience and unexampled thoroughness. The pupil responded well. When he was nine months old, I was invited over for a demonstration in dog-training. The subject gave instant obedience to every command of his owner, executing orders with the precision of a machine. He heeled, he lay down, he got up, he retrieved faultlessly.

When the owner said "Whoa!" the subject, regardless of what he was doing, instantly assumed a stylish point. A fusillade from a cap pistol demonstrated his staunchness to shot. The very paragon of a dog, the owner said, and certainly one that piqued my curiosity. I wanted to see that paragon in the field.

I did. On the opening day I saw him jog unemotionally through three coveys of birds, waiting for his master's inevitable "Whoa!" When ordered to retrieve, the subject pottered around in great perplexity. When his master helpfully tossed a rock in the direction of the dead bird, the dog stepped over the bird and retrieved the rock, immensely pleased with his performance. Be damned if he didn't!

The dog had become an automaton, with no mind of his own. His sole duty was to cater to his master. He had more education than he had sense—like some people. I felt sorry for the owner, sorrier for the dog. Not once during the day did he fail to show instant obedience, not once did he exhibit the slightest inclination to hunt. His record was like the old maid's epitaph: no hits, no runs, no errors.

The pup's training had been so rigorous and so prolonged that he had come to regard yard-work as sufficient in itself, as an end rather than a means. That was hunting, the fulfillment of his mission in life. And therein lies the danger of too much yard-training.

It is best to set up a few fundamentals and insist inflexibly on these. After all the only way a dog can learn to hunt birds is by hunting birds, and the more birds shot over him the better. Nothing in the wide world and all the libraries therein will substitute for birds in training a bird dog. Otherwise, it would be like learning surgery from a textbook or trying to learn to swim from a chart on the blackboard. You've got to get into the water to swim.

Many an inexperienced trainer will chastise a pup for minor misdeeds due solely to the exuberance and curiosity of youth. A puppy's first instincts clamor for expression. If normal and healthy, he has got to busy himself with something. Indeed, he often feels too good for his own good.

When a four-months-old pup points an old hen through the fence, his adoring owner applauds the performance and brags outrageously to his friends. But when the selfsame pup discovers the pristine pleasures of chicken-chasing, an avalanche of abuse descends upon his hapless head.

When the season opens and the precious prodigy points sparrows, grasshoppers, butterflies, a weanling calf or a pickaninny in a cotton patch with equal enthusiasm, his master begins to have misgivings. If the pup continues such wholesale pointing, the outraged owner may twist an ear, which causes excruciating pain, or belabor the culprit with the nearest stick.

Pointing thus becomes associated with pain or disapproval, and if the pup is of a sensitive nature he may develop a neurosis and quit altogether. I have seen many likely youngsters so severely manhandled for what their chagrined owners considered false-pointing that they either showed little zest

Let 'em Fall in Love First

for the job thereafter or gave up pointing altogether as a risky business and one liable to bring down upon their luckless hides the wrath of a capricious master.

After all, it must seem a little strange to a blithesome youngster that, of all the smells and scents and interesting creatures in the teeming world, there is only one his master wants. So let a pup point to his heart's content, and honor his points. You've got to take him seriously if you expect him to take himself seriously. After a while he will learn, with a little chiding on your part, that you are a narrow-minded boss; that you are a specialist who does not shoot butterflies or grasshoppers or pickaninnies in a cotton patch.

What is more natural—indeed inevitable—than that an ambitious and overanxious youngster should try to overhaul a low-flying bird? As natural as for a healthy boy to want to throw rocks at a school-house window or try out his new .22 on the glass insulators on telephone poles.

The dog persuades himself that he can catch a ground-skimming bird, and he almost can. "A poor shot deserves a bird-chasing dog," runs the adage. A pup is especially prone to chase if the gunner is a chronic misser.

Anyway, the dog goes galloping across the field, yipping his fool head off, and you stand there so blazing mad that where you spit no more grass ever grows. When you finally overtake the scapegrace, you firmly resolve to administer so thorough a lesson—either with a hickory stick, the toe of your boot, a check-rope, or a hail of leaden pellets—that it will penetrate to the dog's medulla oblongata, if such he has, and be handed down to his grandchildren.

If the malefactor is a graceless rowdy perhaps no mischief will result. After all, something had to be done. But if he is thin-skinned and sensitive, or if your treatment has been too rigorous . . .

Premature flushing is understandable too. A young dog, palpitating with eagerness and excitement, finds it hard to restrain his ardor. He is within a few precious feet of the skulking quarry. His nostrils are filled with the scent of pulsing bodies. Perchance he even sees them on the ground. He is convinced that a pounce will land him in the midst of the covey. So he pounces, and the bombshell explodes.

Obviously that won't do; so the harassed owner resorts to terrifying language and menacing gestures, picks up the nearest cudgel and makes for the culprit or attaches a stout check-rope to the dog's collar. The next time the dog points, the owner seizes the rope, braces himself and grins with anticipation.

The dog again lunges, and the owner does his manful best to break the rascal's neck. Sometimes he does. At least he somersaults the offender against the ground with a resounding wham. So the feud continues apace. Ultimately such procedure will stop almost any dog from flushing, and will generally leave no ill effects.

But if the dog is high-strung and sensitive, or if he has not been permitted to whet his appetite for hunting first, he may decide that all flushing is a capital offense, and thereafter decline to flush even when ordered to do so. Or he may become bird-shy, nervously circling his coveys at a safe distance through morbid fear of flushing.

Sometimes a nettled owner will throw up his gun and turn loose a broadside at the culprit, running the risk of killing or maiming the dog or of instilling an abiding fear in it thereafter. Many a dog owes his gun-shyness to such harsh measures during the training period; to the fact that he was handled too severely before an unquenchable lust for hunting had been kindled within him.

Often a beginning retriever, finding the bird in his mouth a savory morsel and totally unlike the tasteless old shoe he has been trained on, will yield to his appetite and gulp it down, especially if the bird has been mangled. Although not an unnatural act for a youngster, it is one that calls for summary measures. But if the dog is punished too severely, he may develop a pronounced distaste for retrieving.

Last year I saw a fine young retriever ruined because the hunter, who had borrowed him for the day, was unacquainted

Let 'em Fall in Love First

with one of the dog's peculiarities. The dog had the habit of engulfing a bird in his cavernous jaws, but he always delivered a clean, neat package. You've seen dogs do that. But the borrower, thinking the dog was devouring the bird, kicked him sharply.

The blow landed on the dog's ear, causing intense pain, and the owner has never been able to persuade the dog to pick up another bird since. This was an extreme case, but it often requires a deal of patient work to repair the damage done in one thoughtless moment.

Gun-shyness is often the result of rushing a dog's education. The explosion of a gun is naturally terrifying to a youngster and will sometimes upset him emotionally—unless he is preoccupied with something else when the gun is fired. But if he is interested enough in what he is doing, if he has been allowed to develop a passion for hunting before he is shot over, he will seldom become gun-shy. Either because he never hears the explosion at all, or is more interested than afraid, or he tolerates it as the price to be paid for his fun.

A friend of mine acquired a beautiful dog, a fine natural hunter, that was very gun-shy—if the verdict of successive owners may be trusted—incurably gun-shy. My friend tried all the conventional methods of counteracting the shyness. Meeting with no success, he abandoned the dog to his own devices. Thus neglected, the dog took up rabbit hunting, having himself a grand time chasing cottontails all over the farm. Chancing along one day when the dog was on a sight-race, the owner shot the fleeing rabbit.

To his amazement, the dog not only ignored the gun, but seemed grateful for the timely intercession. Repeating the experiment, he found that the dog continued to ignore the gun, so absorbed had he become in his sport. Consequently the owner hunted rabbits for two weeks. Then, switching hopefully to birds, he was delighted to find not a remnant of the old shyness left. He gradually weaned the dog from rabbit hunting, which is really not hard to do if the trainer has the requisite patience and the dog has the intelligence.

Another man, finding that his dog had a great zest for squirrels, cured him of gun-shyness by hunting squirrels with him. This is a roundabout method of effecting a cure, to be sure. But it will sometimes prove efficacious when other methods fail, and it is certainly inexpensive.

Many a man has found surcease from sorrow by losing himself in a hobby; has found blessed relief from a mental ailment in some absorbing pastime. Rich patients pay psychiatrists handsome fees for switching their worries around for them. You can sometimes cure a man's little worries by giving him bigger ones—sort of a psychological counter-irritant, or escape activity, one might call it. And it often works with men and dogs alike.

Too much interference produces a mechanical or perfunctory hunter, one that potters listlessly around for the sake of appearances. A dog that is perpetually badgered and bossed around will seldom range adequately to find game. Apprehensive of inviting the displeasure of a harsh master, he is reluctant to venture far afield. Nor will he develop any intiative or sense of responsibility, having fallen into the habit of letting somebody else do his thinking for him. He becomes an apron-string dog.

Watch a goody-goody boy, brought up under his mother's apron-strings. When he cuts those strings, he cuts them pretty short. And what happens? First, he is lacking in self-reliance and judgment, never having had to exercise any. Second, he is apt to raise pluperfect hell and make up for lost time. His suppressed desires and long-accumulated grievances will pop out. Same way with dogs.

So let your pup have his fun first. He will make you a better dog later, because a dog hunts best when he loves it. It is zest for the game that makes a champion. To repress a pup too much is to endanger that precious ingredient, enthusiasm. Don't put him in a strait-jacket too soon.

Let 'em Fall in Love First

Let him fall in love with hunting first. Let him become enamored of the spacious fields. Of course, he has got to learn that he is hunting for you and not for himself, but the most painless way you can permanently implant that idea the better.

Why Does a Bass Strike?

To the Biblical trilogy of mysteries that pass understanding I should like to add another, somewhat less Biblical but equally vexatious: why will bass show sovereign contempt for lures fashioned by experts to resemble their natural quarry, and commit battery and assault on some cubistic dido that looks like nothing "in heaven above, in the earth beneath, or in the waters under the earth"?

I sometimes think that the more I learn about bass fishing the less I know. Certain it is that the more I try to pigeonhole old *Micropterus* the less cocksure I become, and the more I follow his devious devices the less complacent I become about my own deductions. After twenty years spent in trying to solve his equation the one fixed conclusion to which I have come is that Emerson hit the nail on the head when he said: "A foolish consistency is the hobgoblin of little minds."

There have been times, "in the morn and liquid dew of

Why Does a Bass Strike?

youth," when I felt that I had arrived at the inevitable plug, or the indispensable fly. I have lived to see my tenderest deductions go a-glimmering, and my fondest delusions knocked into a cocked chapeau. I have long ago learned that the most dogmatic fishermen, indeed the only ones who are altogether sure of themselves, are the youngest. Bass fishing is so *blessedly unstandardized* that after twenty years of experimenting, I am almost back where I started, almost, but not quite, for I do feel that my pleasant researches into bass behavior have led to a few conclusions that are workable, to a sort of irreducible minimum that I can tie to.

Why will bass only too often ignore plugs especially contrived to look like their natural prey, yet fight like the cats of Kilkenny over some outlandish creation that bears not the slightest resemblance to anything they have ever seen before? That such is true almost any old bass fisherman will admit, the adjectival exuberance of tackle manufacturers to the contrary notwithstanding. "Our lures are unbeatable because they are exact replicas of the natural prey of bass." "This plug is a surefire hit because of its remarkable likelike qualities." "Our minnows owe their phenomenal success to the fact that they are perfect reproductions of the bass's favorite food." Such advertisements are so common that he who runs may read.

The whole business of lure-making seems to be predicated on the idea of misleading a bass and deluding him into believing that a gadget bristling with gang hooks and spinners, and painted up like the Fourth of July, is a dish of stewed prunes. The implication is that a bass is at all times a highly selective feeder with a narrow range of gustatory choice, an implication which overlooks two salient facts: that the bass is an omnivorous feeder, perhaps the most omnivorous of game fishes, and that his selectivity is an inconstant quantity.

Some time ago I found in the Congaree swamp (South Carolina) a bassy-looking cypress pond that was alive with bullfrogs. Close observation revealed little evidence of any other kind of food. Concluding that frogs were the chief item on the bill of fare, I proceeded on the theory of "verisimilitude" and fished with frog like lures. I spent the livelong morning giving them the refusal of the cleverest frog imitations in my tackle box, but to little purpose, despite the apparent fact that the pond was teeming with largemouth bass. Finally in desperation I resorted to live frogs, with the same negative results. Then as a forlorn hope I half-heartedly swivelled on a hand-painted "plunker" that looked remarkably like nothing that ever swam, and the cooperation I got during the afternoon amply redeemed the half day of wasted effort. Time and again I have had similar experiences—when large-mouth disdained the reproductions of their natural prey and went for something altogether alien to their experience and appetites.

Last summer while perambulating around in eastern Virginia I located near Richmond a drowned stone quarry that looked awfully good. I was told that it had been stocked with large-mouth years before but that comparatively few had been taken from it. What is the natural food of these fish? I asked myself, proceeding rationally. I soon decided in favor of the perch, with which the sunny water abounded. But my "perch" reproductions failed ignominiously, as did every other regulation bass plug in my collection. Then, out of my flair for experimentation, I procured some live frogs from a neighboring branch and returned. Sticking a large single hook in its mouth, I attached a frog to my casting line and released it.

The big frog headed for the opposite bank of the quarry in a business-like way, drawing out twenty, thirty, forty feet of my line, when the bottom of the pond suddenly erupted and a cavernous mouth gulped it down. I reeled in an eight-pound leviathan. Other live frogs were accorded a similar reception despite the fact that there were no frogs whatever in the vicinity, presumably because of the absence of cover and the sheer granite walls of the quarry. Frogs were undoubtedly caviar to these particular bass yet they struck them in preference to anything else. Bass will some-

Why Does a Bass Strike?

times take frog imitation lures in preference to frogs themselves! Whenever a thing like that happens, all you can say is, *de gustibus non est disputandum:* matters of taste are not to be argued about.

At various times I have fished in ponds in which goldfish seemed to be the most effective bait for bass, in fact the only bait any sizable catch could be made with, yet nobody will insist that goldfish constitute a staple on the large-mouth's regular bill of fare. In many ponds hereabouts the ubiquitous sucker is almost the standard minnow of livebait fishermen, yet this selfsame sucker seems to be as effective in water containing none of its species as in ponds where it exists in such quantities as to afford the principal food supply for bass. And even in the sucker's own water the little gizzard shad, or "nanny" shad as the North Carolinians call it, has the sucker beat. Possibly bass, like human beings, demand something a little "different" on the menu now and then, as a fillet for a jaded appetite!

Down here in South Carolina a bream or red-breast fisherman considers himself among the Lord's anointed if he can take a cage of catalpa worms into the swamp with him, yet the catalpa worm must be a new gastronomic experience for the swamp bream. At certain seasons the grasshopper, dry-fished, is an unbeatable lure for the bluegill which is found in profusion in the recesses of the cypress swamps, yet it is safe to assume that these beautiful fish have had precious few opportunities to lick their chops over such delicacies as grasshoppers. And have you ever tried shrimp for bass? Well, it's rather plebeian, I know, but you'd be surprised! Now will you explain to me how in the whole o' hell and half of Georgy bass two hundred miles from salt water acquired a taste for shrimp?

Such instances can be multiplied almost at will. I grant that some of the cases cited are exceptions, but they are not the sort of exceptions that prove the rule. That always struck me as sublimated poppycock anyway—an exception that proves the rule. While it certainly cannot be urged against a plug that it resembles the natural prey yet I am convinced that this fetish of life-likeness is somewhat overdone. The bass is a voracious and omnivorous feeder, albeit somewhat finicky at times, and I cannot persuade myself that he is so introspective about his diet as commonly supposed.

The selectivity of feeding bass is highly variable, and any discussion of it ultimately involves another question: Why do bass strike at artificial lures anyway? The answer that immediately suggests itself is: because they desire to feed and regard the lure as edible. Yet this is perhaps more often untrue than true. Possibly fifty times out of a hundred a striking bass is *not actuated by the desire to feed,* and is under few delusions about the edibility or inedibility of the quarry. If bass regard some of the crazy gadgets they strike at as food they either have pretty low I.Q.'s or the alimentary immunities of a goat!

What else besides the intent to feed prompts a bass to strike a moving plug? Any one of a number of motives.

Bass, especially pond large-mouth, may attack a cavorting plug out of sheer pugnacity and general cussedness, as a bulldog attacks without provocation, or as a hound chases a rabbit regardless of his gastronomic happiness or unhappiness. *Micropterus* is a belligerent sort of fellow anyway. He carries a chip on his shoulder and is fairly spoiling for a good fight. A gaudily-bedecked minnow played provocatively over his head gets his dander up and he senses the possibility of a good scrap. A plug waltzing and didoing above makes him see red and he attacks with the sole purpose of annihilating this flashy upstart who presumes to invade his domain.

The other day I found a fresh-swallowed eight-ounce gizzard shad in a five-pound large-mouth which had just made three vicious assaults in rapid succession on a crippled minnow played tantalizingly over his head. Did that fellow strike because of his interest in a full dinner pail? Nev-er! Plug casters frequently take bass with sizable frogs, suckers, or pickerel in their maws, gluttonous fellows who have already bitten off more than they can chew before the new target offered itself.

Why Does a Bass Strike?

These bass are not hungry—just cantankerous and spunky.

It is not improbable also that bass sometimes attack a plug through an excess of animal spirits and love of excitement, just as they enjoy doing somersaults and hand-springs in the water even when they are not feeding. In fact when bass are most boisterous in their play they are seldom actually feeding. Like Pandora they are often victims of their own curiosity. Have you ever watched a big fellow idling along behind your plug, blinking quizzically at it, but resisting your every effort to seduce him into striking? He has too much curiosity not to be interested, but too much discretion to pursue the matter too far, so he shilly-shallies back and forth under your plug until you are almost ready for apoplexy. He is not trying to decide which one of his natural victims your lure most resembles. He is simply wondering what the devil that newfangled contraption is anyway!

Under certain conditions a bass may be irritated and goaded into striking. If on occasion he is capable of showing excessive animal spirits, he is also capable of showing a cross-grained and dyspeptic disposition. Now and then you can make him so mad that he will throw discretion to the winds and strike regardless of the consequences. He simply develops a case of nerves. That may be the reason you get a strike on the umpteenth cast in the same water. An acquaintance of mine, while practice-casting down a narrow enclosed run, hung a ten-pound big-mouth on the fourteenth cast. That old hippo is almost bound to have seen the lure from the initial cast on. The crazy gadget prancing and cavorting above him finally got his goat, and he went for it there and then.

Once you have located the hangout of a big bass it is often possible to goad him into striking by working on his nerves and temper, a procedure somewhat ungentlemanly perhaps, but none the less effective. For a program of irritation a surface plug is best, permitting as it does a greater freedom for the maddening maneuvers calculated to inspire the old man's wrath, and affording the caster the added pleasure of seeing the results. A flashy product seems to be more tantalizing than a drab one. A crippled silver flash is a first-class irritator.

The biggest bass I ever took fell a victim of his curiosity and temper. The old warrior had his headquarters under a sunken cypress raft, and he was usually "at home" when I called, but having outlived the impetuosity of youth he was not to be hoodwinked by any ordinary tricks. He had a prodigious curiosity, however, about everything that happened in the precincts of the raft. Whenever I threw into it a few times, the old homesteader would begin idling along behind my minnow, follow it nearly to the boat, then nonchalantly about-face and swim back to his hangout. I got into the habit of making a few overtures to him whenever I passed his "point" on my way up or down the lake. Sooner or later, I resolved, I would catch him off guard and end the feud.

So on one listless day when every fish in the lake seemed to be observing Lent I anchored my boat within casting distance of the raft and decided to dedicate a few hours to my old friend. After a few casts he took up his regular practice of heeling my plugs back to the boat. The water was almost gin-clear, and the spectacle of this enormous big-mouth maddeningly chaperoning my plug back to the boat did my blood pressure little good. In my efforts to pique his curiosity or tantalize him into striking I used every lure I had, putting my plugs through every species of piscatorial acrobatics known. Then I made an accidental discovery that I have used to advantage several times since.

On a long throw to the raft I got a brain-resisting backlash. Disregarding the dead minnow lying over the raft I went to work on that bird's nest, which was tangled up fifty-seven ways from Sunday. In perhaps ten minutes I had the line straight again and started to reel in. When the dead minnow came suddenly to life, the old man, who had evidently been intently watching it all the while, gave the plug a terrific smack and hung himself. The next ten minutes amply repaid me for all the time and energy I had spent in trying to solve the old fellow's equation. Since that accidental discovery I have incorporated the hesitation waltz and 'possum-playing

Why Does a Bass Strike?

tactics as a regular part of the program whenever Barkis is not very willing.

Many non-feeding bass strike through no other motive than self-preservation—the desire to protect their customary habitation and their favorite feeding ground from invasion. As a bass becomes older he is inclined to settle down, often attaching himself to a submerged obstruction and setting up a sort of squatter's sovereignty over adjacent territory. He fancies himself an Alexander Selkirk, "monarch of all he surveys." He hangs out a "Take Notice" sign for trespassers, and woe be unto the luckless transgressor who comes monkeying around his hangout, whether the transgressor be an overgrown sucker, a meddling perch, or a waltzing pikie studded with gang hooks.

Bass, especially pond large-mouth, become creatures of habit in their feeding activities, repairing regularly to the same bushy point or shallow cove-tip to waylay frisking minnows or unwary frogs. When one is lying in ambush for his prey he is as fractious as a setting hen and resentful of all intruders. He is extremely jealous of his favorite feeding preserve and will brook no poaching. He sets up a sort of Monroe Doctrine over that cove-tip and strenuously objects to a prancing plug horning in and messing things up. He is like a hound when he is feeding: a bad risk!

A feeding bass evidently regards a visiting plug as a competitor for the same prey, a competitor that must be disposed of in summary fashion. Possibly he has sense enough to realize that an invading plug jeopardizes his food supply by scaring minnows away. Maybe he simply considers it as an unmitigated nuisance that ought to be abated. Or maybe he is like a dog with a bone in his mouth—disinclined to be bothered. At any rate he will hit a surface plug, properly cast and manipulated, harder and more often when he is feeding under such conditions than at any other time.

He will guard his bed even more savagely and visit retribution upon the head of anything that threatens to molest it, an admirable trait which some degenerates who call themselves fishermen take a sorry advantage of. As everybody knows a bedding bass is not a feeding bass, but because of the zeal with which he protects his bed he may sometimes be betrayed into assaulting a plug drawn vexatiously and repeatedly over the area he is guarding. If a hooked live minnow is dropped into such a bed the male bass will repeatedly nudge it aside, but if minnows are staked to the bed by short lines he will ultimately strike them as the only means of ridding himself of the menace.

Any one of a number of motives, therefore, may be behind the action of a striking bass. If he is actuated by a desire to feed, he is admittedly rather selective and analytical. But if he is striking out of pugnacity, animal spirits, or the necessity of repelling an invader, he is naturally less discriminating, and in such cases whether a lure is a reproduction of a natural quarry seems to be more or less immaterial. The "life-likeness" theory is therefore far from being infallible, overlooking the omnivorousness of the species and being based on the assumption that a striking bass is always a feeding bass.

The Backsliders

City dog-owners envy their country cousins. "Life would be one grand symphony," bemoans the urbanite, "if I didn't have to keep my dogs shut up all summer, if I didn't have to compete in a rationed market for meat-scraps, if my dogs stayed tough-footed and rugged from running loose the year round."

The urbanite surely has ground for envy, especially in these dear and difficult days. Anybody who doesn't envy a farmer in these times is a plain chump. But life in the country is not altogether what bucolic romancers depict it. For the keeper of bird dogs, it is verily a mixed blessing.

True enough, the loose-running country dog will be tough and long-lasting when the season opens—if he survives the hazards of the highway, the larcenous designs of the light-fingered gentry, and especially in the lower South if he survives heart-worm, rabies, venomous snakes, insects and sundry other perils.

But there is another peril more sinister than these, for the gravest danger to a loose-running bird dog is not physical. Unless such a dog has been rigorously trained or is kept under surveillance, or unless his owner is ever so lucky, something might happen of which the owner will be blithely unaware—until the season opens. Then it might be too late.

Such a dog, especially in quail country, is apt to lose his biddableness altogether and become a self-hunter. And when a dog becomes a confirmed self-hunter—

"See that dog?" an irate owner unburdened his mind. "Started out a fine prospect. One of the best. Now he ain't worth a drunkard's promise."

"Why?" I asked, always willing to be enlightened.

"Self-hunting. Fellow who kept him for me let him run loose all summer. Now he's the most incorrigible scapegrace you ever saw."

Veteran hunters throughout the South will tell you the same thing: that many handsome prospects, once infected with the virus of self-hunting, become intractable and worthless.

"Sent my dogs to my farm last summer," a doctor recently told me. "My tenant let 'em roam the country undisciplined. To make 'em tough, he said. When the hunting season opened, two of them had reverted and had to be completely retrained. They'd picked up more bad habits than a delegate to a thieves' convention. One was a total loss."

A friend invited me to Georgia for the opening last year. He had two young dandies which he wanted me to see in action. They were fast, tractable and sure-nosed, he wrote me, and he had insured their hardiness by keeping them in the country.

But the opening day was gall and wormwood to my host. Both stalwarts trailed briskly through a cornfield and pointed in a patch of partridge-peas fifty yards away. Before we had budged from our tracks, they pounced simultaneously atop the skulking covey and scattered the birds to the four winds. Not content with this piece of depravity, they bolted madly

The Backsliders

after the fleeing singles, continuing the chase until they were smack out of sight.

My host stood speechless with wonderment, racking his brain for alibis. Five times in succession those dogs repeated the performance with great gusto. My host whistled. He hollered and stormed. He raised pluperfect hell, singeing off the tops of the ragweed with his blasphemy. But his eloquence was futile. Those dogs had become, in one foot-loose and undisciplined summer, the most intractable crew of pirates I ever saw.

An impressionable young dog with strong hunting instincts and a quick nose will inevitably begin hunting alone if allowed to roam the countryside unattended—especially during the nesting season, when the scent of quail is rank and, to a gifted nose, almost omnipresent. The theory that the body of a brooding quail providentially exudes no odor is far from confirmed.

At first a roving dog may trail and point in the orthodox way, holding steadfastly for the master to come. The point becomes progressively shorter, however, and the incipient self-hunter contents himself with trailing and stalking, at which he becomes adept. Eventually he will point only momentarily or not at all, pouncing upon the quarry with great enthusiasm.

Baffled by the failure of his sudden sally, the dog streaks after the scuttling singles with the fatuous conviction that some day four legs will prove faster than two wings. Sooner or later such a dog will contrive to catch a disabled bird, find a nest and acquire a taste for birds, or slap down a few chicks enmeshed in rank vegetation. Thereafter he hunts for gastronomic pleasure as well as sport.

A self-hunter hunts for himself, and as he jolly well pleases. He is having himself a grand time, and to Gehenna with you and your theories about how it should be done. You are just a fly in the ointment. Sportively oblivious of his responsibilities, he proceeds to see how much fun he can have.

Indeed, a confirmed self-hunter becomes jealous of a gunner, regards him as a competitor, and will deliberately flush to frustrate his rival. All the owner can expect on the opening day is to glimpse his dog from afar a few times, for a dog that hunts for himself during the summer will continue doing so later—and you can lay to that.

The desire to hunt for himself is inherent in a dog and will often pop out when an opportunity presents itself. Hunting for man is, after all, an acquisition, a sort of overlay of instinct. Allowed to go undisciplined for months, almost any young dog may be expected to backslide.

Everybody needs a certain amount of bossing. I require a certain amount of it myself. So do you. Now and then a man or a dog may be so fortified with spirit—or enfeebled by age —as to be unsusceptible to temptation. But the number, sad to say, is far from legion.

A thoughtful old dog will content himself with dozing in the shade of the maples and bargaining with the mistress for an extra scrap of cornbread. Or maybe he will beguile the tedium of the summer by calling on the neighbors. His training and experience are so deep-rooted that he is not likely to become addicted to self-hunting. But a fresh-trained youngster whose venturesome spirit revels in the myriads of scent and the spacious fields about him, who has no one to remind him of his transgressions—well, what can you expect?

Self-hunting is as seductive as sin. Once a dog gets infected with the virus, it is worse than Ten Nights in a Barroom, the melodrama that thrilled and chilled me during boyhood and made me resolve, at the age of ten, never, never to become a drunkard. A resolution that a bad stomach has enabled me to keep.

Self-hunting is contagious, too. One dog will infect another, luring him off into the fields and setting an example in lawlessness, like a roguish cow that incites others to fence-breaking. One self-hunter may ruin a dozen; and once a dog becomes addicted, he is almost unpennable thereafter.

An intractable dog is the devil's recruiting agent. What on this mundane sphere is so utterly worthless, what so complete-

The Backsliders

ly shattering to one's serenity of spirit, what so conducive to intemperance of speech as a lawless and incorrigible dog? Verily, no man is a philosopher when his dog flushes a covey of birds.

Self-hunters are sometimes incurable. Even when curable, they require rebreaking, with emphasis on the "break." Reforming a self-hunter is often more difficult than training a dog anew, since you have to dislodge one set of habits before implanting another.

It is a vexatious business, too, because such a dog's offenses are committed at a safe distance from you. The malefactor is apt to be too far away for physical punishment. To be effective, punishment must follow instantly on the heels of the crime. When a dog flushes birds a hundred yards away, your only resort is to linguistic chastisement, to which the rascal is already impervious.

How can such a renegade be reached at the precise psychological moment? "I can answer that," quite a few hunters will volunteer. "When a lawless dog is otherwise unreachable, the best prescription is a dose of bird-shot." I am aware of the fact that such "rump-stinging" is customary in some parts of the South, but it is a custom more honored in the breach than the observance. Certainly no reputable trainer will recommend such a brutal practice. Anger dethrones the reason, and a mad man is the world's poorest judge of distance.

You occasionally hear of some wayward dog that has been reformed by such treatment, but only silence envelopes those that were maimed or killed; or worse still, in whose lonely hearts a terrible fear of man was implanted. In younger days I impulsively shot a dog that I deeply loved, and spent a long night promising the Lord never to do it again. The dog recovered, but I didn't.

What should the owner of a headstrong dog do? Most such dogs are reclaimable by one method or another, but dogs differ so much that the only safe procedure is to consult an experienced trainer.

There is another reason for restricting a dog's activities

during the summer. A foot-loose dog can be very destructive to nesting quail. The self-hunting vagrant develops a diabolical cunning at finding and despoiling nests. Young quail chicks, too, suffer from his raids, being scattered in heavy clover or weeds and often never rejoining their mothers. An orphaned chick soon succumbs—to loneliness, the first rain, or one of the many awesome perils that confront him.

Many a farmer who is puzzled over a waning quail population will find the answer right under his nose: an untrammeled dog that roams the countryside. Nearly every neighborhood is plagued with two or three such vagabond hunters, for the average farmer seldom pens a dog, either because he is unaware of the resulting damage to both his dog and the bird crop, or because he is indifferent to both, merely boarding the dog for a city acquaintance. Moral: if you send your dog to the country—

There is a good deal of speculation among bird hunters as to the relative destructiveness of hawks, foxes, roving cats and other predators. And speculation it is. My friend, Herbert Stoddard, who has devoted his life to quail research and is the ranking authority, knows as much about this subject as anybody else. Yet amiable Herb will readily admit that there is much he doesn't know.

It is hard to catalogue a wild animal, to dogmatize about the morals and manners of even a field mouse. The difficulty of getting authentic information about wild animals is mainly the difficulty of *observing wildlife unobserved,* over a sufficiently large and varied area and for a sufficiently long time.

In my judgment, the foot-loose dog that roams the countryside during the rearing season ranks high among the arch enemies of quail. For years I have been observing the ravages of such vagrants. I have seen enough evidence of their misdeeds to convict them in any court. The farmer who restricts his dog during the summer not only insures him against self-hunting, but in all likelihood adds immeasurably to the quail crop in his neighborhood.

The Backsliders

So our country cousins have their troubles too. Nature is a good bookkeeper. She looks after her debits and credits, her balances and counterbalances. As Emerson said a long time ago—and as anybody with any gumption knew a long time before that—*compensation compensates.*

Hell-Hound of the Sloughs

The common bowfin, one of the most ubiquitous and ill-esteemed of fish, is really one of the strangest in the world. And one of the most destructive.

The bowfin ranges from the Great Lakes to the Gulf, the variety of his nicknames reflecting his distribution. In the North he is a fresh-water dogfish, though really not a dogfish at all. Elsewhere he is variously known as John A. Grindle, grindle, grindal, brindle cat, cottonfish, blackfish, mudfish, speckled cat, dappled cat, cypress trout. In French Louisiana he is a *chupique, choupiquel,* or *poisson de marais,* which is old French for "fish of the marshes." The most picturesque appellations I have heard are "lake lawyer" and "nigger bass."

The bowfin is a heavy, round-bodied and symmetrically proportioned fish. The females are not only the deadlier, but by far the larger of the species. The male is readily distinguished by a black spot at the base of the tail.

Hell-Hound of the Sloughs

This fish has three striking features: a pronounced dorsal fin, extending from the tail almost to the head; an uncommonly thickset and sinewy tail, and crushing jaws studded with needle-like teeth. Those jaws can whack a two-pound bass or pickerel in two with a single snap, or mutilate your fingers unless you are awfully polite in removing your hook.

For sheer strength, the bowfin is unsurpassed by any fish his size. Every line in his body bespeaks brute strength and ferocity. A big mud has little finesse when hooked, but his initial rushes are like those of a yearling bull run amuck. It is just you against him. As a friend woefully remarked: "You can't play a damned mudfish. He's too much of a hellcat to cooperate with you!"

Although the bowfin will occasionally take a plug, the ordinary rod and reel are hardly recommended for the real juggernauts. After several unhappy encounters with obstreperous specimens, I renounced mine. Too often the line snapped, the reel broke, or I sustained a cracked finger. The bowfin has a genius for snarling a line about submerged debris. If you hook a really big one, forget about the fish and try to save your tackle.

The best method of taking them is by set-lines tied to supple overhanging branches or to springy poles driven into the mucky bottom. Or by trot-lines, provided there is enough resiliency in the base-line.

After experimenting with every bait my imagination could conjure up, I hit upon the inevitable: fresh hog liver. Yessir, an inch cube of fresh bloody hog liver will encompass old Gargantua's downfall at almost any time. But early morning is the best time to seduce him. His sales resistance is lowest between daybreak and nine o'clock, especially on Sunday mornings!

Having worked out my method of attack, I went into the "bowfin business," as my wife good-naturedly chided. During one spring I took a hundred big ones from a deep cove in the Edisto. They ranged from 5 to 13 pounds. During a single day and night, when the water was bowfin-perfect, I caught eleven that weighed 88 pounds. The chairman of the committee tipped the scales at exactly 14 pounds—all mean!

And shall I ever forget that misty daybreak when, in a black and ancient lagoon, I tangled with my champion mud of 18 pounds! That old leviathan stretched across my kitchen table. The marks are still there. After being measured, weighed and adequately admired by my neighbors, he made a Negro family of fourteen very, very happy.

The bowfin is wholly carnivorous, and exceedingly voracious. His unmatched greediness, strength and hardihood make him one of the most destructive of inland fish. He is the ravening wolf of the dark lagoons, the nightmare of the slumberous coves. Skulking in deep water by day, he invades the teeming shallows by night, spreading terror and bloody execution in his wake.

I have lain by black lagoons throughout the night, listening to the frenzied acrobatics of other fish trying to escape these streamlined behemoths. I have seen whole schools of 20-inch pickerel take the air simultaneously to escape the jaws of a big killer.

Fishermen are perennially fussing about their waters being carp-infested, and they have my active sympathy; but the carp is a vegetarian and a pacifist. The worst predators, especially in the South, that I know best, are bowfins and gars. Many ponds and streams have been virtually ruined by the depredations of these ruthlesss cutthroats, and their control is a matter of growing concern.

The bowfin's uniqueness is twofold: his amazing antiquity, ichthyologically speaking, and his peculiar anatomical structure. He is really a prehistoric fish that has managed to outlive his geological age by millions of years. He is the sole survivor of a once-great fish family of the Mesozoic era, the Age of Reptiles—a contemporary of the dinosaur, the pterodactyl and other reptilian nightmares which became extinct millions of years ago. The bowfin may, with considerable propriety, be called the oldest fish in the world. When you look at him, you are looking at a fossil, a living fossil.

Hell-Hound of the Sloughs

Indeed, he is hardly a fish at all. For instance, he is the lucky possessor of a double method of breathing. In addition to gills, standard equipment for fish, the bowfin has a peculiar air-bladder that serves as a lung, giving him a sort of auxiliary respiratory system. When times are good and water is plentiful, he uses his gills. If times are hard and water is scarce, he simply shifts gears and uses his lung.

The bowfin is thus capable of surviving under the most adverse conditions, being able to remain alive for protracted periods in little or no water at all. I have seen big ones in landlocked pools so shallow that their very backs protruded. Mr. Bowfin was apparently unembarrassed.

Back in the mudfish swamps are natives who insist they have seen them "flounderin' around in the muck, with big fish-hawks a-peckin' at their backs." I myself have seen Black River negroes dig through the crust of dried-up canals and pull up wriggling muds. If you don't believe this, meet me there with your hoe!

Down in Louisiana you will hear incredible tales of bowfins having been plowed up alive in the lowlands weeks after floods have receded. While I cannot personally attest to such longevity, the secondary respiratory system of the bowfin does bring such stories within the range of possibility.

Down in the Louisiana back country they will also tell you, if you are credulous enough to listen, that a cooked bowfin will "uncook himself" if left overnight. And that if buried with the proper ritual under a sympathetic moon, a bowfin will invariably convert himself into a live snake!

Is the bowfin edible? It depends upon how hungry you are and whether he has been "processed" or not. I tried it once. I had just come to the deep South and had never encountered doughty old *Amia calva*. A fellow I met in the swamp had a big one tethered out. It was a beautiful, racy-looking specimen, and I admired it extravagantly. The fellow looked at me appraisingly.

"Take 'im if you want 'im," he offered magnanimously.

Thanking my benefactor profusely, I hurried home and invited two preachers to supper. Now, may I say with pardonable pride that I am one of the best fish-cooks in the country—probably the best. My wife and I are unanimous on that subject. It is one of the few unanimities we enjoy.

In baking the handsome carcass, I brought to bear the fruits of twenty years of experience. For two hours I hovered solicitously over that oven. Then I placed the contents, brown and sizzling with butter, in a big platter. 'Twas a culinary masterpiece. In the center of the table I set the platter, blushingly accepting the tributes of my guests. Then I took a carving knife and laid open my masterpiece from stem to stern.

Instantly a nameless effluvium assaulted my nostrils and filled me with a soul-shaking nausea. Stampeding for the great out-of-doors, I promptly "reconsidered" my dinner, my breakfast and, although I won't be dogmatic on this point, probably my supper of the night before. My guests joined in the exercise with gusto. It was then that I understood the munificence of that fellow I had met in the swamp.

This represents the sum-total of my culinary experience with old bowfin. In 1790 an observer wrote feelingly: "They are a soft and sorry fish, and good for nothing; though some eat them for good fish." A statement to which I mightily subscribe.

But if you want to learn how a bowfin can be transformed into a table delicacy, go to Louisiana and Alabama and take a lesson from the swamp folks. In remote lowlands of the deep South, the bowfin is a staple food and a major source of meat supply. He is consumed with gusto by the natives.

In some sections they have evolved a method of processing the rankness out of the bowfin. They often sun-dry and salt-pack them for future use. But the expert processors eviscerate them, salt them, dry them out thoroughly, and subject the carcasses to prolonged hardwood smoking in warehouses. Taste the result and you will never believe it is the "lake lawyer."

Serve this much-smoked product in salad, patties, fishballs; or creamed, baked, or broiled, and you have something not

'Possum up de 'Simmon Tree

"Is that hound any good, Uncle Spiller?" I asked, pointing toward a malevolent-looking brute sniffing at the old darkey's heels.

"Lawdy, Cap'n, if dat dawg had a-been much better de good Marster would a-kept him for to hunt 'possums wid hisself! Dat ole Blue, de high cunstable ob de swamp."

"And what about these others?" I asked, as three churlish-looking varmints emerged from under the cabin.

"Dis here Squaller, and dem two Big Mouf and Snake," he pridefully informed me. "And dar ain't no passel o' dawgs in de county dat's a sarcumstance to 'em, sah. Course I don't mind you speakin' discontemptuous-like about 'em, kase you ain't hunted wid 'em yet."

The dogs were as scurvy and unprepossessing a bunch as I had ever seen. Their ancestry, I felt sure, would have defied a genealogist, but if their family tree had a 'possum up it there would be no complaints from me. Uncle Spiller had such an

Hell-Hound of the Sloughs

even an epicure will turn up his nose at. Indeed, bowfin sometimes finds his way into fashionable restaurants that cater to tourists and outlanders. You might find yourself paying a fancy price for a slice of the old hell-hound of the lagoons—under a frilly French name.

According to Government reports, about a million pounds of bowfin are caught annually. That's right much bowfin. But there is a heck of a lot the Government doesn't know, about fish as well as other things. Most bowfins are taken by people who wouldn't know a statistic from a pillowcase, whose habitations are remote from statistical headquarters, and by citizens who have a marked reluctance toward reporting anything to the Government!

I have lost my boyhood faith in statistics anyway. Vastly more bowfin are caught and eaten in the South, I am certain, than the Government knows about. I am certain of another thing too: not half as many are caught as ought to be caught for the welfare of some of our best fishing waters.

canebrakes with the unfaltering sureness of a child of the swamps.

As we penetrated the depths of the swamp, the black void about us became animate. Night is the true democracy. Innumerable birds flitted uneasily in the inky ceiling overhead. Small animals, disquieted by our passage, scampered noisily away through the underbrush. Once a wild hog, surprised in its lair, emitted an explosive snort and bounded away. Now and then an enormous owl let out a spine-tingling WHOOOOOOOP! that reverberated through the swamp.

Cypress knees loomed grotesquely in the spasmodic flicker of the lanterns, like the snouts of reptilian fossils peering at us from the black muck. Shadows danced eerily. Now and then came the phosphorescent sheen of a decaying stump, whereupon July would mumble, "Dat ole Plat-Eye!" and sidle closer to his grandfather. Finally Uncle Spiller stopped.

"Dis here ole Tom's stompin' ground. Us mout strike 'im and again us moutn't. Luck a funny t'ing," he offered.

"Who is old Tom?" Bill asked.

"Ole Tom de king 'possum uh Inktoe swamp. I been atter him five years, I speck. I done cotch him oncet."

"You caught him once? Why did you turn him loose?" I pursued.

"Didn't tuhn 'm a-loose. Ole Tom, he tuhn me a'loose," he said cryptically. Extending a gorilla-like arm into the region of light, he pointed to a jagged scar at the base of the thumb. "Yassah!" he clucked, "I was a-possumin' dat night, but ole Tom he was a-niggerin'! 'Twas nip an' tuck, sah, and we parted de bes' uh friends."

"Hish!" he interrupted himself. "Hear dat? Ole Blue done struck already!"

A tremulous wail resounded through the night, followed by a series of heavy-throated bellows: "Woo-woo-woo-woo-woo-woo-woo! Woo! Woo! Woo!" Again the tremulous deep-chested wail, and again the staccato sequence of "Woo! Woo! Woo!" from the cavernous throat of old Blue. Each time the rhythm was repeated, the cadences rising and falling on the

'Possum up de 'Simmon Tree

immoderate pride in his mangy pack that I forebore comment. Besides, we were depending upon the old darkey to "chaperon" us on an all-night hunt through the mazes of Inktoe swamp and I was too prudent to incur his displeasure at the outset.

Uncle Spiller is of uncertain antiquity. I have no idea whatever as to his age, but I have nothing on Uncle Spiller: neither has he. He has dried up until he looks like an African mummy. Malaria, rheumatism, and the other "complaints" of the low country have long ago worn themselves out on his leathery carcass and given him up as a bad job.

The old codger looks as if he were about ready for Pilgrim's Progress, but before that night's hunt was over I conceived a profound respect for the stamina that lay wrapped up in that scrawny and ageless body. And he has about him an infectious good nature.

"Old Spiller ain't got but two teefths," he chirruped, "but tank Gawd dey hits."

We also took with us one July, a weazened counterpart of Uncle Spiller, his grandson and the apple of his eye. "Dat pickaninny got monkey blood in he vein!" the old darkey proudly told us. "He is de tree-climbin'est varmint in de swamp. Ain't yer, July?" The little Negro accepted the compliment with gleaming teeth.

I had invited Bill, a "regular" guy who had been *particeps criminis* with me on more than one doubtful venture, and Professor Smathers, a biology instructor in the state university who, I thought, might enjoy the novel experience of a night in the swamps. That half-witted professor! But it was my fault, as Bill reminded me later; I ought to have known better in the first place.

Anyway, our 'possum "safari" was made up, and nightfall found us threading the devious recesses of Inktoe swamp. Within an hour I was hopelessly befuddled as to any sort of direction, but it didn't matter, Uncle Spiller trudged serenely on, leading us over harricanes, windfalls, across glistening streams of black water, and through apparently impassable

'Possum up de 'Simmon Tree

mellow night air. In a few minutes another dog chorused in, then another and still another, their voices merging into the volume of an orchestra. They were presumably following a devious trail, the baying alternately waxing and waning away in the distance.

As if reacting to a galvanic shock, Uncle Spiller suddenly jumped atop a stump, cupped his hands to his mouth, and emitted a penetrating cry that echoed and re-echoed until it died dolefully away in the dismal depths of the swamp:

"YeeeeeeeeeeEEEho!   YeeeeeeeeeeeEEEho!"

As if in response to his encouragement, the tempo of the baying increased.

"Dey's a-trailin', and a-comin' dis way. Dat Snake dar. And dat ole Squaller done open up. Hey, dat ole Big Mouf done chime in! Dat 'possum mos' ready for de kurriner and dat's a fack!"

"What do you mean by *kurriner*?" I asked mystified.

"You know, Cap'n, kurriner. De man whar say you daid afore dey buries you."

The trail was obviously getting warmer and coming toward us. The dogs were now within 200 yards, their voices rising in a clamorous crescendo. Suddenly from the underbrush behind us emerged the pack, with heads down and throats swelling. But why were they coming straight toward us. That was a mystery soon resolved as old Blue trotted importantly forward, thrust his battle-scarred muzzle up the very tree against which Uncle Spiller had been leaning, and wailed disconsolately. The other dogs lunged forward and pandemonium broke loose. The younger dogs set up a clamorous bawling, gnawing at the base of the tree, leaping up the trunk and trying madly for a footing in their frantic efforts to get at the quarry. The old darkey stood with a look of chagrin on his wrinkled face.

"Dar now! Whoever heard o'sich doin's. Leanin' 'ginst a tree wid a 'possum up it. In my younger days, old Spiller would ha smelt dat 'possum hisself." He looked around with a comic seriousness, begging for a spark of credence. "If dem smart-aleck niggers on de oder side de swamp hears 'bout dis, ma hash am settled."

"Come here, July," he ordered. "Shinny up dat tree and shake dat 'possum out."

The little Negro emerged from the shadows and prepared for the ascent. I cast a flashlight beam up the towering sweet gum. The trunk was two feet in diameter, and it was perhaps twenty-five feet to the first limb. At once I became concerned for July's safety, and felt it my duty to protest.

"Uncle Spiller, July can't climb that tree. Nobody but a lumberjack or a . . ."

But the old Negro disdained to hear me, busying himself with his operations. Taking a piece of stout rope from his pocket he tied one end securely to the wrist of July, who promptly embraced the trunk of the tree with his arms. Uncle Spiller then carried the unattached end of the rope around the tree and looped it over the other wrist of July, leaving sufficient play in the cord to permit its being flipped upward or downward at will. The boy was visibly pleased to hold the center of the stage.

"Stand back, gents!" the old darkey ordered in his best showman's voice.

Then, as we stood agape, July extended his feet partly around the tree, thrust his naked toes into the rough bark, and gave a light upward flip of the cord encircling the trunk and attached to his wrists. As the cord caught and tightened his body swung upward perhaps two feet. Quickly repeating the maneuver, he scrambled up another two feet. And in less time than I have taken to describe the performance, he had gained the first limb. Crooking an elbow over the limb, he quickly disengaged the looped end of the cord and scrambled up, disappearing in the thick top.

Meanwhile the varying behavior of the dogs was diverting. The three younger hounds were fairly beside themselves with excitement. While July was scaling the tree, they kept up a frenzied barking which ran the whole gamut from eager whimperings to raucous bellows. They pawed, gnawed the

'Possum up de 'Simmon Tree

bark, and cut all sorts of didoes. But not so with Old Blue. That veteran had lost some of the effusiveness of youth, and he looked with mild tolerance on the antics of his juniors. Indeed, when July prepared to climb, Old Blue nonchalantly stalked off and sat quietly on his haunches, like an elderly gentleman watching his frolicsome children at play. Kindergarden stuff to him! But the second July's voice drifted down, his ears pricked up and he was all 'possum dog again.

"Done found 'im!" The voice of July seemed to float down from nowhere.

"Shake 'im out den," Uncle Spiller called back.

"Done cotch 'im by de tail. Gwyn fling 'im down."

A branch cracked sharply, a heavy body thumped against a limb and came hurtling downward. One of the younger dogs, jealous of his prowess and over-eager to be in on the kill, leaped up and attempted to close in on the body in mid-air—and was knocked flat on his back by the impact. He would remember that lesson. Old Blue had learned it in his youth, but he was nothing reluctant now. Timing his spring to the split-second, he was the first to close in. Then a mad scramble followed, with Uncle Spiller and the dogs in an indiscriminate pile. In a few seconds the old man emerged holding a big, fiercely-grinning 'possum by the tail. I guessed its weight at twelve pounds.

"One fer de bag, an' a nice un, too!"

Before we had finished inspecting the first catch July was down again, descending as he had ascended, and grinning broadly, having verified his grandfather's boast that he had monkey blood in his veins.

The hunt was resumed, and by midnight we had bagged three other sizeable 'possums, having had the good fortune to find two feeding up a persimmon tree. It was a fair start, and we were all in high spirits. Uncle Spiller, walking ahead and carrying the bag of 'possums on his back, broke into song. His voice was falsetto, but his heart was in the right place, and his chantey rang with the melodious and weird cadences peculiar to his race:

"Got ma 'taters,
Got ma rice,
Ain't gwyn worry
'Bout de white man's price,
Got a fat 'possum at home!

Meat outer sight,
Times gittin' tight,
But I ain't gwyn roam,
Cause 'simmons gittin' ripe,
An' I got a fat 'possum at home!"

And in the hunter's triumphant chant was more than the natural ebullience of the race, for the 'possum, especially in times of depression, is of no little economic importance to the Negroes of the lower South. As a source of food the *Didelphis virginiana*, as the encyclopedias call him, is not to be overlooked, and he abounds in the wide-flung lowlands as well as in the hardwood uplands of the South. The darkey may be content with sweet potatoes, rice, and corn meal as weekday rations, but on festive occasions he has got to have a 'possum. It is the pork of the destitute lowlander. In fact, 'possums are sometimes kept in captivity and fattened like pigs.

Along toward 2 o'clock it commenced to get chilly, and Bill began to bemoan his lack of foresight in not bringing along a little something to fortify his courage, the *sine qua non* of an all-night hunting trip. *Sine qua non* is Latin for "not without which," without which Bill was usually not. But the patron saint of 'possum hunters is a regular fellow.

Presently, Uncle Spiller appeared to stumble heavily, falling forward with a vociferous grunt. Regaining his feet, he brushed aside a pile of leaves, exposing, of all things, the protruding top of a wooden keg! The old darkey seemed puzzled. Bill's interest picked up instantly. Kneeling down, he popped the wooden stopper from the bung hole, thrust his nose in like an anteater, and inhaled deeply and feelingly. Then he sat down beside the keg, sighed heavily, and drawled:

'Possum up de 'Simmon Tree

"I'm awful sorry, but I'm plumb tuckered out. I just got to stop here and rest a spell. You all can go on huntin' and maybe I'll overtake you some time or another. If I just had a straw or somethin'," he sighed. It was very touching.

Uncle Spiller's ancient features broke into an expansive grin. Shuffling over to a hollow log, he fumbled around a minute and came up with a long hollow reed. The pious old fraud! It was his own keg, and he had deliberately led us to it. Bill stuck the reed in the keg and commenced drenching himself.

"What is it?" I demanded. But Bill had a one-track mind. After about five minutes he settled back on his haunches and wiped his mouth with the back of his hand.

"Persimmon beer, old son, and of all the persimmon beer I ever sampled . . . well, take a swig and decide for yourself."

Uncle Spiller was immediately bombarded with questions, and his explanations cleared up the mystery of the keg.

"I brung de kaig to de 'simmons stead o' haulin' de 'simmons to de kaig. John Hennery's boy brung me de honey-locusts, and I got de extrys here an' dar. Ole nigger haffa hide kaig in de swamp to keep dem scallions at de house from gittin' it all."

Well, we squatted around the keg and held a caucus, passing the reed from one to another. Bill's judgment stood unimpeached. Cold, sparkling, and mellow, it stole the chill from the frosty air and filled us with a persuasive benevolence and brotherhood. With Professor Smathers, to whom the concoction was new, it was a case of love at first sight. First he knelt down and sucked, then he sat down and sucked, and finally he lay flat on the keg and sucked. Then he took time out to catch his breath and sucked some more, as if he thought it a breach of etiquette to quit before he emptied the barrel.

"Dat gentleman better not drink too much," Uncle Spiller cautioned. "Dat stuff got purgitude in it!"

The professor finally straightened up, his eyes snapping. He was getting "fou and unco happy," as Robert Burns says. Normally of a quiet, retiring nature, he now became highly garrulous, proceeding to deliver to us a grandiloquent lecture on the 'possum, and in his best classroom manner. He descanted at length on its idiosyncrasies, its love life, its intimate family affairs, with numerous references to "nocturnal and arboreal habits," "prehensile tail," and what not. He wound up, or rather unwound with: "It is the only native marsupial in this country. Ain't it a fine marsupial, Uncle Spiller?" he demanded.

The old darkey, who had been visibly impressed, blinked owlishly and apologetically replied:

" 'Possum hash am fust-rate, sah, fer a fact, but I can't say how de *soup* would be, sah."

A distant baying recalled us to the hunt, and we soon came upon the dogs treeing in an uprooted tupelo. The professor, who had a lively interest in affairs now, immediately scrambled up the fallen trunk to find the quarry, protesting that he could outclimb July any day in the week. In a few minutes his flashlight began to play over the thick branches around him. Presently the roving beam stopped on a clump of leaves.

"Ah, I perceive the object of our search, gentlemen. 'Tis an elegant creature. Tail extended and bushy; head tapering and graceful; evidently carnivorous in habit; white longitudinal streaks down its body. Ah, I have it! 'Tis a very, very fine specimen of *Putorius putorius*!" mooned the professor.

We brought up together 200 feet away, panting and brushing the cobwebs from our faces. The light still glowed in the tree lap, and we could hear the indistinct maunderings of the professor.

"Run, you damn fool. That's a polecat!" Bill yelled.

"Run, and miss this specimen? Ah, my good man, that is not the way of science. Your fears are unwarranted. It is true that the *Putorius putorius* may emit a somewhat unpleasant odor from its anal glands, but it is inoffensive unless irritated, and I do not propose to irritate it. Besides, it cannot emit said odor as long as its tail is down, and I shall observe

'Possum up de 'Simmon Tree

the caudal appendage closely. A beautiful specimen!" he murmured rapturously.

Well, he could stay in the interest of science, but in the interest of humanity we couldn't see it that way. We shouted; we coaxed; we cursed; we threatened him with mayhem and manslaughter, and still the professor sat rhapsodizing to that polecat.

"He's drunk as a boiled owl off Uncle Spiller's beer. Why did you bring such an idiot with you anyway? Now what'll we do?" demanded Bill sourly.

In disgust we decided to continue the hunt, hoping the fool would return to his senses and follow. Uncle Spiller had in the meanwhile held the dogs on a leash, explaining that contact with a skunk would so demoralize their sense of smell that they would be worthless the rest of the night.

An hour or so later, during which time we had bagged our fourth and fifth 'possums, we heard someone shuffling through the underbrush. A light flashed on and off. It was the professor and he was carrying a sack and mumbling contentedly. He had evidently caught and sacked a small 'possum without the aid of the dogs, as sometimes happens. Weaving his way into the circle with a fatuous smile on his face, he announced:

"I've got a nice one. Look."

Bill opened the bag and nearly had a stroke. It was that same confounded polecat! Now don't ask me how the professor caught him, or why the polecat did not resent, in his customary manner, the overtures of his captor. I don't know, and, furthermore, I don't give a damn. And the professor doesn't remember. As a matter of fact, the next day, after Uncle Spiller's beer had died out, he indignantly denied the whole business. Anyway Bill picked up the sack, counted one, two, three for our benefit, and hurled it as far into the swamp as he could.

That odoriferous episode over, Uncle Spiller released his dogs again and we straggled on. We had already had a good hunt, but as it turned out, the climax of the night was yet to come.

"De big boys don't move 'round much twell jes befor' day, an' dey don't climb trees much. Dey's too hebby," Uncle Spiller had told us, and his judgment was soon verified.

It was in the intense blackness just preceding daybreak that Old Blue struck again. The trail was hot, and within fifteen minutes the dogs were treeing in a thick windfall. We promptly surrounded the fall to cut off all avenues of escape. The dogs were held back to prevent their closing in too fiercely and mutilating the catch. Snapping on my flashlight I started crawling under the entanglement, worming and bellying my way along until I got to the center. Then I began to play the light around me. All at once the rays caught and held two gleaming pools of fire. Then the beam fell full on an enormous 'possum. He was at bay and in a belligerent mood, his jaws glistening and extended, his breath hissing.

In a voice as casual as I could make it I called the old darkey to me. Scrambling through the windfall he soon squatted by my side. When I flashed the light on again his eyes popped incredulously, and I felt his body grow tense against mine. Old Tom at last!

I continued to hold the light while Uncle Spiller advanced to the attack. Then began the hand-to-hand encounter. It was check and countercheck; maneuver against maneuver; finesse against finesse. It was blackjack against thunder. They were old adversaries, these two, and they respected each other. The Negro found himself repeatedly outsmarted in his efforts to get at the tail. Finally he poked a stick at the hissing jaws and goaded the 'possum into snapping it. Its teeth sank deep and froze to the stick. Then Uncle Spiller made a lightning swoop downward—and came up with both of his huge hands locked about the enemy's throat in such a way that he could not budge his head.

Old Tom was indeed the great panjandrum of the swamp. From tip to tip he was nearly three feet long and must have weighed 25 pounds. The long feud between Negro and brer 'possum was ended, and Uncle Spiller's cup was running over.

'Possum up de 'Simmon Tree

Cocking his shaggy head, he sent an ancient ditty lilting through the mellow night:

> " 'Possum up de 'simmon tree,
> Raccoon on de ground,
> Raccoon said to de 'possum,
> Throw me some 'simmons down!
> Throw me some 'simmons down, Lawdy,
> Throw me some 'simmons down."

His excitement finally subsided, and he brought out a fresh bag to put the prize catch in. The big 'possum had desisted in his efforts to escape, now appearing to be altogether lifeless. Indeed, when Uncle Spiller, as a demonstration, placed him on the ground and released his hold, no signs of life were evident. "No use o' playin' 'possum! You ain't fool nobody," the old negro shouted at his enemy.

Playing 'possum! At least, I smilingly reflected, this amusing little animal has done what few others have done—he has added a picturesque phrase to the English language and got himself into all the dictionaries. How much more vivid and effective is the idiom, "playing 'possum," than the roundabout equivalent, "to dissemble or counterfeit death when endangered or about to be captured."

Day was beginning to break. We had seven 'possums, more than anybody wanted to tote, so we turned our steps homeward. We soon discovered that we had traversed a wide circle, and were agreeably surprised when we emerged into a frost-covered cotton patch within a short distance from Uncle Spiller's cabin, where we had left our car the preceding evening.

Arriving at the cabin, we found that we were expected. Uncle Spiller's granddaughter met us with a gallon of steaming black coffee, the finishing touch to any hunt. We had gotten in our car and started down the lane to the big road when I happened to think that I was taking one 'possum home with me, and that the missus might not know how to cook it. Backing up, I called the old Negro to the car.

"Uncle Spiller, what is the best way to cook a 'possum?"

"Dat very praper question, sah. Hit make a big diffunce. Fust, you hang de 'possum up by de hind feet, lack a hog; den you pull de hide off and entrail 'im; den you wash 'im good and clean; den you builds a good hot fyar in de stove and gits de pan ready; den . . ."

"Then what?" I prompted.

"Den you sends fer me!"

I did.

Hunting Bee-Trees

> "A swarm of bees in May,
> Is worth a load of hay.
> A swarm of bees in June,
> Is worth a silver spoon.
> A swarm of bees in July,
> Is not worth a fly."

This time-honored dictum was as much a part of my childhood legacy as the precious rigmarole about "rich man, poor man, beggar man, thief." How old the dictum is I cannot say, but conveying as it does a prevailing truth, it doubtless goes as far back as bee-keeping itself. And that goes pretty far back.

The antiquity of bee-keeping is attested by numerous allusions in classical literature and legend, and by various references to the subject in the Bible. Samson, for instance, once propounded a riddle that gave the Philistines a seven-day headache: "Out of the eater came forth meat; out of the strong came forth sweetness." The answer was a swarm of bees that had set up housekeeping in the carcass of a lion. Even in ancient times bees apparently had the habit of establishing themselves in the most surprising places.

Bee-tree hunting is still the favored outdoor pastime with thousands of Americans in various sections of the country, but notably up and down the Appalachian cordillera.

"If your time is worth more than a dollar a day, you can't afford to hunt bee-trees," remarks a treatise on bee-keeping. Yet many experienced hunters find it a source of income as well as enjoyment. I have run into gnarled backwoodsmen who have found and cut as many as twenty-five bee-trees in a year. Down in the Ozarks you "hear tell" of old-timers who eke out a livelihood by hunting bee-trees.

Up in the Blue Ridge Mountains of Virginia I once met a grizzled veteran they called Sourwood Bill who, according to neighborhood report, had found and cut a thousand trees in his life. And Buck Goodson, another hunter who has rambled the foothills of Piedmont Virginia in quest of bee-trees for the better part of fifty years, tells me he has found more than five hundred—as many as fifteen in a single day.

Bee-trees are hunted for two reasons—the honey store and the bees themselves. The quality and quantity of the honey taken naturally varies with several factors. It may range from five pounds to a hundred, or in extreme cases one hundred and fifty pounds. And it may be almost inedible, or have a flavor and clarity unequalled by the product of domestic bees.

The bees captured are ordinarily more valuable than the honey. The majority of so-called wild bees are absconding swarms that have simply reverted to nature. Occasionally I have run into a tree colony of apparently pure Italians, although wild bees are usually hybrids, though none the less productive. They are easily domesticated, become docile with the least decent handling, and are easily reconciled to their new habitation. Of the dozen hives in my backyard apiary at present, ten colonies were taken from the woods, yet they

Hunting Bee-Trees

averaged one hundred pounds of first-class honey apiece last season.

Infrequently I run across a woods colony of little black bees. These diminutive daughters of war are not exactly distinguished for their hospitality, but they are marvellous little honey factories. And they can earn a livelihood under circumstances that would baffle most domestic colonies.

The season to hunt for bee-trees depends on whether one is interested primarily in getting the honey or capturing the bees. If bees are the main consideration, the tree should be cut before the honey flow sets in, say along in May or June, in time for the captured colony to rehabilitate itself and lay up sufficient stores to see them through the winter. If honey is the main object, the tree should be cut toward the end of the honey flow, along in September or October, making allowances for variations of season and climate.

As to the best locality in which to hunt for trees, there is no substitute for common judgment. Two or three general observations, however, might not be amiss. Hunt within reasonable proximity to domestic colonies, unless you are intent on procuring the original black bee, since escaping swarms comprise the majority of wild bees; and in timber containing sizable trees, since larger and older trees are more likely to afford the necessary hollows and crevices that recommend themselves to reconnoitering scouts. Cliffs and "hog back" ridges near running streams are usually a good bet, especially if the section abounds in sourwood.

Roughly speaking, there are three methods of locating bee trees, the first of which is too elementary to call for enlargement. It consists simply in "giraffing" up at every likely-looking tree in the woods. Such a hit-or-miss affair is scorned by the real bee hunter, who commonly relies upon one or two other methods.

The most effective way of determining the probable location of a tree is by observing the line of flight of watering bees. During the spring and summer, bees require an abnormal amount of water for raising their young, and being creatures of habit, they water pretty regularly in the same place, which is seldom more than half a mile from the tree. But you must keep your eyes peeled for sandbars and sunlit openings. There is no dilly-dallying with a drinking bee. She fills up quickly and hits for home.

The other method differs from that already mentioned in that the observer follows the flight of nectar-gathering bees rather than watering bees. It calls for a silly-looking but efficient little contraption known as a "bee box," which may be variously contrived. Probably the simplest way to make such a contraption is to take an ordinary cigar box and cut a circular hole about the size of a half-dollar in the top; then place a tin slide or shutter over this opening to permit its being closed at the will of the operator. On the cover attach a smaller box, something like a chalk container, from which the bottom has been removed. Arrange a sliding glass cover for the second box, and your equipment is ready.

Now place a piece of empty comb or small bee-feeder containing sweetened water or diluted honey in the cigar box. Put a few drops of oil of anise into the sweetened water or on the comb, and smear a little of the oil inside the cigar box.

Thus appointed, the hunter betakes himself to bee-tree territory and exposes his bait. Or he may capture a nectar-gathering bee that he chances to see, enclose the bee in the cigar box and close the slide. The imprisoned bee is held in the lower compartment until he has had an opportunity to fill up on the bait and absorb the odor of the oil of anise. Then the hunter places the bee box on some stationary object within convenient view, and permits the bee to enter the top compartment by means of the attached slide. Next he withdraws the glass slide on top and permits the imprisoned bee to escape.

After circling about to orientate herself for the return trip, the released bee flies directly to her tree to unload. The course of her successive flights may be easily marked. Within a few minutes the released worker will return to the box, bringing other bees that have been attracted by the scent of anise oil.

Hunting Bee-Trees

By sprinkling a pinch of flour on the back of a visiting bee and timing the interval between her visits, the approximate distance of the tree may be determined. It is estimated that a worker bee requires eight minutes for a round trip of half a mile.

If trouble is experienced in locating the tree, the visiting bees may be cross-lined by moving the box some distance away and trapping more bees. Where the two established lines of flight intersect, there will be your bee-tree.

Once the tree is found it is ordinarily felled, the hollow trunk or limb containing the bees split, and the honey removed. When their home is demolished, and the honey removed, the bees soon settle nearby. They can be hived and moved as easily as a swarm of domestic bees. If they are disinclined to settle or become obstreperous, they may be subjugated by means of a smoker.

Sometimes, however, a bee-tree cannot be cut. The owner may register an objection. The location of the tree may render cutting inadvisable, or its size may make it impracticable. In such cases the quickest procedure is to remove the limb in which the bees are holed up.

It may happen that neither of these methods may be followed. Bees may be in a trunk rather than a limb. Or they may set up squatters' sovereignty in a valuable shade tree that the owner does not wish mutilated. They may establish themselves in a tree in a public park, or in a private dwelling, or even in a church. What then? Can they be removed without damage to the premises?

They can, and with relatively little difficulty. Not only that, but the honey can be removed as well, without even "scratching the surface" of the premises. The secret is a simple and inexpensive little device known as a "bee-escape."

A few months ago a swarm of bees took an apartment in a historic live oak in a southern city. It was a magnificent tree, but admiring it close-up was not altogether to be recommended because of the venomous temper of the bees. The oak was, of course, untouchable. Mutilating even a part of it was out of the question. So harried park officials besought the services of a veteran bee-tree hunter.

A few weeks later the hunter had the colony of bees in his own backyard and a quantity of honey in his pantry, without having scratched the bark of the majestic tree.

The trick was accomplished as follows: a light platform was erected under the hollow limb harboring the colony of bees. On the platform, as near the flight-hole as possible, was placed a hive containing a nucleus, made by "stealing" two or three frames of bees along with a queen or queen cell, from another colony. Then the operator inserted over the flight-hole a bee-escape, a little one-way-street device resembling a funnel that permits bees to come out but not to go in. Having so done, he left his apparatus to take care of itself.

As the bees emerged from their old home and found it impossible to reenter, they gradually took up residence in the new hive occupied by the nucleus, to which they were a welcome addition. Within three weeks practically all the bees had deserted the old homestead, only the queen and a few retainers remaining in the tree. The operator then returned, removed the bee-escape, filled his smoker with sulphur and destroyed the queen and her retainers.

But what about the honey? The bees, with their customary frugality, took care of that. Once the queen had been destroyed and the bee-escape removed, they proceeded to reenter the former habitation and ransack its treasures, which they straightway transported to the new hive.

Whenever a professional bee hunter finds a tree he wishes to take later, custom requires that he place his initials or a cross on the tree to signify priority. Common law originally entitled the marker of such a tree to possession of the bees. Some hunters, however, regarding such a sign as an invitation to unscrupulous prowlers, refrain from so advertising their finds. One shaggy old hunter of my acquaintance, who wouldn't know an ethic if he met it in the middle of the road, follows the dubious practice of putting his initials on every likely-looking hollow tree he sees, whether it has bees

Hunting Bee-Trees

or not. His explanation sounds plausible: "Got everything to gain and nothin' to lose. If bees ever take up thar, hit's my tree; if'n they don't, hain't no harm done."

The first question asked whenever the subject of bee-tree hunting comes up is: "Don't you get stung?" As a matter of fact, bees are fascinating and relatively harmless insects. There is little occasion for being stung, provided you know how to handle them. I once asked Sourwood Bill about being stung, and his answer was characteristic: "Now and then mebbe, but a feller's liable to git stung in any business these days."

Stop-off for Turkeys

One December morning found me bogged down on a solitary country road in one of the back provinces of Virginia. There I was, my car as muddy as a tank emerging from battle, wheels mired down to the axle, a tire stripped off in the scrimmage, and an over-heated motor gasping like an asthmatic Missouri mule. Two hours in the mudhole left me physically and linguistically exhausted.

Time was precious. I had driven all night to keep an appointment with half a dozen cronies who were gathering the next day at an old plantation in South Carolina for our annual week of bird hunting. Now I thought of the wide, broom-straw fields of the Low Country, bathed in the soft glamour of Indian summer, of the hickory fire, hissing away in the big living room of the old homestead, of the convivial crowd already dribbling into camp for the hunt. Under the circumstances, such thoughts did not add measurably to my happiness.

Stop-off for Turkeys

Finally I abandoned the car and struck out by shanks' mare over the frozen ground. An hour later, I was bargaining with a farmer for the use of a white mule I saw dejectedly nibbling at honeysuckle in a near-by lot. The farmer was busy killing hogs, but guessed he could stop.

Three hours later my car was sorrowfully reposing in the front yard of the farm house, looking like the wreck of the Hesperus. The motor was as dead as an ex-politician. A neighborhood mechanic obligingly came over and performed an autopsy, mentioning two or three damaged parts. Then, to add insult to injury, he said he would have to go to town for the parts, and would not be able to install them before the next morning.

You can talk all you want about taking things philosophically, but when you have a long-planned trip upset by some trivial circumstance, it's precious little good philosophy will do you. Certainly it is a poor substitute for a Low Country bird hunt.

With rather poor grace, I am afraid, I engaged a room at my enforced habitation and proceeded to catch up with my sleep.

At nightfall, my farmer friend, a wiry and keen-eyed little fellow by the name of Pankey, called me down to supper. We sat down to fresh pork sausage, crackling bread, and ice-cold buttermilk, with a big jar of damson preserves in the center of the pine table.

"Hep yourself, young fellow. Thar's plenty more whar this come from," he invited. Then, passing me a big platter of sausage cakes, he added: "Take one, brother. Take two, take three, take the whole damned plateful if you want to. Got another razorback shoat in the pen that wants killin'."

But the invitation was hardly necessary. After gargantuan helpings of sausage cakes and crackling bread, I began to feel a kindlier interest in humanity.

"By the way, do you have any birds in this country?" I asked.

"If you mean partridges, no great shakes. Country hereabouts too grown-up, and not enough farming, I reckon. Thar's a sight of squirrels, though, and a smatterin' of deer, and by the way, what do you say to a turkey hunt tomorrer mornin'? You got to pass the time while your car's bein' fixed, anyway."

"Turkeys? Suits me," I readily assented.

"Got a field of corn down on the creek flat I haven't shucked yet. Still standin' in the shock. Last week I noticed turkey tracks around the shocks where they'd been peckin' at the corn. I been layin' off to sneak down thar, and tomorrer mornin' just suits, young fellow. Thar's one bodacious old gobbler on the place I been after for years."

"That's a bargain," I agreed.

"I'll get you up at 4 o'clock. That bein' the case, we'd better quit jawin' and turn in now."

Almost before I got to sleep, it seemed, something was pulling at my leg. I sat up in bed and blinked sleepily at a man holding a lantern in one hand and what appeared to be a pair of heavy drawers in the other. I shook my head groggily and looked again. It was not an apparition, but my friend Pankey.

"Hit's 4 o'clock, brother, and cold enough to freeze the tail off'n a brass monkey. Wife says you'd better put these here on, and it ain't a bad idee. Pretty nigh zero outside, and we'll be settin' still in a blind, you know."

For that matter, it was pretty nigh zero inside, and I began to repent of the promise I had made. I looked curiously at the drawers Pankey proffered me. They were long and heavy and warm.

"But I'm bigger than you are, Mister Pankey. Your drawers won't fit me," I protested.

"I know, but—" Pankey awkwardly shifted feet and grinned, "but you won't have any trouble gettin' into these here, sir. You see, they ain't exactly mine, but if it's all right with you—" And my little friend bowed apologetically and backed from the room.

Puzzled at his odd demeanor, I held the garment up to the

Stop-off for Turkeys

lantern light, and I saw the cause of the man's embarrassment. He had brought me a pair of his wife's drawers! For although Pankey was of rather meager stature himself, his spouse certainly was not. Before the day was over I was grateful for the odd generosity of my little host, and the proportions of his wife.

When I got downstairs, I found a pot of scalding black coffee, hot biscuits, and sizzling sausage cakes waiting for me. The coffee was so hot it seared all the way down, but from the way mine host drenched down five cups of it he must have been fire-proofed inside.

As we were leaving the yard, I noticed a small, nondescript dog sniffing at Pankey's heels.

"What kind of dog is that?" I asked.

"He's part spaniel, I think they call it, part bird dog, and part, well, I'd rather not say. Anyway, Hopper has got a whole lot of dog in him and he ain't bad for turkeys, sir."

Hopper was hardly prepossessing in appearance. He looked as if he had been sired by a syndicate, and perhaps the least said of his ancestry the better, but he was such an alert, friendly little animal that I saw no objections to taking him along.

By 5 o'clock we were looking down on a small, moon-drenched flat that was hedged in on three sides by a pine ridge that loomed darkly against the horizon, and on the fourth side by the sinuous run of a creek and a laurel cliff beyond. At intervals of a hundred feet or so, stood the pyramids of corn stalks, dark on the silvery landscape below us. Pankey proceeded to initiate me into the mysteries of his kind of turkey hunting.

"Take this here lantern," he said, "and find yourself a shock of corn with plenty of tracks around it. Worm your way under the shock and fix yourself up comfortable for a good spell. Be sure you're holed up so they won't see you, and don't dislodge the stalks so they'll look suspicious. Then make a good peephole through the corn, facin' the creek. 'Long about daybreak, or mebbe a little later, a flock of turkeys ought to fly down from that ivy cliff and start feedin' in the field. I'll be squattin' in another shock not far away."

Following instructions, I got down on hands and knees, and burrowed three or four feet into the shock. Then I arranged a loop-hole, facing the creek, and made myself as comfortable as possible. Hooper, trusting little nondescript that he was, curled himself amiably at my feet and went to sleep. My cubbyhole was warm and dry, and I soon began to feel drowsy.

I dozed fitfully, awaking perhaps an hour later to find it still dark. Clouds were racing ominously across the face of the moon, at times obscuring it entirely and enveloping the little flat and surrounding ridges in intense blackness. Why, I wondered, did the indefatigable Pankey drag me out of bed at least two hours before a turkey or anything else could see how to eat? I dozed off again.

When I awoke, a dismal day was breaking. The sky was leaden and overcast. From the dry cornstalks above me came the soft patter of rain, freezing as it fell. A marrow-chilling wind began to cut through the base of the shock, showing scant respect for even the voluminous flannels the obliging Pankey had supplied me with. But for the drawers, however, I should have frozen then and there.

On an ordinary bird hunt, cold weather is exhilarating. If you are properly dressed, a little exercise will make you as warm as an oven. But to squat like a Buddha in a sleet-covered corn shock, with a frost-bitten wind playing "Pop Goes The Weasel" up and down your backbone, and your feet and legs dead from sitting in a cramped position for hours, is not my idea of comfort.

Huddling miserably in my refuge like a rabbit in a wet hollow, I waited. At 9 o'clock, there had been no sign of turkeys. Nothing but sleet and frozen silence. No use of being a chump any longer, I decided. I would roust out friend Pankey, if he had not already left, and go to the house to thaw out.

But just as I started to push my way out, my eye caught a

Stop-off for Turkeys

movement that sent hot blood racing through my veins, and made me forget my miseries. Down from the laurel cliff and across the frozen creek flew a big gobbler. As I looked, the old fellow was joined by six others. Halting circumspectly at the edge of the flat 150 yards away, the birds cocked their beady heads and critically surveyed the field. Then, with an imperial old gobbler in the vanguard, the flock spread out fan shape and started into the field. It made me shiver to think how near I had come to spilling the beans.

Pecking desultorily along, the flock of two gobblers and five hens headed straight toward my blind in the center of the corn patch. Where was Pankey? I berated myself for not noticing what part of the field he had holed up in. Would he intercept the drove before they got to me and spoil my chance? Rather selfishly, I hoped he had ensconced himself in a shock to my side or rear, anywhere but in front. Crouching ready to shoot, I cautiously elevated my gun into the narrow opening.

But before the lead gobbler came within shooting distance, the flock drifted toward the left and out of sight. Through the small aperture between the stalks I could see only the area directly in front of me. I considered changing positions for a better view, but knowing the turkeys were feeding upfield, I feared any movement on my part might dislodge a part of the wind-blown shock, and put the flock to instant flight. I could do nothing but wait and hope for one to cross directly in front. Surely Pankey would shoot any minute now. Then I could tumble out and take pot luck at the flock.

Presently I heard the crunching of feet on the sleet-covered ground and the noise of a turkey feeding at a shock behind me. Craning my head around, I tried to peer through the stalks. If I could locate the turkey I might, by exercising enough caution, manage to reverse the barrel of my gun. But I found it impossible to see at all through the two-foot thickness of corn stalks that walled me in. If I had been in the field alone, I think I should have rushed out pell-mell and taken my chances with any luckless laggard within range, but I had no wish to jeopardize Pankey's chances.

Suddenly, on the outside of the very shock under which I crouched, I heard a movement that froze me into immobility, and would have made my hair stand on end if I hadn't been bald-headed. A turkey was industriously pecking away at my back, clucking contentedly as it plucked corn from a protruding ear not more than three or four feet from me.

What should I do? It was a foolish and tantalizing predicament—I was almost close enough to grab a wild turkey, yet wondering how the devil I could get a shot.

Then it occurred to me that Pankey, perhaps not remembering where I had hidden, might send a salvo of No. 3's rattling through the corn stalks into my back. That possibility hardly added to my comfort.

My indecision was abruptly relieved as I heard the reverberating thunder of Pankey's old chokebore. Scurrying feet crunched the sleet. The moment had come. Jumping bolt upright through the shock of corn, I made for the open field, with Hopper at my heels.

About 150 feet away, a turkey hen was streaking for the protection of the pines. Throwing up my 20, I saluted her, but she adroitly sidestepped behind a shock just as I squeezed the trigger, and I missed. Maybe the left barrel would redeem me. Facing about, I targeted at a big gobbler that had lifted from the upper end of the field and was raw-hiding it for a cliff across the creek.

It was a gambler's shot, too far for even the No. 3's in the left barrel to tell consistently. The old fellow soared majestically on across the flat. Apparently I had made a clean miss. If I just hadn't lost my head over that hen! But, down near the creek, the gobbler seemed to falter and sideslip suspiciously. As I watched, he glided down into a clump of ivy and vanished. Had I made a hit after all? I raced for the creek, a wild thrill surging through me. Ahead of me Hopper was high-tailing it like a dirty streak across the field. Before

Stop-off for Turkeys

I reached the creek, he had bounded across, scrambled up the bank, and scampered into the laurel like a cottontail.

I floundered through the laurel as fast as I could, but running through that stuff was next to impossible. I fought my way for 100 yards and stopped to listen. I could hear nothing of turkey or dog. I crossed the cliff, and dropped into a small ravine beyond. And there, under a big pine, a sight met my eyes that I shall not forget.

A big gobbler was struggling valiantly to disengage a leg from the desperate grip of Hopper, flailing the little dog unmercifully with his heavy wings. In spite of the punishment he was absorbing, Hopper held on resolutely. He had caught a tartar. A slightly wounded old gobbler has a terrific interest in self-preservation, but if the little dog regretted his bargain, there was nothing to show it. I rushed into the panting melee and administered the *coup de grâce*. Even after the turkey's struggles had subsided, I had to persuade Hopper to release his adversary's leg. Then, a bit groggy from the mauling he had taken, he followed me back into the corn field. At the creek Pankey met me with a hen he had dropped with the first shot.

When I pulled up at the Low Country plantation the next afternoon, I found the gang had assembled, but they were hardly in what you would call a convivial frame of mind. A cold rain had been falling for two days, keeping them out of the field. They had worn out their tempers and the only pack of cards on the premises. After salutations and back slappings had been duly exchanged, I returned to the car and brought in the big gobbler. Rations were running low, and the gobbler was a windfall.

Then they gathered around a hickory fire to hear how it was done. I spun a beautiful yarn, studiously avoiding any allusion to mudholes, women's underwear, corn shocks, or a tough-jawed little mongrel by the name of Hopper.

Postscript

In 1977, when rumors that I was about to become President of the University of South Carolina reached my father, he said to me "If you go to South Carolina, see if you can get them to reprint any of those wonderful books by Havilah Babcock."

He was referring to four books that collected Dr. Babcock's humorous essays on hunting and fishing, most of which had previously been published in *Field and Stream* or other magazines. Head of the University's English Department for many years, Havilah Babcock was perhaps the most widely read scholar the South has ever produced, although there is no doubt that most of his readers did not think of what they were doing as reading the work of a scholar: they supposed themselves to be having fun.

During our first few weeks of residence in the President's House on the famous "Horseshoe" of the University of South Carolina, my wife and I discovered that in the Palmetto State Babcock was famous not only as a writer of wise and witty little pieces on hunting and fishing but also as a teacher of English Composition. Innumerable alumni spoke to us of Dr. Babcock's legendary course on vocabulary-building known as *I Want a Word*. It was obvious that they could not forget either the teacher or the lessons they learned from him. About a hundred yards away from the house that is now our home, the initials HB are set in the bricks of the Horseshoe. They stand for Havilah Babcock and they look as if they've been there since the days when the nearby buildings served as hospital wards during the Civil War, although they were laid in the 1950s by enthusiastic students and alumni who neither asked or needed official permission to commemorate in this way the Virginian who became the most popular professor in the history of the University of South Carolina.

Tales of Quails 'n Such was first published in 1951 in New York by Greenberg. Having been out of print for more than twenty years, it is now reissued not to please me or my father but as part of an effort to satisfy the thousands of people who insist that a universe in which the Babcock books cannot be bought is unsatisfactory. It is now a historical document, and I have no doubt that a person as extraordinarily sensitive to the changing nuances of words as Havilah Babcock would rephrase a few of his references to blacks, but the author no longer has the opportunity to revise his words, and who else would dare to alter the work of so masterly a wordsmith?

James B. Holderman
July 4, 1985